NOLO® Products & S...

⇨ Books & Software

Get in-depth information. Nolo publishes hundreds of great books and software programs for consumers and business owners. Order a copy—or download an ebook version instantly—at Nolo.com.

⇨ Legal Encyclopedia

Free at Nolo.com. Here are more than 1,400 free articles and answers to common questions about everyday legal issues including wills, bankruptcy, small business formation, divorce, patents, employment and much more.

⇨ Plain-English Legal Dictionary

Free at Nolo.com. Stumped by jargon? Look it up in America's most up-to-date source for definitions of legal terms.

⇨ Online Legal Documents

Create documents at your computer. Go to Nolo.com to make a will or living trust, form an LLC or corporation or obtain a trademark or provisional patent. For simpler matters, download one of our hundreds of high-quality legal forms, including bills of sale, promissory notes, nondisclosure agreements and many more.

⇨ Lawyer Directory

Find an attorney at Nolo.com. Nolo's consumer-friendly lawyer directory provides in-depth profiles of lawyers all over America. From fees and experience to legal philosophy, education and special expertise, you'll find all the information you need to pick the right lawyer. Every lawyer listed has pledged to work diligently and respectfully with clients.

⇨ Free Legal Updates

Keep up to date. Check for free updates at Nolo.com. Under "Products," find this book and click "Legal Updates." You can also sign up for our free e-newsletters at Nolo.com/newsletters/index.html.

1st edition

Nonprofit Fundraising Registration

The 50-State Guide

by Stephen Fishman, J.D.

FIRST EDITION	OCTOBER 2010
Editor	DIANA FITZPATRICK
Cover Design	SUSAN PUTNEY
Book Design	TERRI HEARSH
Proofreading	ANI DIMUSHEVA
Index	SONGBIRD INDEXING
Printing	DELTA PRINTING SOLUTIONS, INC.

Fishman, Stephen.
  Nonprofit fundraising registration : the 50 state guide / by Stephen Fishman. -- 1st ed.
    p. cm.
  Summary: "This 50-state guide provides the information a nonprofit needs to register
to fundraise legally in any state"--Provided by publisher.
  ISBN-13: 978-1-4133-1273-7 (pbk.)
  ISBN-10: 1-4133-1273-X (pbk.)
  ISBN-13: 978-1-4133-1301-7 (e-book ed.)
  ISBN-10: 1-4133-1301-9 (e-book ed.)
  1. Fund raising--Law and legislation--United States--States. 2. Nonprofit
organizations--Registration and transfer--United States--States. 3. Charity laws and
legislation--United States--States. 4. Incorporation--United States--States. I. Title.
  KF1389.5.F57 2010
  346.73'064--dc22

                            2010021160

Please note

We believe accurate, plain-English legal information should help you solve
many of your own legal problems. But this text is not a substitute for
personalized advice from a knowledgeable lawyer. If you want the help of a
trained professional—and we'll always point out situations in which we think
that's a good idea—consult an attorney licensed to practice in your state.

Acknowledgments

Many thanks to:

Diana Fitzpatrick for her outstanding editing

Terri Hearsh for book design

Melody Englund for the index.

Table of Contents

B Supplemental State Forms for the URS 285

Your State Fundraising Registration Companion

Life has never been easy for nonprofits, but today it seems to be harder than ever. As if the ongoing struggle to raise funds weren't hard enough, there are increased government compliance burdens to deal with as well. As you probably already know, a few years ago the IRS rewrote and expanded the reporting requirements for the annual information return that nonprofits must file—Form 990. Among other things Form 990 now requires numerous disclosures about compliance with state nonprofit laws, including those concerning nonprofit fundraising registration.

Thirty-nine states plus the District of Columbia require nonprofits that solicit donations in their jurisdictions to register with a state agency. These laws have been on the books for years, but most nonprofits largely ignored them. Now, however, given the increased interest of the IRS and many states in this area, this is no longer an option.

Unfortunately, state fundraising registration can be a confusing and expensive process. Every state has its own rules and forms. Just figuring out which states your nonprofit must register in can be a nightmare. You can hire a professional firm to register for you—something that many large nonprofits do. However, this will be expensive—it can cost at least $5,000 to $7,000 to pay a professional firm to register your nonprofit in all 40 jurisdictions. This doesn't count the registration fees, which can be another $2,700 to $3,000. If you don't want to spend that kind of money, this book is for you.

In the past, if you wanted to comply with the various states' fundraising registration requirements yourself, you'd have to hit the law books and study the charitable solicitation laws and rules of as many as 39 different states plus the District of Columbia. This book, the first of its kind, has done that work for you. It shows you how to register your nonprofit in any or all of the 40 jurisdictions that require it. It explains:

- what the IRS wants to know about your registration practices
- what type of solicitations trigger registration requirements
- how to determine which states your nonprofit must register in

- exemptions from registration
- the impact of Internet fundraising on registration requirements
- strategies you can use to reduce the number of states in which you must register, and
- how to streamline the registration process by using the Unified Registration Statement.

It also includes an appendix with detailed summaries of the fundraising registration laws of all states—a huge amount of information reduced to an easily digestible form. A separate chapter covers the state laws that require many out-of-state nonprofit corporations to qualify to do business outside their home state.

By using the information provided here, you should be able to confidently register your nonprofit in every state that requires it.

State Regulation of Nonprofit Fundraising

Fundraising is the life blood of all nonprofits. Without gifts from donors, most nonprofits would cease to exist. Fortunately, Americans have proven to be generous givers. In 2008 alone, nonprofits raised over $307 billion in donations, including over $229 billion from individual donors. Not surprisingly with so much money at stake, there are many laws and government agencies that regulate nonprofits. First and foremost among these is the IRS, which is in charge of granting nonprofits their exemption from federal income taxes and making sure that they follow federal tax rules.

However, while the IRS's role is vital to all nonprofits, it is not the only player in the nonprofit regulation game. All states have nonprofit corporation laws governing nonprofit corporations organized within their state. States also have consumer protection laws intended to protect the public from all forms of fraud, including fraudulent fundraising by nonprofits and professional fundraisers.

This book deals with a particular subset of state nonprofit laws related to fundraising by nonprofits. Thirty-nine states and the District of Columbia have enacted laws—often referred to as "charitable solicitation acts"—that specifically regulate fundraising by nonprofits and the professional fundraisers they hire. These laws are primarily intended to protect donors from fraud by nonprofits in their fundraising efforts. They require nonprofits to register with a state agency before engaging in any fundraising activities in that state and to file periodic reports with the state. They also prohibit fraudulent or deceptive fundraising practices, regulate professional fundraisers, and impose penalties for violations.

Clearly, there is a need to protect the nonprofit community, particularly donors, from abuses related to how money is raised. While most nonprofits are legitimate and deserve to be generously supported, according to the Federal Trade Commission, 1% of all charitable donations are misused or collected using fraudulent or deceptive practices. That amounts to over $3 billion every year. In addition, because of the obligations imposed on nonprofits by these fundraising laws, it is crucial for nonprofits to understand and comply with them before engaging in any fundraising in a state that has a charitable solicitations act.

RESOURCE

Need additional information on other laws affecting nonprofits? For information on IRS tax laws that affect nonprofits and their tax-exempt status, see *Every Nonprofit's Tax Guide*, by Stephen Fishman (Nolo). For more on consumer protection and other state laws regulating nonprofits, contact your state's charity regulator. A list of state charity offices can be found at the National Association of State Charity Officials website at www.nasconet.org/agencies.

Charitable Solicitation Laws—The Basics

All nonprofits should have a basic understanding of the charitable solicitation laws of every state where they plan to solicit donations. These laws impose registration and periodic filing requirements on nonprofits that solicit contributions in that state and regulate certain fundraising-related activities. Charitable solicitation acts vary from state to state which can make this a difficult task for a nonprofit that fundraises in numerous states. In the hopes of creating some uniformity among states, two national organizations, The National Association of Attorneys General (NAAG) and the National Association of State Charity Officials (NASCO), created *A Model Act Concerning the Solicitation of Funds for Charitable Purposes*. You can download a copy of the model act from the NASCO website at www. nasconet.org.

Most states included the basic provisions from the model act when they created their own solicitation laws. Reading through the model act will provide a good overview of what most state solicitation acts look like. However, most states also included their own variations in the law and define key elements of the act differently. For example, while all states require nonexempt nonprofits to register with the state charity agency, the type of financial information that must be disclosed varies from state to state—some states require audited financial statements, while others do not.

State Solicitation Acts Apply to All Nonprofits— Not Just 501(c)(3) Organizations

State solicitation acts regulate fundraising activities by all types of tax-exempt nonprofits. Nonprofits that obtain their tax-exempt status under Section 501(c)(3) of the Internal Revenue Code are the most common type of tax-exempt nonprofit. They include organizations like the Red Cross and United Way and a myriad of others that perform charitable work and whose activities are also heavily regulated by the IRS because of their tax-exempt status. However, there are 27 types of tax-exempt nonprofits other than 501(c)(3) organizations. Unless they are specifically exempted, the state charitable solicitation rules apply to these organizations whenever they solicit donations from the public for educational, philanthropic, humanitarian, scientific, patriotic, social welfare or advocacy, public health, environmental conservation, civic, law enforcement, public safety, or any other charitable purpose.

The most common of these non-501(c)(3) organizations are social welfare organizations which must be operated exclusively to promote social welfare. These include, for example, volunteer fire companies, homeowners associations, and advocacy organizations such as the League of Woman Voters. Other types of nonprofits include membership organizations created primarily to benefit their members such as social and recreational clubs, business leagues (chambers of commerce), fraternal organizations (college fraternities or membership lodges), cooperative organizations, and credit unions.

When we use the word "nonprofit," we are referring to all types of tax-exempt organizations.

States With Charitable Solicitation Acts

State	Charitable Solicitations Act
Alabama	Alabama Code §§ 13A-9-70 and following
Alaska	Alaska Statutes §§ 45.68.010 and following and 9 Alaska Administrative Code § 12.010
Arizona	Arizona Revised Statutes §§ 44-6551 and following
Arkansas	Arkansas Code Annotated §§ 4-28-401 and following
California	California Government Code §§ 12580-12599.7; California Code of Regulations, Title 11, §§ 300-307; 311; 999.1
Colorado	Colorado Revised Statutes §§ 6-16-101 through 6-16-104
Connecticut	Connecticut General Statutes §§ 21a-190a, and following
Dist. of Columbia	District of Columbia Code Annotated §§ 29-301.01 and following
Florida	Florida Statutes §§ 496.402 and following
Georgia	Georgia Code Annotated §§ 43-17-1 and following
Hawaii	Hawaii Revised Statutes §§ 467B-A and following
Illinois	760 Illinois Compiled Statutes §§ 55/1 and following
Kansas	Kansas Statutes Annotated §§ 17-1760 and following
Kentucky	Kentucky Revised Statutes Annotated §§ 367.650; 367.657 and following
Louisiana	Louisiana Revised Statutes Annotated §§ 51:1901-1902; Louisiana Administrative Code, Title 16, Part III, § 515
Maine	Maine Revised Statutes Annotated, Title 9, Chapter 385, §§ 5001-5018
Maryland	Maryland Annotated Code, Business Regulation Article, §§ 6-101 through 6-205; §§ 6-401and following
Massachusetts	Massachusetts General Laws Chapter 12, §§ 8e and 8f; Chapter 68, §§ 18 through 35
Michigan	Michigan Compiled Laws §§ 400.271 through 400.292
Minnesota	Minnesota Statutes Annotated, §§ 309.50; 309.515; 309.52; 309.53
Mississippi	Mississippi Code Annotated §§ 79-11-501 through 79-11-511

States With Charitable Solicitation Acts (cont'd)

State	Charitable Solicitations Act
Missouri	Missouri Revised Statutes, Title XXVI, §§ 407.450 through 407.462
New Hampshire	New Hampshire Revised Statutes Annotated, Title 1, §§ 7:21 through 7:32b
New Jersey	New Jersey Statutes Annotated §§ 45:17A-18 and following
New Mexico	New Mexico Statutes Annotated §§ 57-22-1 and following
New York	New York Executive Law, Article 7a, §§ 171-a through 177, Not-For-Profit Corporation Law §§ 101 and following
North Carolina	North Carolina General Statutes §§ 131 F-2 through 131f-8
North Dakota	North Dakota Century Code, Chapter 50-22
Ohio	Ohio Revised Code Annotated §§ 1716.01 and following, Ohio Revised Code §§ 109.23 through 109.32
Oklahoma	Oklahoma Statutes Annotated §§ 18-552.1 through 18-552.6
Oregon	Oregon Revised Statutes Annotated, Volume 3, §§ 128.610 and following
Pennsylvania	10 Pennsylvania Statutes, Chapter 4B, §§ 162.1 through 162.7
Rhode Island	Rhode Island General Laws §§ 7-6-1 and following
South Carolina	South Carolina Code Annotated §§ 33-56-10 and following
Tennessee	Tennessee Code Annotated §§ 48-101-501 and following
Utah	Utah Code Annotated §§ 13-22-1 through 13-22-15; Utah Administrative Code, Rule R152-22-1 through R152-22-5
Virginia	Virginia Code Annotated §§ 57-48 through 57-61.1; Virginia Administrative Code, Title 2, §§ 5-610-10 through 5- 610-40
Washington	Washington Revised Code Annotated of §§ 19.09.020 and following; Washington Administrative Code §§ 434-120-100 through 434-120-175
West Virginia	West Virginia Code §§ 29-19-1 through 29-19-6
Wisconsin	Wisconsin Statutes §§ 440.41-440.42; Wisconsin Administrative Code, Chapter RL 5

States With Charitable Solicitation Acts (cont'd)
Notes: Idaho and Vermont have charitable solicitations laws, but they do not require nonprofits to register with the state. Texas only requires public safety charities to register. Delaware, Indiana, Iowa, Montana, Nebraska, Nevada, South Dakota, and Wyoming have no special charitable solicitation statutes and no registration or reporting requirements for charitable organizations engaged in fundraising.

Now let's look at some of the key provisions that are found in most state solicitation acts.

Registration Requirement

The cornerstone of state charitable solicitation laws is the requirement that nonprofits must register with a state agency—typically the secretary of state or state attorney general—before soliciting donations from that state's residents. The details on when you must register and what is involved in the registration process are covered in Chapter 2, "An Overview of the Fundraising Registration Process."

Requiring out-of-state nonprofits to register is intended to accomplish two main purposes:

- give the public easy access to important information about charities soliciting donations in their states, and
- provide useful information to the state agencies that are responsible for protecting the public from fraudulent fundraising practices.

Much of the information required in the state registration process is already provided to the IRS and is readily available on private websites such as GuideStar. However, by making these disclosures a legal requirement under state law, the states can hold nonprofits and their professional fundraisers liable if they lie or omit information. This gives nonprofits a strong incentive to provide complete and accurate information.

Public Access to Information

A donor needs accurate and current information to assess a charitable organization and determine if it is worthy of a donation. State registration laws require soliciting nonprofits to disclose important information about their finances, including the amount they spend on professional fundraising; the backgrounds of their directors, officers, and employees; the nature of their activities; and whether the organization has been in trouble in the past.

The registrations are available online so donors can check them before giving money and decide if the organization looks like a legitimate charity and if they approve of how it spends its money—whether it goes primarily to its stated charitable purpose or if too much goes to administrative or fundraising or other costs.

Help for Law Enforcers

Registration information also helps state law enforcers to bring enforcement actions against nonprofits that flout the law. For one thing, state fundraising registrations let the state charity agency know that a nonprofit is soliciting, or intends to solicit, in the state. The registration has the current names and addresses of an organization's directors and officers, as well as those who are responsible for maintaining custody of donated funds. It also discloses the identities of professional fundraisers employed by nonprofits.

Exemptions from Registration

All states exempt certain types of nonprofits from registration. These usually include educational institutions, hospitals, religious entities, and organizations with limited annual income. However, the definitions for each of these organizations vary greatly from state to state so an organization that is exempt in one state may not fall within another state's definition of exempt. We go over each state's exemption requirements in Appendix A.

Annual Financial Reporting

In all states, annual financial reporting is coupled with the registration requirement. Indeed, in most states the two are combined—that is, both are filed together at the same time. The financial report contains detailed financial information on the organization including its balance sheet, statement of support, revenue, expenses, and statement of functional expenses broken into program, management, and general categories. In most states, the annual financial reporting requirement can be satisfied by providing a copy of the organization's completed and filed IRS Form 990 or 990-EZ for the prior year. However, in some states, larger nonprofits are required to file audited financial statements. These statements, prepared by an independent certified public accountant, may be more reliable than the self-reported amounts on Form 990 or 990-EZ. Annual financial reporting requirements for all states are covered in Appendix A.

Unfair and Deceptive Practice Provisions

State solicitation acts contain provisions prohibiting the use of any unfair or deceptive acts or practices when soliciting charitable donations. Here is the list of banned practices contained in the Model Charitable Solicitations Act, which many states follow (to some extent):

- using any unfair or deceptive acts or practices
- using any representation that implies the contribution is for or on behalf of a charitable organization, or utilizing any emblem, device, or printed matter belonging to or associated with a charitable organization, without first being authorized in writing to do so by the charitable organization
- using a name, symbol, or statement so closely related or similar to that used by another charitable organization that the use thereof would tend to confuse or mislead a solicited person
- misrepresenting or misleading anyone in any manner to believe that the person on whose behalf a solicitation or charitable sales promotion is being conducted is a charitable organization or that the proceeds of such solicitation or charitable sales promotion will be used for charitable purposes if such is not the fact
- misrepresenting or misleading anyone in any manner to believe that any other person sponsors, endorses, or approves such solicitation or charitable sales promotion when the other person has not given

consent in writing to the use of his or her name for these purposes, and

- using or exploiting the fact of registration so as to lead any person to believe that such registration in any manner constitutes an endorsement or approval by the state.

Disclosure Statements

Twelve states require nonprofits to provide a written notice, called a disclosure statement, to prospective donors. The 12 states are Colorado, Florida, Georgia, Illinois, Maryland, Michigan, New Jersey, New York, Pennsylvania, Virginia, Washington, and West Virginia. Among other things, the disclosure statement must inform anyone being solicited that information about the nonprofit can be obtained from either the state or the nonprofit itself. Most of these states require that the notice be included on every printed solicitation and every written confirmation, receipt, or reminder of a contribution. However, two states (North Carolina and Washington) require that their notices always be provided at the point of solicitation.

Each state's disclosure statement is worded differently. As a result, nonprofits that solicit from a large number of states or nationally may have to include up to 12 different disclosure statements in their solicitation materials.

The required disclosure statements for each of the 12 states are included in Appendix A under the state information. Here are examples of two of the required disclosures:

- **Georgia.** All nonprofits in Georgia must include the following disclosure statement on every printed solicitation and every written confirmation, receipt, or reminder of a contribution:

  > A full and fair description of [*name of charity*] and its financial statements are available on request at the address indicated above.

- **Florida.** All nonprofits in Florida must include the following disclosure statement on every printed solicitation and every written confirmation, receipt, or reminder of a contribution:

A COPY OF THE OFFICIAL REGISTRATION AND FINANCIAL INFOR-
MATION MAY BE OBTAINED FROM THE DIVISION OF CONSUMER
SERVICES BY CALLING TOLL-FREE, 1- 800-435-7352 WITHIN THE
STATE. REGISTRATION DOES NOT IMPLY ENDORSEMENT, APPROVAL,
OR RECOMMENDATION BY THE STATE.

Rules for Professional Fundraisers, Solicitors, and Consultants

In addition to regulating nonprofits, state solicitation laws also have rules
governing professional fundraisers, solicitors, and consultants who help
nonprofits raise money. These rules differ from those that govern the charitable organizations soliciting on their own behalf, but they are intended for
the same purpose—namely, to prevent any fraud or abuse when soliciting
money from donors. In the case of professional fundraisers, the laws are
also intended to protect nonprofits from professional fundraisers misusing
donor funds they receive on behalf of the nonprofit or misrepresenting the
organization in the solicitation of funds.

If your nonprofit hires outside professionals and companies to help
with fundraising, you need to know about your state's rules governing
professional fundraisers. This includes, for example, hiring a telemarketing
firm to call prospective donors, paying a fundraising firm to conduct a
door-to-door campaign, or using a direct marketing firm to help plan a
direct mail campaign.

This book does not cover the registration or other legal requirements for
professional solicitors and consultants. For more information on your state's
requirements, contact your state's charity regulator. A list of state charity
offices can be found at the National Association of State Charity Officials
website at www.nasconet.org/agencies.

Semantic Confusion

First, there is a good deal of confusion about the terms used to describe
outside fundraisers because they differ from state to state.

Professional fundraisers. As used in this book, a professional fundraiser is any outside professional person or company hired by a nonprofit to help with fundraising. These are independent contractors who hire themselves out to nonprofits—they are not employees of their nonprofit clients. There are two basic types of professional fundraisers regulated by the states:

- professional solicitors, and
- fundraising consultants.

Professional solicitors. Depending on the state, professional solicitors may also be called paid solicitors, professional fundraisers, professional commercial fundraisers, professional fundraising firms, paid fundraisers, or commercial fundraisers. Whatever they are called, these people or companies are paid by nonprofits to solicit contributions directly from the public. This may be through telemarketing, door-to-door soliciting, event marketing, or any other type of direct solicitations.

Fundraising consultants. Fundraising consultants are also called fundraising counsel (though they are not attorneys) or professional fundraisers. Unlike professional solicitors, fundraising consultants have no direct contact with the public. Instead, they help a nonprofit plan or manage a fundraising campaign. Direct marketing firms often fall into this category. An outside grant writer hired as an independent contractor to help write a grant request would also be a fundraising consultant.

State Registration and Other Requirements

Because they deal directly with the public and may obtain access to cash or personal credit card information, professional solicitors are regulated very closely by the states to guard against misrepresentations and fraud. Forty-five states require professional solicitors to register or be licensed by a state agency. The only states that do not require registration are Montana, Nebraska, Nevada, Texas, and Wyoming.

Solicitors may also be required to file annual financial reports with the state regarding charitable solicitation activities conducted during the preceding year. Most states have other rules governing solicitors' activities, such as requiring them to disclose their identity as such before soliciting donations or having to disclose their fundraising expenses and ratios upon request.

Most states also require professional solicitors to enter into written contracts with the nonprofits they work for and post a bond before commencing work in a state (generally $10,000 or $20,000). They are also subject to extensive record-keeping requirements.

Because fundraising consultants typically do not have direct contact with donors, they are not as strictly regulated as professional solicitors. However, 28 states require fundraising consultants to register.

If You Hire Outside Fundraising Help

If your nonprofit hires an outside professional solicitor or fundraising consultant, you should always make sure it has complied with all of the legal requirements of the state or states where the funds will be raised. First, make sure the person or company is registered, if required. Although it is the solicitor's or consultant's obligation to register, in some states a nonprofit that hires an unregistered solicitor or consultant can be subject to fines or penalties.

Also, you should always have a written contract with a professional fundraiser. Many states will require you to include copies of all such contracts when you register or renew your registration. Failure to do so could result in your registration being rejected.

The Federal Trade Commission has prepared a useful guide for nonprofits that hire fundraising professionals called "Raising Funds? What You Should Know About Hiring a Professional." It is available on its website at www.ftc.gov/bcp/edu/pubs/business/resources/bus32.shtm.

 CAUTION
All required filings under state solicitation acts are public records. This includes not only the application for registration, but annual reports and contracts as well. In most states, the public can view or obtain copies of all of these records through a state website. These documents and the IRS Form 990 are heavily relied on by potential donors and others seeking information about a nonprofit. Make sure you carefully and accurately complete these forms and filings and do everything you can to make sure your organization's good works and responsible spending are reflected in these public records.

An Overview of the Fundraising Registration Process

This chapter covers the basics about state registration—who needs to register, who is exempt, how you register, and the registration application forms. It also discusses some strategies you can use to decrease your nonprofit's registration burden. After reading this chapter, you should have a good idea of the states where your nonprofit may need to register and what the process will involve. Then, you can use the Appendix at the end of the book to find the specific registration rules for all 50 states.

Who Needs to Register?

Thirty-nine states and the District of Columbia require nonprofits that are not exempt to register with a state agency before soliciting contributions from state residents. Basically, the rule is that any nonprofit that makes, or intends to make, a charitable solicitation within a state that requires registration must register with that state. "Charitable solicitation" is defined broadly to include any request for a contribution by a nonprofit or someone working on its behalf in which:

- an appeal is made for a charitable purpose
- the name of a charitable organization is used, or
- a statement is made that implies that all or part of the contribution will be applied to a charitable purpose or donated to a charitable organization.

The registration requirement is triggered by asking for donations—it is not necessary that your nonprofit actually receive a donation. That means you must register in any state before you actually solicit there (except for California where you have 30 days from the time you receive your first contribution to register). The only exception to this general rule is for nonprofits that fall within an exemption from registration.

In most cases, it will be pretty obvious when your nonprofit is making a charitable solicitation—you'll be asking for money and a charity or charitable purpose will somehow be involved. For example, a nonprofit would have to register if it had a booth at a shopping center manned by volunteers asking for donations to help Haitian refugees. But registration would not be required if the volunteers were merely offering to register people to vote and not asking for contributions.

Charitable solicitations don't always have to involve asking for a donation. Offering to sell a product or service that includes a representation that all or part of the money received will be devoted to a charitable organization or charitable purpose is considered a charitable solicitation and triggers the registration requirement. This includes cases where nonprofits sell merchandise or services themselves—for example, operating a nonprofit thrift shop. It also includes "commercial coventuring" or "cause marketing" where a nonprofit teams up with a for-profit business to market an image, product, or service with the promise that part of the proceeds will go to the nonprofit. One well known example is the partnership of Yoplait's "Save Lids to Save Lives" campaign in support of the nonprofit organization Susan G. Komen for the Cure. The company packages specific products with a pink lid and promises consumers that it will donate ten cents to the nonprofit for each lid turned in. If sales are nationwide, then the Susan G. Komen for the Cure would have to register in every state that requires registration. Of course, this can be done on a much smaller scale. For example, in 2010 the San Francisco nonprofit Save the Bay received the proceeds from two days of sales of vanilla cupcakes by a local bakery. This would only trigger a registration requirement for Save the Bay in San Francisco where the organization was already registered because that is its home state.

CAUTION

Do you have a "Donate Now" button on your website? Using the Internet and email to solicit contributions from a state's residents can trigger registration requirements—it depends on the circumstances and the state's rules. This complex topic of Internet and email fundraising is covered in Chapter 4, "Internet Fundraising and State Registration: A Match Made in Hell."

Legal Definition of Charitable Solicitation

Most states have patterned their charitable solicitation laws on a model law developed by the National Association of Attorneys General in 1986. This model law defines solicitation as follows:

'Solicit' and 'solicitation' mean the request directly or indirectly for money, credit, property, financial assistance, or other thing of any kind or value on the plea of representation that such money, credit, property, financial assistance, or other thing of any kind or value, or any portion thereof, will be used for a charitable purpose or benefit a charitable organization. Without limiting the scope of the foregoing, these words shall include the following methods of requesting or securing such money, credit, property, financial assistance or other thing of value:

(1) Any oral or written request;

(2) The making of any announcement to the press, over the radio or television or by telephone or telegraph concerning an appeal or campaign by or for any charitable organization or purpose;

(3) The distribution, circulation, posting or publishing of any handbill, written advertisement or other publication which directly or by implication seeks to obtain public support;

(4) The sale of, offer or attempt to sell, any advertisement, advertising space, book, card, tag, coupon, device, magazine, membership, merchandise, subscription, flower, ticket, candy, cookies or other tangible item in connection with which any appeal is made for any charitable organization or purpose, or where the name of any charitable organization is used or referred to in any such appeal as an inducement or reason for making any such sale, or when or where in connection with any such sale, any statement is made that the whole or any part of the proceeds from any such sale will be used for any charitable purpose or benefit any charitable organization.

A solicitation shall be deemed to have taken place whether or not the person making the same receives any contribution.

Who is Exempt From Registration?

All states exempt certain types of nonprofits from their registration require-ments. In some cases, this is because they are already heavily regulated by other state agencies—nonprofit hospitals and educational institutions for example. In the case of religious institutions, states don't want to interfere with the free exercise of religion. In the case of very small nonprofits, it's because they are relatively harmless and it's not worth the trouble.

If your nonprofit is fortunate enough to fall into one of the exempt categories, your registration burden will be greatly lessened or even eliminated. Unfortunately, determining whether your nonprofit is exempt can be difficult. The list of exempt nonprofits varies from state to state. Thus, a nonprofit can be exempt in one state but not another. For example, a nonprofit that receives contributions under $25,000 per year is exempt from registering in New York, but not in California. See the "State Exemptions From Registration" chart below.

This means that you will have to look at the laws of each state to see if an exemption applies to your nonprofit. Moreover, the exempt categories are often defined differently in different states. For example, in most states, only accredited educational institutions are exempt. However, in Alabama, for example, there is no requirement that the school be officially accredited to be exempt.

In addition, in 12 states, exemptions are not automatic—a nonprofit must have its exemption confirmed by the state charity office. This involves filing an application and providing proof that your nonprofit qualifies for the exemption. This requirement is often not strictly enforced, but it is still the law. Some states also require nonprofits that are exempt to pay a fee.

TIP

Ask for help. If you're not sure whether your nonprofit qualifies for an exemption in a particular state, you may ask the state charity agency to confirm that your organization is exempt. You'll need to submit a letter explaining why you think your nonprofit is exempt and proof that you qualify for the exemption. For example, if your nonprofit is a religious corporation, you should submit a copy of your articles of incorporation. If you're exempt because you are a small nonprofit, provide a copy of recent financial statements.

Common exemptions from registration include:

Small nonprofits. Twenty-eight states exempt nonprofits that have annual gross revenues of less than a specified amount. In 12 states, the threshold amount is $25,000. But the amount varies in other states—from as high as $50,000 in Connecticut to as low as $1,500 in the District of Columbia. In most states, your nonprofit cannot qualify for this exemption if you use professional fundraisers. That is, all your fundraising must be done by unpaid volunteers. However, the rules vary on this as well. In some states, you can use salaried staff to do some fundraising whereas this would disqualify you from the exemption in other states. In addition, in some states, only nonprofits that are totally unpaid volunteer organizations can qualify for the exemption. You will have to check the Appendix for each state's rules.

It is important to take note of how the annual ceiling is calculated by the state in question. In most states, it works like this:

- the ceiling applies to the total annual contributions your nonprofit receives from residents of all states, not just the state in question
- you need not count government grants or contracts toward the ceiling, and
- bona fide membership dues, fees, and similar payments don't count because they aren't charitable contributions.

However, not all states follow this pattern. For example, in New York, you only count contributions from New York state residents and you must include government grants. Again, you'll have to check each state's particular rules.

If your contributions go over the state's annual limit during the year, you'll need to register with the state—usually within 30 days.

A few states also exempt nonprofits that receive contributions from less than a specified number of state residents. For example, Michigan exempts nonprofits that receive contributions from ten or fewer people during the year.

Finally, keep in mind that 11 states—including three of the largest—have no exemption for small nonprofits. These include:

- California
- Florida
- Illinois
- Kentucky

- Louisiana
- Missouri
- New Hampshire
- North Dakota
- New Mexico
- Oregon, and
- Utah.

Thus, for example, no matter how small your nonprofit is, it will have to register to solicit donations in California, unless it is exempt on some other basis.

Religious organizations. All states except Arizona exempt churches and other tax-exempt religious organizations from their registration requirements. Indeed, the charitable solicitations laws of 14 states don't apply at all to religious organizations. These states are: District of Columbia, Florida, Georgia, Kentucky, Maine, Michigan, Mississippi, New Hampshire, New Mexico, New York, North Carolina, North Dakota, Tennessee, Virginia, and Washington.

National organizations with chapters or affiliates. If a nonprofit is a national or regional 501(c)(3) organization with unincorporated chapters or affiliates in multiple states, the individual chapters may not need to register if they are covered by the national organization's group registration with the IRS. The parent organization must file a consolidated Form 990 for its subordinate organizations. In some states, however, group registration is available only when the parent nonprofit has its principal office in the state. Of course, the parent organization must register in all states where there are chapters and where money is raised.

Hospitals. Fifteen states exempt nonprofit hospitals and some other types of health organizations from registration. However, the list of that health-related organizations that are exempt varies from state to state.

Educational institutions. Thirty-four states exempt educational institutions. The definition of "educational institution" differs from state to state, but most states exempt any type of accredited educational institution. Additionally, many states exempt foundations and support groups established by exempt educational foundations. In some states, this exemption is limited to cases where the institution only solicits funds from its students and alumni, faculty, trustees, and their families.

Membership nonprofits. Twenty-four states exempt nonprofits that solicit funds only from their members. These may include fraternal, patriotic, social, or alumni organizations.

Political groups. Eighteen states exempt political parties, candidates for federal or state office, and political action committees who are required to file financial information with federal or state elections commissions.

Appeals for a specific person. Twenty-four states exempt charitable appeals made on behalf of a specific person, provided that the fundraising is conducted by unpaid volunteers. Most states require that all the money collected be handed over to the person, but a few permit some deductions for expenses.

> **EXAMPLE:** When a police officer in Boulder, Colorado is killed in the line of duty, several residents of the town establish a fund in his name to collect money for his wife and children. They solicit donations door-to-door and during television interviews. These individuals are exempted from having to register under Colorado's charitable solicitations law.

Other exemptions. Depending on the state, various other types of organizations may be exempt—for example, nonprofit libraries, museums, historical societies, veterans groups, labor unions, trade associations, nonprofit credit-counseling agencies, volunteer firefighters, ambulance associations, rescue squad associations, and senior citizen centers. Some states even exempt certain named organizations such as the Red Cross, Boy Scouts, Girl Scouts, YMCA, and Junior League.

Why Register?

If your nonprofit solicits charitable contributions in a state that requires registration and is not exempt, then it is required by law to register there. Nevertheless, until recently, all but the largest nonprofits that solicited contributions nationwide tended to ignore state registration requirements. Indeed, some experts estimate that as many of 90% of all nonprofits failed to register in one or more states even though they were required to do so by state law. Typically, nothing happened because most states lacked the manpower and desire to enforce their registration laws. However, the game has changed. New IRS requirements now make it imperative for all nonprofits to comply with state registration laws. If you don't, you risk unwanted attention and scrutiny from the IRS and states, and potential problems with donors.

The IRS Wants to Know

In the past, the IRS did not ask for information from nonprofits about whether they were in compliance with state registration requirements or what states they were registered in. However, this changed in 2007 when the IRS adopted new, radically different Forms 990 and 990-EZ. These are the annual information returns that nonprofits file each year with the IRS. Both of these forms now require nonprofits to provide information to the IRS about their state registration. With these new reporting requirements, nonprofits must now disclose to both the IRS and the general public whether they are complying with state registration requirements.

For a detailed discussion of the IRS, Form 990, and state registration, see Chapter 3, "The IRS and State Registration."

It's the (State) Law

All but eleven states have laws requiring nonprofits to register before soliciting in their state. If you don't register in a state where you are required to, you are breaking that state's law and you could be subject to fines and other penalties. These fines can be substantial. In Pennsylvania, it's a minimum $1,000 fine for failing to register. Moreover, the state may order your nonprofit to cease soliciting donations within the state until you register there.

Although in the past most states have not taken action against nonprofits for failing to register, things may change with the revised Form 990 and 990-EZ. The new IRS interest in state registration has brought the issue to the forefront and states may be more interested now as well. In addition, information is more readily available through the Form 990 and 990-EZs and states may use this information to start enforcing their registration laws. In one recent case, the state of Florida filed suit against a small Tampa Bay area police charity that failed to register. The suit asked the court to impose a $10,000 civil penalty and to prohibit the charity from seeking donations until it complied with the law. The charity ultimately settled the case by registering and paying a $1,000 fine.

Even before the recent IRS changes, some states actively went after nonprofits that failed to register. A state could find out about an unregistered nonprofit through an inquiry about the nonprofit from a member of the public or someone seeking to file a complaint against it. In looking into the matter, the state office might find that the nonprofit was not listed as registered in its records. And, a state could always decide to proactively go after out-of-state nonprofits soliciting within its borders. Some budget-strapped states may come to view registration fees as a potentially lucrative source of income and start going after nonprofits more aggressively than they have in the past. The New York Attorney General's office collected over $500,000 in fines and fees after an investigation in 2004 in which it identified and went after approximately 12,000 nonprofits that had failed to register properly. In 2009, the state of Washington sent letters to 39,000 Washington-based nonprofits demanding that they register. Basically, you never know when your nonprofit might get caught in a state's net—especially now that registration information is more readily accessible through the 990 filings.

Funders, Donors, and Auditors May Ask

Foundations, government agencies, and other sophisticated funders know about state registration requirements. Any of them may ask you whether you have properly registered in the states where you are raising funds and may even want proof of it. Not complying with state registration laws may make your nonprofit look like an amateurish operation that doesn't deserve funding.

It also won't look good for less sophisticated donors if it gets out publicly that your organization has broken the law by failing to comply with state registration laws. Some states are posting the names of nonprofits that fail to register on the Internet.

Most donors are looking for organizations that they can trust—after all, they are turning over their money to you. Being a law-abiding citizen seems like a minimum threshold that most people would expect from a nonprofit that is asking them for their money and support.

Finally, financial auditors also are become increasingly aware of state registration requirements. They may require that your nonprofit register or mention that it has not done so in their audit reports.

> **CAUTION**
>
> **Your board members can be held personally liable.** Unlike many other debts and liabilities of a nonprofit, if your organization is fined for failure to register with a state, your board of directors can be held personally liable for those fines. Many state solicitation laws provide that a nonprofit cannot reimburse its directors, officers, or employees for such fines. Don't put yourself in the position of having your board members personally responsible for fines that you can avoid by registering.

It's a Fundraising Tool

If failing to register looks bad, complying with your registration responsibilities looks good. Your nonprofit may never state or imply that registering with a state means that that state endorses your organization. However, many nonprofits list on their websites all the states in which they have registered. This helps show potential donors that your nonprofit is a responsible organization that operates in multiple states.

Charitable Contributions May be Jeopardized

Legally speaking, your nonprofit does not have the right to solicit contributions in any of the 39 states that require registration until it has, in fact, registered. Any contribution you solicited and received while you were not registered is in legal jeopardy. If a court determines that your nonprofit failed to register, it can order that it make restitution—that is, give back any of the contributions it received during that time. If a donor—or, perhaps the heir of a donor who made a large gift by will—discovers that you failed to register, that person could bring a court action to get back or set aside the gift. This has actually happened.

When Should You Register?

A nonprofit is legally required to register with a state *before* it solicits contributions there. Remember, the registration requirement is triggered by asking for donations; it is not necessary that your nonprofit actually receives a donation. (The only exception is California where you have 30 days from your first solicitation to register.) Ideally, you should start the registration process at least two or three months before your nonprofit starts to solicit donations in a state. You want to be sure to finish all your state registrations before your nonprofit has to file its Form 990 or 990-EZ with the IRS. These forms must be filed within 4½ months after the close of your nonprofit's fiscal year. If your nonprofit uses the calendar year, that means your fiscal year ends on December 31st and your 990 forms are due by May 15th of the following year.

If You're Out of Compliance

What if your nonprofit has already solicited donations in one or more states where it should have registered but failed to do so? Most nonprofits are in this boat. You should go ahead and register where you need to. Depending on the state, your nonprofit may have to pay a fine. The size of the fine usually depends on how long you've been soliciting in the state and how much you've collected from state residents. In New York, for example, the fine is up to six years of registration fees that should have been paid in prior years. So the sooner you register the better.

However, many states want to encourage nonprofits that are not in compliance to register. Thus, if your nonprofit acts in good faith and quickly registers after discovering registration is required, the state charity office may decide not to fine you or only impose a minimum fine. Some states even establish periodic amnesties in which all nonprofits are allowed to register late without having to pay a fine—for example, New York state had an amnesty during the first half of 2010.

Newly-Formed Nonprofits

If you're in the process of forming your nonprofit, don't wait until you receive your IRS determination letter to register. This can take some time to arrive. Instead, you should register in all states where you intend to solicit contributions and are not exempt right after you file your IRS Form 1023, *Application for Recognition of Exemption*. Most states will require you to submit a copy of the filed form with your application. Then, when you get your IRS determination letter recognizing your tax-exempt status, send a copy to the state charity registration agency.

Where Must You Register?

Small nonprofits that only fundraise locally may only be required to register in one state (typically their home state). Larger nonprofits that fundraise on a national basis may have to register in many states—often in all 39 that require registration, plus the District of Columbia.

State of Domicile

Unless your nonprofit is exempt or located in one of the few states that doesn't require registration, you'll always need to register in your home state (also called the state of domicile). This is the state where your principal office is located. This should be the very first state you register in, and you should do so as soon as you can. As stated above, if your nonprofit is new, you need not wait until you receive your determination letter from the IRS—do it when you file your IRS Form 1023, *Application for Recognition of Exemption*.

Any State Where You Fundraise

Your nonprofit will also have to register in any state with charitable solicitations laws if it solicits contributions there or intends to do so. This is true whether or not your nonprofit has a physical presence in the state, such as an office or volunteers working there. It doesn't matter whether your nonprofit solicits the donations itself, or you have volunteers, professional fundraisers, or others do so on your behalf—provided they do it with your knowledge and permission. Either way, your nonprofit will have to register before any solicitations are made.

Charitable solicitations don't need to be made in person—they can be made in writing or through other media forms that don't involve physical presence or contact. Examples of the type of contacts that would trigger a registration requirement include:

- direct postal mail to addresses within the state—for example, sending state residents fundraising letters, brochures, or newsletters soliciting donations
- telephoning people located in the state
- purchasing advertising in any newspaper or other publication that circulates in the state, or on any TV station or radio station that airs in the state
- advertising in national media, whether on radio, television, magazines, or other means that reaches state residents
- holding or publicizing fundraising events that occur in the state, such as dinners, dances, parties, raffles, auctions, concerts, walk-a-thons, or golf tournaments
- door-to-door solicitations or other person-to-person contacts in the state, or
- placing donation boxes in the state.

Using the Internet and email to solicit contributions from a state's residents may also require registration in that state, but not always. Internet and email fundraising is covered in Chapter 4, "Internet Fundraising and State Registration: A Match Made in Hell."

> ### Is Applying for a Grant a Charitable Solicitation?
>
> In most states, applying for a grant from the government or from another nonprofit is a charitable solicitation requiring registration. Your nonprofit should be registered before applying for a grant in a state. But there are some exceptions, particularly for government grants.
>
> In the following states, requesting a government grant or contract is not considered to be a charitable solicitation: Alabama, Florida, Kentucky, Maine, Maryland, Minnesota, Mississippi, New Jersey, North Carolina, Pennsylvania, Virginia, or Wisconsin.
>
> In the following states, requesting a grant from a tax-exempt nonprofit, including a family or community foundation, is not considered to be a charitable solicitation: Florida, Maine (charitable and educational foundations only), and North Carolina.

How Do You Register?

Unfortunately, there is no single national registration application that works in every state. Instead, your nonprofit must individually register with each state where it is required to do so, following that state's particular requirements. These requirements differ from state to state—sometimes dramatically—so the more states you fundraise in, the more work you will have. Even the name for registration varies depending on what state you're in—in some states, it's called a registration statement; in others, it's called a license, solicitation permit, or certificate.

Registration usually consists of two parts: an initial registration application and an annual renewal or financial reporting requirement.

First Things First—The Initial Registration

All states with solicitation laws require nonprofits that want to fundraise in their state to file an application with a state agency. Usually, you will need to file the application with the state attorney general's office or the secretary of state's office. This initial registration application asks for organizational and financial information about your nonprofit. The application must be signed under penalty of perjury by a principal officer of the nonprofit, such as the president or chief financial officer. Many states require two signatures. The registration is a public record, and in most states is made freely available to the public from a state-run website.

In most states, you will have a choice as to whether to use the multi-state application form or the state's own application form.

The multi-state form (URS). Having to register in multiple states (as many as 39 plus the District of Columbia) can be a terrible burden for a nonprofit. Imagine having to fill out 39 different registration applications. Fortunately, there is an easier way. The National Association of State Charity Officials ("NASCO") has created a single registration form that can be used to register in multiple states. Using the multi-state form, called the Unified Registration Statement ("URS") can save time. Currently, 34 states and the District of Columbia accept the URS. However, as many as 16 of these states require that you also file supplemental state forms with your URS. For more information on the URS, including detailed guidance on how to complete the form, see Chapter 5, "The Unified Registration Statement."

The individual state forms. Almost all states with registration requirements have their own application form that is different from the URS. Your nonprofit can always choose to use a state's individual registration form instead of filing the URS. While it may seem like it would be easier to use a single multi-state form if you are registering in multiple states, the state forms are often shorter and simpler than the URS. So even if you are registering in more than one state, it may be easier to use the individual state forms.

Contents of application. The information required on the application varies depending on whether you use the URS or a state form, and whether a state that accepts the URS requires supplemental information. Typically, you'll have to provide the following information:

- contact information for the nonprofit
- the organization's legal status—corporation, trust, or unincorporated entity
- names and addresses of the nonprofit's officers and directors
- whether the nonprofit is tax exempt and the purpose for which it was formed

- the purpose or purposes for which the contributions to be solicited will be used
- how donations will be solicited—for example, whether a professional fundraiser will be used
- figures on fundraising costs
- a financial report for the prior fiscal year, if any
- whether the nonprofit has registered in other states and if so, which ones
- the names of the individuals who will be responsible for taking custody of the contributions and distributing them, and
- disclosure of any injunction, judgment, or administrative orders against the nonprofit because of its fundraising practices.

In addition, almost all states require nonprofits to submit copies of their articles of incorporation, bylaws, IRS determination letter, and most recently filed Form 990 or 990-EZ. Many require copies of fundraising contracts as well.

Application fee. All but six states charge a registration fee, which also varies from state to state. Some states charge on a sliding scale, based on the size of the nonprofit. The fees range from as little as $10 to as high as $425 or more. See the "State Registration Fees and Population" chart later in this chapter. To register in every state would cost at least $2,700 in fees.

Renewal Registration

The initial registration is only the beginning of the state compliance process. In all but six states—Alabama, Illinois, Minnesota, New Mexico, New York, and Oregon—your registration will expire after a specified time. The expiration date varies from state to state. Typically, it is either one year after the registration is issued, at the close of the calendar year, or at the close of your fiscal year. So you will need to periodically renew your registration within a certain time period before the existing registration expires. Most states charge a fee for the renewal, which is often the same as the initial registration fee.

How to renew. To renew, you'll need to complete a renewal application. In all but two states, you must use the individual state renewal forms. In two states you can use the URS to renew your registration. You'll also need to include copies of any changes to the documents you filed with your initial registration, such as amendments to your articles of incorporation or new contracts with fundraisers.

Filing deadlines. The filing deadline for renewals varies from state to state. See the "Renewal and Financial Reporting Deadlines" chart below. Thus, if your nonprofit is registered in multiple states, you'll have to keep track of several different deadlines. Thirteen states time their due dates for the renewal financial report to coincide with the deadline for filing Form 990 or 990-EZ with the IRS—4½ months after the end of your nonprofit's fiscal year. If your nonprofit uses the calendar year, this means it is due by May 15th. Almost all states will allow your nonprofit to obtain an extension of time to file the renewal. The procedure to do so differs from state to state. In several states, you must first file IRS Form 8868, *Application for Extension of Time to File an Exempt Organization Return,* to obtain an extension. In others, you'll have to fill out an extension request form; in some states, you can do it online.

Annual Financial Reporting

All states also require registered nonprofits to submit an annual financial report. However, in a few states very small nonprofits are exempted from this requirement. For example, in California, nonprofits with annual revenues and assets less than $25,000 are not required to file a financial report. But they must still file a renewal.

Technically, under most state solicitation laws, annual financial reporting is separate from initial registration and renewal registration. However, in most states, the renewal and annual financial report are combined—that is, both are filed together at the same time—and the same deadline applies to each. Although Alabama, Illinois, Minnesota, New Mexico, New York, and Oregon don't require registrations to be renewed, they do require annual financial reports. Moreover, even in these states you are required to keep the state charity agency apprised of major changes, such as amendments to your articles of incorporation.

Contents of report. In most states, you can satisfy the annual financial reporting requirement by simply providing a copy of your organization's completed and filed IRS Form 990 or 990-EZ for the prior year. You submit it along with your renewal application. However, a few states won't accept the 990 Form and require that you restate the financial information on their state forms. In Colorado, for example, you must complete an online state form.

Audited financial statements. In 19 states, larger nonprofits (in terms of annual income) must prepare and submit annual financial statements audited by an independent certified public accountant (CPA). This requirement varies from state to state. In Massachusetts, for example, an audited financial statement is required if a nonprofit has gross annual revenues of $500,000 or more, while in New York, audited statements are required for nonprofits with annual revenue of over $250,000.

Filing deadlines. In almost all states, the deadline for filing the annual financial report is the same as the deadline for filing the renewal registration. See the "Renewal and Financial Reporting Deadlines" chart below.

Formulating a Registration Plan

Registration is time consuming and expensive, so you'll likely want to register in as few states as possible. This requires some careful planning. Obviously, because registration can be burdensome and expensive, you'll want to register in as few states as legally required. There are a number of strategies you can use to reduce the number of states where your nonprofit must register.

Are You Exempt?

Your nonprofit could be exempt from registration in all or most states where it would otherwise be required to register. For example, if your nonprofit's annual revenue is less than $25,000, it will be exempt in 27 states. Churches and other religious organizations are exempt in all states except Arizona. Educational institutions are exempt in 34 states. If your nonprofit falls into one of the exempt categories summarized in the following chart, turn to Appendix A to check the laws of the state in which it is domiciled and all the states where it targets donors. You may not have to register in any state.

State Exemptions From Registration

Alabama

Dollar Exemption: $25,000

Exempt entities:
- Religious institutions
- Educational institutions
- Membership organizations
- Political organizations
- Appeals for individuals
- Veterans organizations
- Volunteer firefighters
- Ambulance companies
- Rescue squads

Alaska

Dollar exemption: $5,000

Exempt entities:
- Religious institutions
- Political organizations

Arizona

Exempt entities:
- Political organizations
- Government agencies

Arkansas

Dollar exemption: $25,000

Exempt entities:
- Religious institutions
- Educational institutions
- Political organizations
- Appeals for individuals
- Government agencies
- Health organizations

State approval of exemption required

California

Exempt entities:
- Religious institutions
- Educational institutions
- Political organizations
- Government agencies
- Health organizations
- Cemetery corporations

Colorado

Dollar exemption: $25,000

Exempt entities:
- Political organizations
- Appeals for individuals
- Health organizations

Connecticut

Dollar exemption: $50,000

Exempt entities:
- Religious institutions
- Educational institutions
- Government agencies
- Health organizations
- PTAs

District of Columbia

Dollar exemption: $1,500

Exempt entities:
- Religious institutions
- Educational institutions
- Membership organizations
- American Red Cross

State Exemptions From Registration (continued)

Florida

Exempt entities:
- Religious institutions
- Educational institutions
- Membership organizations
- Political organizations
- Appeals for individuals
- Government agencies

Georgia

Dollar exemption: $25,000

Exempt entities:
- Religious institutions
- Educational institutions
- Membership organizations
- Political organizations
- Appeals for individuals
- Professional associations
- Volunteer firefighters
- Hunters, fisherman, and target shooters

Hawaii

Dollar exemption: $25,000

Exempt entities:
- Religious institutions
- Educational institutions
- Membership organizations
- Government agencies
- Health organizations

Illinois

Exempt entities:
- Religious institutions
- Educational institutions

- Membership organizations
- Political organizations
- Appeals for individuals
- Veterans organizations
- Volunteer firefighters
- Nurseries for orphan infants
- PTAs
- Boys clubs

State approval of exemption required for religious organizations only

Kansas

Dollar exemption: $10,000

Exempt entities:
- Religious institutions
- Educational institutions
- Membership organizations
- Appeals for individuals
- Health organizations
- 10-person exemption
- Many others—see Chapter 3

Kentucky

Exempt entities:
- Religious institutions
- Educational institutions
- Membership organizations
- PTAs and student groups

Louisiana

Exempt entities:
- Religious institutions
- Educational institutions
- Health organizations
- All nonprofits that don't use professional solicitors

State Exemptions From Registration (continued)

Maine

Registration still required—see Chapter 3

Dollar exemption: $10,000

Exempt entities:
- Religious institutions
- Educational institutions
- Membership organizations
- Appeals for individuals
- Health organizations
- 10-person exemption

Maryland

Dollar exemption: $25,000

Exempt entities:
- Religious institutions
- Educational institutions
- Membership organizations
- Appeals for individuals
- Volunteer firefighters
- Nonprofits that only receive grants

State approval of exemption required

Massachusetts

Dollar exemption: $5,000

Exempt entities:
- Religious institutions
- Membership organizations
- Appeals for individuals
- Several named organizations—see Chapter 3

Michigan

Dollar exemption: $8,000

Exempt entities:
- Religious Institutions
- Educational Institutions
- Appeals for Individuals
- Veterans Organizations
- Government Agencies
- Health Organizations
- 10-person exemption
- PTAs
- Advocacy groups
- Private foundations
- Child-care providers
- Service clubs

State approval of exemption required

Minnesota

Dollar exemption: $25,000

Exempt entities:
- Religious institutions
- Educational institutions
- Membership organizations
- Appeals for individuals
- Private foundations

State approval of exemption required

Mississippi

Dollar exemption: $25,000

Exempt entities:
- Religious institutions
- Educational institutions
- Membership organizations

State Exemptions From Registration (continued)

- Appeals for individuals
- Volunteer firefighters
- Humane societies

State approval of exemption required (except religious organizations)

Missouri

Exempt entities:
- Religious institutions
- Educational institutions
- Membership organizations
- Political organizations
- Health organizations
- All section 501(c)(3) organizations
- Section 501(c)(7) social and recreational clubs
- Section 501(c)(8) fraternal and benevolent organizations

State approval of exemption required

New Jersey

Dollar exemption: $10,000

Exempt entities:
- Religious institutions
- Educational institutions
- Local units of registered parent organizations

New Mexico

Exempt entities:
- Religious institutions
- Educational institutions
- Appeals for individuals

New York

Dollar exemption: $25,000

Exempt entities:
- Religious institutions
- Educational institutions
- Membership organizations
- Political organizations
- Appeals for individuals
- Veterans organizations
- Government agencies
- Law enforcement support groups
- Historical societies
- Volunteer firefighters
- Volunteer ambulance service organizations

State approval of exemption required

North Carolina

Dollar exemption: $25,000
- Religious institutions

North Dakota

Exempt entities:
- Religious institutions
- Educational institutions
- Political organizations
- Appeals for individuals

Ohio

Dollar exemption: $25,000

Exempt entities:
- Religious institutions
- Educational institutions
- Membership organizations

State Exemptions From Registration (continued)

Oklahoma

Dollar exemption: $10,000

Exempt entities:
- Religious institutions
- Educational institutions
- Membership organizations
- Appeals for individuals

Oregon

Exempt entities:
- Religious institutions
- Educational institutions
- Membership organizations (Oregon mutual benefit corporations)
- Government agencies
- Unincorporated organizations
- Oregon child care agencies
- Trustees of certain charitable remainder trusts
- Cemetery corporations

Pennsylvania

Registration may still be required

Dollar exemption: $25,000

Exempt entities:
- Religious institutions
- Educational institutions
- Veterans organizations
- Health organizations
- PTAs
- Volunteer firemen
- Ambulance associations
- Rescue squad associations
- Nonprofit senior citizen centers and nursing homes

Rhode island

Dollar exemption: $25,000

Exempt entities:
- Religious institutions
- Educational institutions
- Membership organizations
- Appeals for individuals
- Veterans organizations
- Health organizations
- Several others—see Chapter 3

South Carolina

Dollar exemption: $20,000 and $7,500

Exempt entities:
- Religious institutions
- Educational institutions
- Membership organizations
- Political organizations
- Appeals for individuals
- Veterans organizations
- Government agencies

State approval of exemption required (must apply every year)

Tennessee

Dollar exemption: $30,000

Exempt entities:
- Religious institutions
- Educational institutions
- Political organizations

State Exemptions From Registration (continued)

- Health organizations
- Volunteer fire departments
- Rescue squads
- Local civil defense organizations
- Community fairs, county fairs, district fairs, and division fairs

Utah

Exempt entities:
- Religious institutions
- Educational institutions
- Membership organizations
- Political organizations
- Appeals for individuals
- Government agencies
- Volunteer fire departments
- Rescue squads
- Local civil defense organizations
- Nonprofit broadcast media

State approval of exemption required

Virginia

Dollar Exemption: $5,000

Exempt entities:
- Religious institutions
- Educational institutions
- Membership organizations
- Political organizations
- Appeals for individuals
- Health organizations
- Nonprofits supported by grants
- Red Cross
- Nonprofits that solicit in five or less counties

- Nonresident organizations with registered affiliates
- Labor groups
- Tax-exempt trade associations

State approval of exemption required (except religious institutions, political groups, Red Cross)

Washington

Dollar exemption: $25,000

Exempt entities:
- Religious institutions
- Educational institutions
- Political organizations
- Appeals for individuals

State approval of exemption required

West Virginia

Dollar exemption: $25,000

Exempt entities:
- Religious institutions
- Educational institutions
- Membership organizations
- Appeals for individuals
- Health organizations

Wisconsin

Dollar exemption: $5,000

Exempt entities:
- Religious institutions
- Educational institutions
- Membership organizations

Register in Your Home State

Your nonprofit should always register in your home state, unless you are exempt or the state does not require registration. If your nonprofit is locally based, this might be the only state in which you have to register.

Register Where You Solicit

You must also register in any other requiring states where you solicit funds from residents of that state and are not exempt from registration. This includes any state where your nonprofit hires professional fundraisers.

New York and New Jersey—Special Rules

New York and New Jersey don't follow the Internet fundraising rules that most states use. (See the discussion on the Charleston Principles in Chapter 4, "Internet Fundraising and State Registration: A Match Made In Hell.") If your nonprofit has an interactive website—that is, a website with a donation button or other means of accepting online contributions—you may need to register in New York and New Jersey, even if you don't directly solicit donations in those states. These states don't follow the Charleston Principles discussed in Chapter 4. In their view, any nonprofit website with a donation button is a charitable solicitation requiring registration. See Chapter 4 for details. The only way to avoid registering in these two states is to include a disclaimer on your website explicitly stating that you do not accept donations from residents of those states. See "Strategies to Avoid Registration," below.

States You Don't Have to Worry About

The following 11 states do not require nonprofits to register because of their charitable solicitation activities within their states.

- Delaware
- Idaho
- Indiana
- Iowa
- Montana

- Nebraska
- Nevada
- South Dakota
- Texas (requires only "public safety" charities to register)
- Vermont
- Wyoming

In addition, you likely won't have to register in Missouri because it exempts most types of nonprofits from registration, including all Section 501(c)(3) organizations. Also, only nonprofits that use professional fundraisers must register in Louisiana.

However, if your nonprofit is a corporation and it engages in intrastate business in any of the above states, it will have to qualify to do business in the state (assuming it is not your nonprofit's home state). This requirement is totally separate from charitable fundraising registration. It involves filing an application with a state official—usually the secretary of state—and appointing a registered agent to accept legal papers on your behalf. See Chapter 6, "Qualifying to Do Business Outside Your Home State," for a detailed discussion of this topic.

Keep Track of Renewal and Financial Reporting Dates

Your registration is only good if it's current. All states require that registered nonprofits file annual financial statements, while all but five require that registrations be renewed, usually annually. Failure to timely renew and/ or file the financial report will usually result in your registration no longer being considered legally valid by the state. If your nonprofit continues to fundraise despite its lapsed registration, it could be fined by the state or the state could even order it to stop fundraising until it renews its registration.

Unfortunately, the time to renew a state fundraising registration and/ or file the financial report varies from state to state. Be sure to calendar all the dates when renewal registrations must be filed in the states where your nonprofit has registered. Most of these deadlines can be extended by asking for permission from the state agency involved. Review the rules for each state in Appendix A.

Renewal and Financial Reporting Deadlines		
	Deadline to File Renewal	Deadline to File Annual Financial Report
Alabama	none	90 days after end of fiscal year
Alaska	September 1	combined with renewal
Arizona	September 1	combined with renewal
Arkansas	anniversary date of initial registration	May 15
California	4.5 months after end of fiscal year	combined with renewal
Colorado	4.5 months after end of fiscal year	4.5 months after end of fiscal year
Connecticut	5 months after end of fiscal year	combined with renewal
District of Columbia	staggered dates—renewal every 2 years	combined with renewal
Florida	anniversary date of initial registration	none
Georgia	renewal every 2 years based on anniversary date of initial registration	combined with renewal
Hawaii	none	4.5 months after end of fiscal year
Illinois	none	6 months after end of fiscal year
Kansas	6 months after end of fiscal year	combined with renewal
Kentucky	December 31	combined with renewal
Louisiana	anniversary date of initial registration	combined with renewal
Maine	November 30	September 30
Maryland	6 months after end of fiscal year	combined with renewal
Massachusetts	4.5 months after end of fiscal year	combined with renewal
Michigan	6 months after end of fiscal year	combined with renewal
Minnesota	none	6.5 months after end of fiscal year

Renewal and Financial Reporting Deadlines (continued)		
	Deadline to File Renewal	Deadline to File Annual Financial Report
Mississippi	anniversary date of initial registration	combined with renewal
Missouri	none	2.5 months after end of fiscal year
New Hampshire	none	4.5 months after end of fiscal year
New Jersey	6 months after end of fiscal year	combined with renewal
New Mexico	none	6 months after end of fiscal year
New York	none	4.5 months after end of fiscal year
North Carolina	4.5 months after end of fiscal year	combined with renewal
North Dakota	none	September 1
Ohio	4.5 months after end of fiscal year	combined with renewal
Oklahoma	anniversary date of initial registration	combined with renewal
Oregon	none	4.5 months after end of fiscal year
Pennsylvania	4.5 months after end of fiscal year	4.5 months after end of fiscal year
Rhode Island	anniversary date of initial registration	combined with renewal
South Carolina	4.5 months after end of fiscal year	4.5 months after end of fiscal year
Tennessee	6 months after end of fiscal year	combined with renewal
Utah	anniversary date of initial registration	combined with renewal
Virginia	4.5 months after end of fiscal year	combined with renewal
Washington	4.5 months after end of fiscal year	combined with renewal
West Virginia	anniversary date of initial registration	combined with renewal
Wisconsin	July 31	6 months after end of fiscal year

Minimizing Your Registration Requirements

Unless you receive at least $250 in donations each year from a state's residents, it makes no sense to register there because the cost of registration will exceed the value of the donations your nonprofit receives from the state. Nevertheless, if you're not careful, your nonprofit will be legally required to do so anyway. Indeed, you may be legally required to register in states where you don't receive contributions from any residents at all. Remember, it's asking for contributions, not receiving them, that triggers the registration requirement.

Where Is It Worthwhile to Register?

If your nonprofit has been in operation for a while, carefully examine your fundraising history to examine which states the bulk of your contributions come from. If, like most nonprofits, your nonprofit is a local or regional organization that only receives donations from residents of one or a small handful of states, it may only make sense to register in those few states. On the other hand, you may want to register in many states if your nonprofit actively fundraises nationally by sending email or other fundraising materials to residents of all or many states.

If your nonprofit is new or has a limited fundraising history, the two charts below may be helpful. They show the registration fees and populations of all states that require fundraising registration. The first is in alphabetical order, the second is according to population in descending order.

Examining these charts, you can see that almost half the population of the United States resides in just ten states that require registration: California, New York, Florida, Illinois, Pennsylvania, Ohio, Michigan, Georgia, North Carolina, and New Jersey. You might conclude that it's only worthwhile to register in these larger states. Or, you might want to cast your registration net wider and include all states with populations over 5 million. There are only 20 such states. Certainly, unless it's your home state or you intend to solicit there, there would seem to be little reason to register in a very small state like North Dakota with a population under 700,000.

State Registration Fees and Population (alphabetical)			
State	Initial Registration Fee	Renewal/Annual Report Fee	Population
Alabama	$25	$25	4,708,708
Alaska	$40	$40	698,473
Arizona	None	None	6,595,778
Arkansas	None	None	2,889,450
California	$25	$0–$300	36,961,664
Colorado	$10	$10	5,024,748
Connecticut	$50	$50	3,518,288
District of Columbia	$303	$303 (every two years)	599,657
Florida	$10–$400	$10–$400	18,537,969
Georgia	$35	$20	9,829,211
Hawaii	$10–$750	$10–$750	1,295,178
Illinois	$15	$15	12,910,409
Kansas	$35	$35	2,818,747
Kentucky	None	None	4,314,113
Louisiana	$25	$25	4,492,076
Maine	$50	$25	1,318,301
Maryland	$0–$200	$0–$200	5,699,478
Massachusetts	$35–$250	$35–$250	6,593,587
Michigan	None	None	9,969,727
Minnesota	$25	$25	5,266,214
Mississippi	$50	$50	2,951,996

State Registration Fees and Population (alphabetical) (cont'd)

State	Initial Registration Fee	Renewal/Annual Report Fee	Population
Missouri	$15	$15	5,987,580
New Hampshire	$25	$75	1,324,575
New Jersey	$30–$250	$30–$250	8,707,739
New Mexico	None	None	2,009,671
New York	$25	$10–$25	19,541,453
North Carolina	$0–$200	$0–$200	9,380,884
North Dakota	$25 ($85 for out–of–state nonprofits)	$10	646,844
Ohio	$0–$200	$0–$200	11,542,645
Oklahoma	$15	$15	3,687,050
Oregon	None	$10–$200	3,825,657
Pennsylvania	$15–$250	$15–$250	12,604,767
Rhode Island	$90	$90	1,053,209
South Carolina	$50	None	4,561,242
Tennessee	$50	$100–$300	6,296,254
Utah	$100	$100	2,784,572
Virginia	$100–$325	$30–$325	7,882,590
Washington	$20	$10	6,664,195
West Virginia	$15–$50	$15–$50	1,819,777
Wisconsin	$30	None	5,654,774

State Registration Fees and Population (by population)			
State	Initial Registration Fee	Renewal/Annual Report Fee	Population
California	$25	$0–$300	36,961,664
New York	$25	$10–$25	19,541,453
Florida	$10–$400	$10–$400	18,537,969
Illinois	$15	$15	12,910,409
Pennsylvania	$15–$250	$15–$250	12,604,767
Ohio	$0–$200	$0–$200	11,542,645
Michigan	None	None	9,969,727
Georgia	$35	$20	9,829,211
North Carolina	$0–$200	$0–$200	9,380,884
New Jersey	$30–$250	$30–$250	8,707,739
Virginia	$100–$325	$30–$325	7,882,590
Washington	$20	$10	6,664,195
Arizona	None	None	6,595,778
Massachusetts	$35–$250	$35–$250	6,593,587
Tennessee	$50	$100–$300	6,296,254
Missouri	$15	$15	5,987,580
Maryland	$0–$200	$0–$200	5,699,478
Wisconsin	$30	None	5,654,774
Minnesota	$25	$25	5,266,214
Colorado	$10	$10	5,024,748
Alabama	$25	$25	4,708,708

State Registration Fees and Population (by population) (cont'd)

State	Initial Registration Fee	Renewal/Annual Report Fee	Population
South Carolina	$50	None	4,561,242
Louisiana	$25	$25	4,492,076
Kentucky	None	None	4,314,113
Oregon	None	$10–$200	3,825,657
Oklahoma	$15	$15	3,687,050
Connecticut	$50	$50	3,518,288
Mississippi	$50	$50	2,951,996
Arkansas	None	None	2,889,450
Kansas	$35	$35	2,818,747
Utah	$100	$100	2,784,572
New Mexico	None	None	2,009,671
West Virginia	$15–$50	$15–$50	1,819,777
New Hampshire	$25	$75	1,324,575
Maine	$50	$25	1,318,301
Hawaii	$10–$750	$10–$750	1,295,178
Rhode Island	$90	$90	1,053,209
Alaska	$40	$40	698,473
North Dakota	$25 ($85 for out–of–state nonprofits)	$10	646,844
District of Columbia	$303	$303 (every two years)	599,657

Strategies to Avoid Registration

Unless your nonprofit is exempt from registration in a state that requires registration, there is only one way to avoid having to register there: You must not solicit contributions in that state. This means you must not ask for donations from state residents in writing, in person, or through the media (including the Internet). Moreover, you must not hire fundraisers to solicit on your behalf in the state. This can require a good deal of care and discipline. For example, if your nonprofit has a newsletter distributed by postal mail or email that contains an appeal for contributions, you have to make sure you don't send it to residents of states in which you haven't registered.

If, like most nonprofits, your nonprofit has an interactive website—that is, a website that contains a "donate" button or other means of accepting online donations—you should place a disclaimer on it making it clear that you do not accept donations from residents of the state or states in which you do not want to register.

Here's an example of a disclaimer used by one charity on its website:

The following states have been identified as "no donations" states:

Arizona	Maine	North Dakota
DC	Michigan	Pennsylvania
Florida	Mississippi	Rhode Island
Georgia	New York	South Carolina
Illinois	North Carolina	Tennessee
Kentucky		

Donations from "no donations" states will be refused.

If your nonprofit accepts online donations, you should consider using donation software that permits you to block donations from residents of the states you select. This software can even eliminate selected states from the pull-down menus donors must use to make their contributions. Such software is available from www.etapestry.com, www.clickandpledge.com, www.donorperfect.com, and other vendors. You can find reviews of many donor management software packages at the website www.techsoup.org.

Instead of accepting online donations through your own website, you could do so through a website operated by a donor-advised fund such as www.networkforgood.org or www.justgive.org. As discussed in "Using Charity Portals to Receive Donations" in Chapter 4, donations received through these sites should not give rise to a duty to register for you.

The IRS and State Registration

t wasn't long ago that the Internal Revenue Service (the "IRS") essentially had no involvement whatsoever with fundraising registration by nonprofits. Solicitation laws are state laws, enforced by state agencies, and there was no crossover or hook for the IRS to get involved in these state matters. Things changed when the IRS revised the annual information report that nonprofits are required to file each year. In that report—the Form 990 or Form 990-EZ—the IRS included items that now require nonprofits to answer questions about their fundraising activities and registrations. It is still up to the states to enforce their charitable solicitation laws but the IRS has become indirectly involved by asking questions about these matters on the IRS annual report. Now your nonprofit could suffer unpleasant consequences either by not registering properly with a state or by failing to provide accurate information about its registrations with the IRS.

Filing IRS Information Returns

All nonexempt nonprofits are required to file a form each year with the IRS. For the smallest nonprofits (those with under $50,000 in gross receipts in 2010 and later), this is simply an electronic postcard with minimal information. All others must file an information return—either the dreaded Form 990, or its less burdensome cousin, the Form 990-EZ.

An information return is just what it sounds like: a tax form that gives the IRS detailed financial and other information about your nonprofit. It helps show the IRS how your nonprofit spends its money, conducts its operations, and whether it is in compliance with the tax laws that govern tax-exempt organizations.

These 990 returns are a big deal for nonprofits. If they aren't filed properly, you risk having to pay IRS sanctions and could even lose your tax-exempt status. They have always played an important role in the state registration process—even before the IRS forms asked about registration matters. All states except Alabama, Colorado, and Hawaii require nonprofits that have filed a Form 990 to include a copy of the Form 990 with their initial registration application. In addition, all states either require nonprofits to file their Form 990 as part of their annual financial reporting process or permit the form to be filed instead of other financial statements. Thus, most state charity agencies will have copies of your nonprofit's annual 990 filings. If they don't, the 990s are publicly posted and easily available for anyone to access and read. So you can assume that state charity agencies will have access to your Form 990—either because you will have provided it to them as part of their registration process or because it is publicly available.

In the past, the IRS did not ask for information from nonprofits about their state fundraising registrations. Then, in 2007, the IRS adopted a new, radically different Form 990 and 990-EZ. These forms now contain questions that directly address registration. For the first time, the IRS has inserted itself into what was purely a matter between you and the states where you solicited funds.

Which Form Do You File?

The disclosures you are required to make regarding state registration differ depending on which information return you file. Larger nonprofits file Form 990, which is a long, complicated form that asks for extensive information about a nonprofit's finances, governance, and other issues. Smaller organizations have the option of using the shorter and simpler Form 990-EZ instead.

Very small nonprofits—those with annual receipts of less than $50,000 in 2010 and later—are not required to file Form 990 or 990-EZ. These (smallest) nonprofits have the option of filing a brief electronic postcard called the Form 990-N which does not ask for any information on state registration. Nonprofits were first required to use the new Form 990 and 990-EZ for their 2008 tax year (filed in 2009). The requirements for filing the new revised annual reports will be phased in as follows:

Form 990 Filing Requirements	
2009 Tax Year (Generally Filed in 2010)	**Form to File**
Gross receipts $25,001 to $499,999 Total assets less than $1.25 million	990-EZ
Gross receipts $500,000 or more Total assets $1.25 million or more	990
2010 Tax Year and Later (Filed in 2011 and Later)	**Form to File**
Gross receipts "normally" $50,000 or less	990-N (electronic postcard)
Gross receipts $50,001 to $199,999 Total assets less than $500,000	990-EZ
Gross receipts $200,000 or more Total assets $500,000 or more	990

Is Your Nonprofit Exempt?

Most nonprofits that have been recognized as tax-exempt by the IRS must file an annual information return with the IRS. However, certain organizations are exempt from this annual filing requirement, including the following:

Religious organizations. The largest group of nonprofits that is exempt from any IRS informational filing requirement is churches and religious organizations. This exemption covers:

- any church (including synagogues, mosques, and temples); an interchurch organization of local units of a church; a convention or association of churches; or an integrated auxiliary of a church (such as a men's or women's organization, religious school, mission society, or youth group)
- schools below college level affiliated with a church or operated by a religious order
- any exclusively religious activity of any religious order, or
- religious missions in foreign countries.

Subsidiaries of other nonprofits. A nonprofit that is a subsidiary of another larger nonprofit is exempt from the IRS information filing requirement if the parent nonprofit files a consolidated return for its subordinate organizations, including the particular subsidiary nonprofit. For example, individual Boy Scout troops usually do not file their own information returns—they are covered by the Boy Scout parent organization's filing on behalf of all its subsidiary organizations.

A parent organization may file on a subsidiary's behalf only if the subsidiary nonprofit is covered by the parent's group exemption letter from the IRS. In addition, each subsidiary nonprofit covered by the exempt group must give the parent written authority each year for inclusion in the group return.

Parent nonprofits do not have to file a consolidated return for their subsidiaries—they can require them to file their own returns. Whether they do so or not, a parent nonprofit must file its own separate return. If you're not sure whether or not your parent organization will include you in a group return, contact the main office of the parent group and ask.

Nonprofits not registered with the IRS. Any nonprofit that hasn't applied to the IRS for recognition of its exemption from federal income taxes is exempt. Nonprofit organizations that receive less than $5,000 in income each year don't have to file Form 1023 to obtain tax-exempt status and they don't have to file an information return.

Federal corporations and state institutions. This exemption applies to tax-exempt federal corporations such as federal credit unions, and to state and local agencies or other entities such as a state colleges or universities or state hospitals.

Foreign nonprofits. Foreign nonprofits, including those located in United States possessions, need not file an information return if their annual gross receipts from sources within the United States are normally less than $25,000.

Private foundations. These entities file IRS Form 990-PF each year, instead of one of the 990 forms discussed in this chapter.

> TIP
> **Look at your IRS determination letter.** If your nonprofit has received a determination letter from the IRS recognizing its tax-exempt status, the letter should state whether your nonprofit is exempt from filing an information return.

The New Form 990

The new Form 990 has two questions related to state registration. This may not sound like much, but the implications are enormous. One of the questions is on the main part of the form that everyone must answer. The other question is on one of the schedules so only organizations required to complete that schedule must answer the second question.

Part VI, Line 17

The first question about state registration is contained in the main part of the Form 990 which all nonprofits are required to complete. Part VI of the form contains a series of questions about governance, management, and disclosure policies related to your nonprofit. Line 17 of Part VI asks you to: "List the states with which a copy of this Form 990 is required to be filed."

Notice that this item doesn't ask *where* you have filed a 990—it asks *where you are required* to file a Form 990. In effect, this is asking you to list the states where you are supposed to file the form. This means you are supposed to name all the states where you would be required to file a Form 990 because of your activities in those states—regardless of whether or not you have actually registered there.

All but three of the 39 states that have fundraising registration— Alabama, Colorado, and Hawaii—require that you file a copy of your Form 990 each year as part of their financial reporting process. If your nonprofit solicits charitable contributions nationwide, it should list at least the following states: Alaska, Arizona, Arkansas, California, Connecticut, Florida, Georgia, Illinois, Kansas, Kentucky, Louisiana, Maine, Maryland, Massachusetts, Michigan, Minnesota, Mississippi, New Hampshire, New Jersey, New Mexico, New York, North Carolina, North Dakota, Ohio, Oklahoma, Oregon, Pennsylvania, South Carolina, Tennessee, Utah,

Virginia, Washington, West Virginia, and Wisconsin. You are not allowed to say "all states."

Your nonprofit doesn't need to register in Louisiana unless it employs professional fundraisers there. If you don't, you need not list Louisiana. And your nonprofit is likely exempt from registration in Missouri, which exempts all tax-exempt 501(c)(3) organizations. Thus, you probably don't have to list Missouri either.

If your nonprofit does not solicit contributions nationwide, you only need to list those states in which you do solicit. Of course, these should include all the states where your nonprofit has already registered. If you are soliciting contributions in states where you have failed to register or where your registration has lapsed, you should list those states too—this item asks for the states where you are required to register. However, you should immediately file registration applications in all those states.

Schedule G

For some nonprofits, the Form 990's interest in state registration doesn't end with the Line 17 question. Certain nonprofits must also complete Schedule G to Form 990, *Supplemental Information Regarding Fundraising or Gaming Activities.* This schedule requires you to provide detailed information about your nonprofit's fundraising expenses. However, not all nonprofits must file this schedule and there's a good chance that your nonprofit will be one of those lucky ones.

Who must file Schedule G? Only nonprofits that report payments of more than $15,000 for expenses for "professional fundraising services" must complete Part I of Schedule G, the portion asking about state registration. You report how much you pay for professional fundraising services in your Form 990, Part IX, *Statement of Functional Expenses*, lines 6 and 11(e).

"Professional fundraising services" includes more than hiring a professional fundraiser to run a fundraising campaign. The IRS says that it includes any service "requiring the exercise of professional judgment or discretion consisting of planning, management, preparation of materials (such as direct mail solicitation packages), provision of advice and consulting regarding solicitation of contributions, and direct solicitation of contributions." This includes just about any outside person your nonprofit hires to help you plan your fundraising activities or to actually solicit contributions. Some examples the IRS provides in the Schedule G instructions include:

- contracting with a business to supply printing and mailing services
- hiring a single fundraiser to advise on and coordinate direct mail fundraising
- contracting with a consultant to perform data analysis of solicitation efforts
- retaining a fundraiser to conduct a feasibility study for a capital campaign, or
- hiring a fundraiser to plan and produce programming for a media campaign.

However, professional fundraising services do not include purely ministerial tasks, such as printing, mailing services, or receiving and depositing contributions to a charity.

Line 3: Where are you registered? If you do have to file Schedule G, you will have to answer the following item which appears on Line 3: "List all states in which the organization is registered or licensed to solicit funds or has been notified it is exempt from registration or licensing." For this item, you will need to list all the states where you have actually registered to fundraise or have been notified by the state that you are exempt.

Unlike Line 17, this doesn't ask where you *are required* to register—only where you *are* registered or have been notified that you are exempt. The states you list here as the ones you are registered in should match those listed in Line 17—the ones where you are required to register. If they don't, it will be clear that your nonprofit has failed to register in one or more states where it is required to do so. The IRS won't take any action against you for this because it does not enforce the state registration laws. But any state regulator or donor or any other person who examines the form will be able to see whether you have complied with your registration responsibilities.

If you have failed to register in all the states in which you are required to file Form 990, but are in the process of doing so, be sure to explain this on the form.

Line 3: Where are you exempt? Line 3 also asks you to list all the states that have notified your nonprofit that it is exempt from registration. Ordinarily, a state will notify your nonprofit that it is exempt only if you apply for an exemption from the state charity agency and it is granted. Only 12 states require you to apply for an exemption: Arkansas, Illinois (religious organizations only), Maryland, Michigan, Minnesota, Mississippi, Missouri, New York, South Carolina, Utah, Virginia, and Washington. If you've applied for and received an exemption in one or more of these states you should list them in Line 3.

The other states do not require you to apply to have your exemption approved. Rather, they leave it up to you to decide whether or not you qualify for the exemption. The form does not require you to list these states. Thus, the fact that a particular state is not listed as exempt here does not necessarily mean your nonprofit is not exempt in that state.

However, most states will tell you if you qualify for an exemption if you ask them in writing. List any state for which you have done so and have been notified that you are exempt.

The New Form 990-EZ

Form 990-EZ, the simpler information return, also asks about state registration. Line 41 of the form directs the nonprofit to: "List the states in which a copy of this return is filed." Thus, unlike Form 990, this item does not ask you to list where the form is *required* to be filed—only where you have actually filed it.

The following 28 states require that Form-EZ be filed as part of the registration or renewal process, or accept it as an annual financial report: Arkansas, California, Connecticut, Florida, Georgia, Hawaii, Illinois, Kansas, Kentucky, Maine, Maryland, Massachusetts, Michigan, Minnesota, Mississippi, New Hampshire, New Jersey, New York, North Carolina, North Dakota, Ohio, Oregon, South Carolina, Tennessee, Virginia, Washington, West Virginia, Wisconsin.

If you have not filed your 990-EZ in a state where you should have filed it because of your fundraising activities there, you should not list that state here. However, this could be a red flag if your nonprofit is actively and visibly engaged in fundraising in any of the above states and has not registered. You should register in any such states as soon as possible. Schedule G does not present any state registration disclosure issues for Form 990-EZ filers because—unlike Form 990 filers—they are not required to complete the portion of the schedule that asks about state registration.

IRS Penalties for Filing Inaccurate Forms

You must file a complete and accurate Form 990 or 990-EZ. This means reading the questions carefully, and completely and accurately answering the question that is asked. Not having carefully read the question (for example, listing where you *have filed* instead of where you *are required* to file) is not likely to go over well with the IRS. You don't want to find yourself in the position of having to convince the IRS that your response was complete and accurate—you just misread the question.

If you have failed to register in some states and are concerned this will be evident by your responses, you are better off explaining why or what actions you are taking to remedy the situation as opposed to trying to obfuscate the truth with answers that are not 100% responsive to the question asked. You have a legal duty to accurately and completely report to the IRS in your Form 990 or Form 990-EZ and the IRS can take action against you for failing to do so. The IRS can't take any action if it realizes you have failed to register in a state where you are required to register. It will be up to the state to pursue you (which up until now states have shown little interest in doing).

The consequences for failing to file an accurate and complete Form 990 or 990-EZ with the IRS can be harsh and include the following:

Penalties against your nonprofit. You could be charged a penalty of $20 a day, up to the lesser of $10,000 or 5% of your annual gross receipts. Nonprofits with annual gross receipts exceeding $1 million are subject to a penalty of $100 a day, up to a maximum $50,000 penalty. The penalties begin to accrue on the date your Form 990 or 990-EZ was due and last until you file a complete form.

Penalties against responsible people. If you do not furnish correct information, the IRS can send a letter setting a timeframe in which you need to fix the problem. After that period expires, the person (individual) who was responsible for complying with the IRS request and failed to do so can be charged a penalty of $10 a day, up to a maximum penalty of $5,000 for any one return.

Loss of tax exemption. Beginning in 2010, any nonprofit that fails to file Form 990 or 990-EZ for three consecutive years automatically loses its tax exemption. Because failure to file an accurate return is considered the same as filing no return at all, a nonprofit that fails to file an accurate return for three consecutive years could lose its tax exemption.

In the past, the IRS rarely, if ever, took away a nonprofit's tax exemption solely because it failed to file information returns. Much more serious misconduct was required. However, the new rules place a greater emphasis on filing accurate returns than ever before. As written, the rules give the IRS no choice but to revoke the tax exemption of any nonprofit it finds has failed to file accurate returns for three straight years. The moral: file complete and accurate returns with the IRS. If you discover you've made a mistake, file an amended return. If you haven't registered in states where you are required to register, take action to remedy the situation but don't lie about it on an IRS information return.

Internet Fundraising and Registration: A Match Made In Hell

The Internet has revolutionized nonprofit fundraising and has had an equally big impact on fundraising registration. In the past, only large nonprofits could afford to fundraise outside their home state—usually by conducting extensive telephone or direct mail campaigns. Smaller nonprofits typically would only fundraise locally, or, at most, statewide. Thus, it was only the larger nonprofits that had to worry about registering outside their one state. Small nonprofits usually never had to deal with the expensive and time-consuming burden of multi-state registration.

Today, however, even the smallest nonprofit can reach a nationwide audience through an inexpensive website or email, and collect contributions from donors located anywhere in the country. Consequently, many small nonprofits that have never had to deal with registration other than in their home state must now figure out where and how to register in multiple states.

Website Fundraising— What Are the Boundaries?

Save Historic Eureka (SHE) is a small California nonprofit dedicated to helping preserve historic buildings located in Eureka, California. SHE has a website that explains its mission and contains a "donate now" button allowing it to directly collect contributions from donors' credit cards. Sam, a resident of Pittsburgh, Pennsylvania, happens to find the SHE website while surfing the web. He is so impressed with SHE, he sends it a $25 donation. This is the only donation SHE has ever received from Pennsylvania. Does SHE have to register in Pennsylvania?

If you read the charitable solicitation laws of Pennsylvania literally, the answer to this question is "yes." The law states that "[a]ny direct or indirect request for a contribution … that is … distributed … by press, telegraph, television or any other media" constitutes a charitable solicitation requiring registration in the state. Obviously, using the Internet to solicit contributions falls into the "any other media" category.

The charitable solicitation laws of almost all other states are the same as, or similar to, Pennsylvania's. Read literally, they require any nonprofit that has a website that includes a donate button (or any other charitable solicitation) to register with the state even if it has no actual physical presence within that state, makes no direct fundraising efforts there, and even if they receive no contributions from state residents. If the law was applied in this way, even small nonprofits like SHE, in the example above, would have to register with every state charity office simply because it has a website that asks for a contribution. This would work an enormous burden on small nonprofits.

Fortunately, most state nonprofit regulators realize that it is impractical (and likely unconstitutional) to literally apply their solicitation laws to all Internet fundraising. Thus, most states do not require a nonprofit to register in a state simply because it has a website that can be viewed there. Unfortunately, determining when a website requires registration can be complex.

Some Guidelines to Follow— The Charleston Principles

In 2001, the National Association of State Charity Officials (NASCO) issued detailed guidelines on when the existence of a website alone should give rise to an obligation to register with a state. These guidelines are called the Charleston Principles because they were adopted during a NASCO meeting in Charleston, South Carolina. Under these guidelines, registration in a state is required only if:

- the nonprofit's website is used to make charitable solicitations, and
- the nonprofit has sufficient fundraising contacts with state residents, whether through the website or by other means.

Thus, under the Charleston Principles, you do not need to register with a state simply because you have a website that people in the state can view. Something more is needed, such as sending a fundraising email to state residents, applying for grants from private or government funders in the state, or making telephone solicitations there. In the words of NASCO, "the ultimate … question, roughly put, is 'Has someone purposefully directed a charitable solicitation to a resident of our state?'"

However, it is important to remember that these guidelines are not legally binding on any state. They merely represent the "informal, non-binding advice of the NASCO Board of Directors to NASCO members." NASCO is not a government agency—it is a nonprofit membership organization for state charity officials. Nevertheless, with some important exceptions noted below, most states follow the Charleston Principles (more or less). Two states—Colorado and Tennessee—have incorporated the principles directly into their charitable solicitations law. Two states—New York and Jew Jersey—do not follow the principles. You can download a free copy of the principles from the NASCO website at www.nasconet.org.

By answering the following questions, you can determine whether the Charleston Guidelines require you to register your nonprofit in a particular state because of your website. Of course, the fact that the existence of your website does not by itself require your nonprofit to register does not mean it won't be required to register for other reasons—for example, because you send postal mail to prospective donors in the state or conduct a telemarketing campaign there.

Does Your Website Solicit Donations?

The first consideration is whether your nonprofit uses its website to solicit charitable contributions. As explained in Chapter Two, "charitable solicitation" is defined broadly to include any instance where a nonprofit asks for money or property (or to sell a product or service) and an appeal to a charitable purpose is made, the name of a charity is used, or it's implied that all or part of the money will be used for a charitable purpose or donated to charity. Obviously, any website with a "donate now" button or other link from which a donation can be completed is asking for contributions.

Of course, not all nonprofit websites are used to solicit contributions. Maintaining or operating a website that is used solely to provide program services through the Internet does not, by itself, require registration. This is true even if unsolicited donations are received because of information obtained from the website. So a website used solely to provide the public with information or other services, and not to solicit donations, would not require registration.

If your website is not being used to make a charitable solicitation, it does not require that you register with the state charity office. And you do not need to read any further.

Always Register in Your State of Domicile

Nonprofits that solicit through a website are always required to register in the state where they have their main office. This is called the state of domicile. This is true whether the Internet solicitation methods it uses are passive or interactive as described below. Moreover, registration is required even if the Internet solicitations are conducted by another entity with which the nonprofit contracts, such as a professional fundraising company.

Is Your Website Interactive?

It's when a nonprofit is not domiciled within a state that things get complicated. The first thing you must consider is whether your website is interactive. An interactive website is one that allows you to directly accept contributions (or sell a product or service involving an appeal to charity). For example, if your website allows users to donate by providing their credit card information or using electronic funds transfers from online payment vendors such as PayPal, then your site is interactive. In this context, "interactive" means that the entire transaction can be immediately completed online. It doesn't matter whether you (the nonprofit) collect and process donors' credit card information or whether the transaction is completed through the use of linked or redirected sites, such as www.4Charity.com, www.contribute.com, or www.clickandpledge.com. Moreover, your website will be considered interactive if it has this capacity, regardless of whether donors actually use it.

The fact that your website is interactive does not necessarily mean you must register. The Charleston Principles require a nonprofit with an interactive website to register only if it:

- specifically targets state residents for contributions, or
- receives substantial contributions from state residents on a repeated and ongoing basis through or in response to the website solicitation.

Thus, under these principles, a nonprofit with an interactive website need not register in a state in which it is not domiciled if it carefully avoids making any solicitations in the state and receives little or no money from there.

CAUTION

New York and New Jersey don't follow the Charleston Principles. In their view, any nonprofit with an interactive website is making charitable solicitations and must register in their states. This is true even if the nonprofit does not specifically target state residents or receive substantial contributions from them.

Targeting state residents. A nonprofit specifically targets state residents if (1) its website expressly or impliedly requests contributions from them, or (2) it directly solicits them through other means such as advertising, telephone contacts, or email (but see the discussion of email below).

> **EXAMPLE:** Homeward Bound, a St. Louis nonprofit that delivers meals to the needy, has a website with a donate button. It regularly sends fundraising emails to residents of Illinois, though it receives few contributions from there. Homeward Bound must register in Illinois because it has an interactive website, and is specifically targeting Illinois residents with fundraising solicitations (the emails).

On the other hand, a nonprofit that operates on a purely local basis, or within a limited geographic area, does not target states outside its operating area if its website makes it clear that its fundraising focus is limited to that area.

> **EXAMPLE:** Save Our Streets (SOS) is a small nonprofit dedicated to raising funds to help upgrade the streets and roads of Pittsville, Pennsylvania. It has a two-page website with a donate button. The website calls on all residents of Pittsville to chip in to help the city repair the streets. It makes clear that all funds collected will be used for that local purpose only. SOS has made no effort to raise funds from anyone other than Pittsville residents. Even though SOS has an interactive website that can be viewed by people throughout the

United States, under the Charleston Principles, it need not register outside of Pennsylvania.

Substantial contributions. Even if your nonprofit does not specifically target the residents of a state, under the Charleston Principles, it will still have to register there if it has an interactive website and receives substantial contributions from residents of that state. Unfortunately, what constitutes "substantial contributions" is not made clear in the principles. Both the total amount received and number of contributors from the state must be considered.

The principles include an example in which the threshold is at least one hundred online contributions from state residents and at least $25,000 in total online contributions from the state in the year. However, this is just an example. Each state is free to set its own numerical limits. In Colorado, for example, a nonprofit receives contributions on a repeated and ongoing basis if it receives at least 50 online contributions from Colorado residents at any time in a year; and it receives substantial contributions if it receives $25,000 or 1% of its total contributions, whichever is less, in online contributions from Colorado residents in a fiscal year. In Tennessee, the limits are 100 or more online contributions at any time in a year, and $25,000 in annual online contributions. Most states, however, have not adopted a specific numerical threshold for determining when online contributions from state residents are sufficiently substantial and repeated to require registration.

EXAMPLE: Blackout Theatre, a nonprofit theater company located in Lexington, Kentucky, has an interactive website. Blackout actively fundraises only in Kentucky, and has never sent a fundraising email or other solicitations outside the state. Last year it received $4,000 in donations from Tennessee residents—primarily people who attended one or more of its theater events. Blackout did not need register in Tennessee because its total contributions from there were well under the state's $25,000 annual limit. This year, however, Blackout received $30,000 in donations from Tennessee, including a $20,000 grant from a private foundation located in Nashville. Blackout must now register in Tennessee.

TIP

Use a disclaimer to avoid registration requirements. If your nonprofit's website clearly indicates that it is not seeking contributions from residents of a particular state, then the website alone does not give rise to a registration requirement in that state. Thus, one easy way to avoid having to register in a state because of your website is to include a disclaimer on the site saying that your nonprofit does not accept donations from residents of the state.

If Your Website is Non-Interactive

Your nonprofit's website is non-interactive if it contains a solicitation, but donors cannot complete their donation online through the site itself or through a link on the site. A non-interactive website gives rise to an obligation to register if it meets the requirements for an interactive website discussed above—specifically targeting state residents or receiving substantial contributions. However, because the contribution cannot be entirely completed online, additional ties to the state are necessary to require registration there. Specifically, one of the following two additional conditions must be present:

- the non-interactive website specifically invites further off-line activity to complete a contribution—for example, by providing a postal address where contributions can be sent, or a telephone number to call to make a donation, or
- the nonprofit has other contacts with state residents—for example, it sends them email, advertises, or takes other steps to drive traffic to its website, or it takes other steps to direct its message specifically to persons physically located in the state.

EXAMPLE: Taplight, a California-based nonprofit, tracks lobbyist contributions to politicians. It has a website, but does not accept online donations. Its website, therefore, is non-interactive. However, the website contains an address to which donors can send contributions by postal mail. Taplight has never targeted residents of Georgia—it has never sent any fundraising email there, advertized there, or made any other solicitation directly to Georgia residents; and it has never received any contributions from Georgia. It need not register in

Georgia. On the other hand, Taplight has sent fundraising emails to prospective donors in Illinois so it must register in that state because it has targeted donors there by sending emails to them.

> CAUTION
> **Follow-up fundraising contacts may require registration.** Even if your nonprofit is not initially required to register in a state because of its website, it can easily end up having to do so if it receives a donation from someone in that state who visits the site. The initial donation won't require registration, but any direct follow-up requests for donations to the state resident by postal mail, telephone, email, or other means will give rise to a duty to register in the donor's state.

EXAMPLE: The Sons of Texas is a Texas-based nonprofit that has never solicited in Massachusetts. Joe, a Boston resident, happens on the nonprofit's website and mails in a small contribution. The nonprofit places Joe on its mailing list and sends him periodic emails requesting further donations. Sons of Texas must now register in Massachusetts because it has solicited contributions there.

Crossing State Lines by Email

Under the Charleston Principles, if you solicit charitable contributions by sending emails to a resident of a state, you are treated the same as if you had solicited that person by telephone or direct mail, if you knew, or reasonably should have known, that the recipient was a resident of, or was physically located in, that state. Of course, email addresses normally don't include geographic information about the recipient's physical location. So your nonprofit may send emails to prospective donors without knowing where they reside. In this event, the email is not treated as a charitable solicitation unless you should have known where the recipient was located.

However, in many cases, you know or should know the geographic location of the people to whom you are sending emails. For example, the Charleston Principles provide that a nonprofit should have known where an email recipient resided if the person previously made an online donation

The Charleston Principles Flowchart

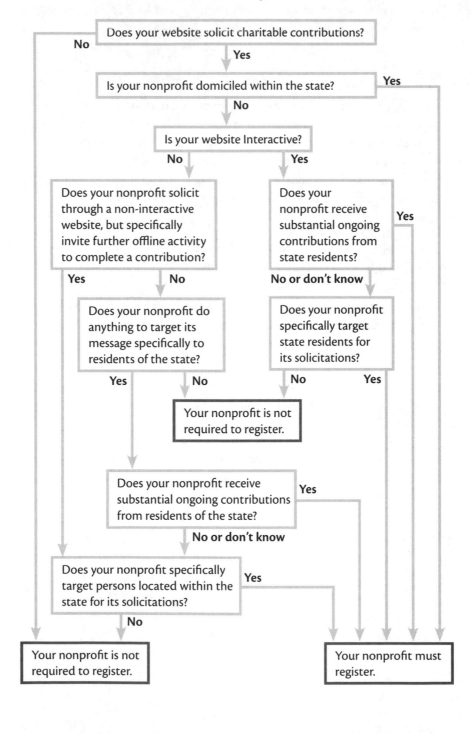

and the nonprofit received the donor's billing address as part of the credit card transaction. Similarly, a nonprofit should know an email recipient's state if the person provided a zip code—while signing up for an e-newsletter or to download material from the nonprofit's website.

Using Charity Portals to Receive Donations

Charity portals or gateways are websites that contain a directory of nonprofits to which the public may contribute. They accept and process donations from visitors on behalf of the charities listed and then distribute the money to them. Their job is to attract lots of traffic to their site and encourage visitors to make contributions to the nonprofits listed. One of the best known charity portals is Network for Good, which is operated by a donor-advised fund—a tax-exempt nonprofit that exists to distribute funds to other nonprofits. Another portal is www.justgive.org, which is also a donor-advised fund. Donors can use these websites to make online contributions to virtually every tax-exempt nonprofit in the United States.

Technically, when a donor contributes through a website like www. networkforgood.org, the donation is made to the Network for Good donor-advised fund, not to the nonprofit to which Network for Good ultimately forwards the money. For this reason, the donor's credit card statement lists Network for Good as the payee. Under federal law, a donor who gives money to a donor advised fund can recommend to the fund the charity to which he or she wishes the money to go to, but the fund has the final say over the distribution. If a valid charity is recommended, the recommendation is almost always followed. However, the donor-advised fund, not the donor, has ultimate control of the funds.

Donor-advised funds like Network for Good and www.justgive.org have usually already registered in all the states where they are required to register. It seems likely that a nonprofit that receives money from such a fund would not have to register in a state for that reason alone. Indeed, the Charleston Principles indicate as much. They provide that in such situations "states should consider whether, as a matter of prosecutorial discretion, public policy, and the prioritized use of limited resources" it makes sense to require such nonprofits to register.

Soliciting Through Online Social Networks

Online social networks such as Facebook, Twitter, MySpace, and YouTube have taken the nonprofit world by storm. Many nonprofits send out Twitter messages every day to inform the world of their doings, while over 30,000 nonprofits have Facebook pages.

Under the Charleston Principles, if you use these websites to solicit contributions and you meet the requirements for an interactive or non-interactive website discussed above, then you would have to register. For example, if your nonprofit's Facebook page contains a "donate now" button, you would be soliciting contributions through the page. Under the Charleston Principles, the Facebook page would be an interactive website. You'd have to register if your nonprofit targeted a state's residents or received substantial contributions.

On the other hand, if you use a website like Facebook or Twitter or one of the others only to provide the public with information about your mission or activities and not to solicit contributions—either expressly or impliedly—then you wouldn't need to register.

> **EXAMPLE:** Warming Planet, a nonprofit that seeks to help halt global warming, sends out weekly Twitter messages announcing new developments in scientific research on global warming throughout the world. Such informational messages wouldn't constitute charitable solicitations.

What about "viral" fundraising where, on their own initiative, members of the public use software to create their own individual pages on websites such as Facebook to solicit donations from family, friends, co-workers, and others? No one in authority has yet addressed this question, since this form of fundraising is so new. However, if the nonprofit is not directly involved in the solicitation, it seems logical that it should not have to register.

> **EXAMPLE:** Nancy, a Facebook user with an interest in global warming, urges all her friends on Facebook to donate money to the nonprofit Warming Planet. Since this was done without Warming Planet's knowledge or consent, it shouldn't constitute a charitable solicitation by the nonprofit.

The Unified Registration Statement

Registering your nonprofit to fundraise in multiple states is burdensome—no question about it. First, you need to figure out which states you have to register in. That alone is a difficult task—simply accepting donations through your website can trigger registration requirements in certain states. Once you figure out where you may have to register, you need to look at that state's rules to see whether you fall within an exemption. Then, imagine having to fill out as many as 40 different registration applications. That could be a nightmare. Fortunately, there is an easier way: a unified registration form that can be used to register in multiple states. This chapter goes over this form—the Unified registration Statement (URS)—and how to complete it, including line-by-line instructions.

The Unified Registration Statement

As its name implies, the Unified Registration Statement (URS) is a fund-raising registration application form designed to be used in any state that chooses to adopt it. It was created by the National Association of State Charity Officials (NASCO) and the National Association of Attorneys General as part of their Standardized Reporting Project. The purpose was to help simplify the registration process by creating one application form that could be used in any state. As shown in the chart below, 36 states allow nonprofits to use the URS when they register to fundraise in their state.

While having a single application form to register in multiple states can reduce the pain of registering, it is not a panacea. For one thing, as many as 16 states that accept the URS also require nonprofits to submit additional forms and documents along with it. This tends to lessen, if not destroy, the purpose of a uniform form. Moreover, because the form was designed to include all the information that might be required by any state, the URS is longer and more difficult to complete than many of the states' application forms. That's why, if you're registering in only one or two states, you probably won't want to bother with the URS. In addition, in all but six states, you can only use the URS for your initial registration. You have to use the individual state forms to renew your registration or file your annual financial reports as required by the different states.

States That Accept the URS	
State	**Special Conditions**
Alabama	None
Alaska	None
Arizona	None
Arkansas	State Consent for Service Charitable Organization form must also be filed
California	Nonresident nonprofits only
Connecticut	None
District of Columbia	D.C. Basic Business License application form must also be submitted
Georgia	State Control Persons form must also be submitted
Illinois	Certificate of Authority to Transact Business from the Illinois Secretary of State must also be submitted
Kansas	Form FS must be submitted if no Form 990
Kentucky	None
Louisiana	None
Maine	1st page of Maine Application for Licensure as an Exempt Charitable Organization must be attached
Maryland	None
Massachusetts	Nonresident nonprofits only
Michigan	Some applicants must also submit Michigan Statement of Functional Expenses form
Minnesota	Minnesota Supplement to Unified Registration Statement form must also be submitted
Mississippi	State Annual Financial Statement Report Form must also be submitted
Missouri	None
New Hampshire	None
New Jersey	None
New York	None
North Carolina	None
North Dakota	North Dakota Charitable Organization Registration Statement must also be submitted

States That Accept the URS (continued)	
State	**Special Conditions**
Ohio	Online registration optional
Oregon	If applicant registers solely in Oregon, the state application form, Form RF-C, Registration for Corporation, should be used instead of URS
Pennsylvania	Online registration optional
Rhode Island	Online registration optional
South Carolina	None
Tennessee	Online registration optional State Summary of Financial Activities must be submitted
Utah	State Supplement to Unified Registration Statement must also be submitted
Virginia	None
Washington	Washington State Unified Registration Addendum form must also be submitted
West Virginia	State Unified Registration Statement Supplement must also be submitted
Wisconsin	Applicants may also have to submit a state financial report or affidavit

States That Don't Accept the URS	
State	**Special Conditions**
California	Nonprofits located in the state must use state form
Colorado	Online filings only
Florida	None
Hawaii	Online filings only
Maine	Exempt nonprofits (as defined by state law) must use state form. (Nonexempt nonprofits can use URS.)
Massachusetts	Nonprofits located in the state must use state form
New Mexico	Online filing only
Oklahoma	None

Despite these drawbacks, if you need to register in a lot of different states—particularly if you're doing it all at once—you'll likely want to use the URS. However, using the URS is never mandatory. You're always free to use a state's individual registration form instead.

The URS Registration Process—Step by Step

You can download (for free) the URS registration kit from the Multi-State Filer Project website at www.multistatefiling.org/index.html. The kit includes the URS form, detailed instructions, copies of the supplementary forms required by several states, checklists, and an appendix with summaries of all the states' registration requirements. However, don't rely on the appendix included with the Multi-State Filer Project kit—it was out of date at the time this book was published. Instead, refer to Appendix A in this book for information on each state's specific filing requirements and Appendix B for copies of the supplemental forms required in thirteen states. These supplemental forms are state-specific forms that must be filed with the URS in addition to any governing or other documents, such as articles of incorporation or a Form 990.

Now let's go through the steps you need to take to complete and file your URS application:

Step 1: Complete one copy of the downloaded application form, leaving the reporting year line, Item 17, and the signature lines blank.

Step 2: Make a photocopy of the completed form for each state in which you want to register.

Step 3: For any state that requires it, complete the reporting year line at the top of the form and Item 17.

Step 4: Download and complete any required state supplemental forms. Supplemental forms are required by Arkansas, District of Columbia, Georgia, Maine, Michigan, Minnesota, Mississippi, North Dakota, Utah, Washington, West Virginia, and Wisconsin. Copies of these forms are included in Appendix B to this book. To make sure this is still the most up-to-date version of the form, check the state websites listed in Appendix A and make sure it is the same version as the one in the appendix.

Step 5: Have each separate application form signed—and, if necessary, notarized—depending on each state's requirements (see Appendix A for each state's signature requirements).

Step 6: Collect and attach any documents that must accompany the application—typically, copies of articles of incorporation, bylaws, IRS determination letter, or filed IRS Form 990s. Each state's requirements are listed in Appendix A and are summarized in the checklist at the end of this chapter.

Step 7: Write a check for each state's prescribed registration fee, if any (again—see Appendix A for the amount of the fee and who to you need to make it out to).

Step 8: Mail your registration packages to each state's administering agency. (See Appendix A for the name of the agency and the mailing address.)

How to Complete the URS

Now let's take a look at the URS form itself. It's not particularly long or complicated but you need to fill it out completely and accurately. Remember, this will be a public document available for anyone to view. We'll go through the form and provide some tips and point out some pitfalls you'll want to avoid. A copy of the URS form is included in Appendix B. You can refer to the form as we go line by line through it.

Top of the Form

Initial or renewal. Check the box for "Initial Registration" if this is your first time registering in the state. If you're using the URS to renew your registration, check "Renewal/Update." Only Kentucky, Louisiana, Michigan, Mississippi, Minnesota, and Ohio permit you to use the URS to renew your registration.

Reporting year. Leave this item blank when you first complete the application. You are supposed to insert here the state-specific date for the registration period covered by your URS. You need to provide a date here only if you are using the URS to renew a previous registration, or your initial registration is for a state with a fixed-date reporting cycle—that is, all registrations in the state end on a specific date. Registrations end on a fixed date in the following states:

- Alaska (September 1)
- Arizona (September 1)
- Kentucky (December 31)
- Maine (November 30)
- Utah (January 1, April 1, July 1, or October 1, depending on your initial filing date)
- Wisconsin (July 31)

If the state has one-time only registration, insert "N/A" in the reporting year line. The following states have one-time only registration: Alabama, Hawaii, Illinois, Minnesota, Missouri, New Mexico, North Dakota, and Oregon.

Filer EIN. Fill in your organization's federal Employer Identification Number (EIN).

State. (Complete this step on each state's copy.) Specify the state where this particular URS application will be sent.

State ID. (Complete this step on each state's copy.) If this is a renewal or update, specify the state-specific identification (a unique file, license, or identifying number) your organization has been assigned by the state to which you are submitting this copy of the URS. If it's your initial application, leave this item blank.

Contact Information (Items 1-5)

Item 1. Provide your nonprofit's legal name. If your nonprofit is a corporation, your legal name is the name that appears in your articles of incorporation. This may be different from the name you use in your day-to-day operations. If you used a different legal name in a prior URS filing, state that name or any other names your organization may be identified or known as in the "previous name" space. Under "other names," list any distinctive names such as the name of a particular campaign or any other names the organization uses for solicitation purposes (for example, "The Oakland New Library Project" of the Friends of the Oakland Library).

Item 2(A) and (B). Provide your street address in item 2(A) and your mailing address, if different (usually a PO box), in item 2(B).

Item 3. Provide the information requested, including your organization's email and website address if they are used to provide information to or communicate with the public.

Item 4. For this item, you must attach a list with the complete names and addresses of all your other offices, chapters, branches, and/or affiliates. For Kansas, Maine, Mississippi, and Tennessee, you must specifically state in that state's application the offices, chapters, branches and/or affiliates for that state.

Your Legal Status (Items 5-6)

Item 5. List the date your nonprofit was incorporated and the state of incorporation. The date will be in your articles of incorporation. Also, insert the end date for your nonprofit's fiscal year—for example, if you use the calendar year, insert "December 31."

Item 6. Most nonprofits are corporations, but not all. If your nonprofit is not incorporated, list in item 6 the type of organization it is and the date it was formed. Most nonprofits that are not incorporated are unincorporated associations. If this is the case for your nonprofit, insert "unincorporated association" in item 6.

Do You Have a Rap Sheet? (Items 7A-D)

This is where the URS starts to get serious. Items 7A though 7D all ask questions about whether your nonprofit has run into any trouble with the government in the past. If you answer "yes" to any of these questions, you must attach a written explanation. Keep in mind that all the information you provide will be a public record and will be freely available for anyone to read on a state website. You will want to carefully explain why your nonprofit may have encountered problems in the past.

Item 7A. Check the appropriate box as to whether your organization has ever been enjoined or prohibited from soliciting donations by a government agency or court. This covers any state, not just the one you are applying to.

Item 7B. Check the appropriate box as to whether your organization has ever had its registration denied or revoked. Again, this covers any state, not just the one you are applying to.

Item 7C. This item asks whether your nonprofit has "been the subject of a proceeding regarding any solicitation or registration." The word "proceeding" in this context means a court case or any type of investigation or legal or administrative action by a government agency involving your nonprofit's fundraising or registration. Presumably, the intent of this question is to discover whether your nonprofit was investigated or otherwise subject to government action, without having had your registration denied or revoked, or having received an injunction or other legal order preventing you from soliciting.

For example, you would not have been involved in a proceeding if a secretary of state's office sent your nonprofit a letter informing you that your annual renewal was overdue. But you would have been the subject of a proceeding if a state charity agency investigated your nonprofit and imposed a fine because your renewal registration was late.

Item 7D. Check the appropriate box as to whether your organization has ever entered into a voluntary agreement of compliance with a government agency or in a court or administrative case. A voluntary agreement of compliance comes about where a government agency or court finds that something your nonprofit is doing is illegal, and you agree in writing to stop doing it.

Previous Registrations (Items 7E-F)

Item 7E. This item asks if you have applied for, but not yet received or completed, your registration or exemption from registration in any state. If you answer "yes" to this item, you must attach a "written explanation" regarding the states where your registration or exemption is not yet complete. This means you would list all the states where you have sent in an application for registration and those where you have requested an exemption. You should include the date of the request and that its status is pending. Only 12 states require you to apply for an exemption. You should not include states where you are exempt but are not required to apply for exemption.

Item 7F. This item asks if you are registered with or have obtained an exemption from any state or agency. If you answer "yes" to this item, you must attach a list of all the states showing the ones where you are registered and the ones from which you have obtained an exemption. Include the name of the registering agency, the date of registration or exemption, the registration numbers, and any other names under which your organization is or was registered or exempted.

Previous Solicitations (Item 7G)

Item 7G. This item asks if you have solicited funds in any state. This apparently innocuous item can be quite dangerous. If you answer "yes" and you are applying for an initial registration, you must give the specific date when you began soliciting in that state. In almost all states with charitable solicitation laws, you are supposed to register before you solicit in the state. (The only exception is California where you have until 30 days after you receive your first donation to register). If you solicited in a state before you registered there, the state agency may require you to pay a late fine and/or file a separate registration for the prior years when you when supposed to have registered.

If you answer "no" to this question but intend to begin soliciting, you must give the approximate date that you expect to start soliciting in that state. This date should be some time after the date you expect to complete your registration.

Your IRS Status (Items 8-9)

Item 8. This item asks whether your nonprofit has been recognized as tax-exempt by the IRS. If so, you should have a determination letter from the IRS. You need to specify the IRS code section number for your exempt status (for example, "501(c)(3)" or "501(c)(4)"). Most states require you to provide a copy of your determination letter with your state registration application.

Item 9. This item asks if your exempt status has ever been denied, revoked, or modified. Check the appropriate box and attach a written explanation if your answer is "yes." The IRS should have provided you with an explanation for its action that you can use here.

How You Solicit Contributions (Item 10)

Item 10. Check all the appropriate boxes that describe any methods of solicitation you use. In the blank "Other" space, specify any solicitation method you use that is not listed. This would include Internet fundraising or any type of solicitations you do through a website. Also, if you raise money by operating or sponsoring games of chance, such as bingo or casino nights, you must state that here, specifying the name of the game or event. If you list games of chance, be sure to make clear what states these are used in. Many states have special legal requirements for nonprofits that operate such games.

Describe Your Purposes and Programs (Items 11-12)

Item 11. The National Center for Charitable Statistics has developed a system for classifying nonprofits called the National Taxonomy of Exempt Entities (NTEE). There are 26 major groupings for nonprofits under the NTEE system. Select the code letter that best describes your organization's primary purpose or field of endeavor. If no single code is adequate, you can enter a second or third code. The codes are:

- **A** Arts, culture, humanities
- **B** Educational institutions & related activities
- **C** Environmental quality, protection & beautification
- **D** Animal related
- **E** Health—general & rehabilitative
- **F** Mental health, crisis intervention
- **G** Disease, disorders, medical disciplines
- **H** Medical research
- **I** Crime, legal related
- **J** Employment, job related
- **K** Food, nutrition, agriculture
- **L** Housing, shelter
- **M** Public safety, disaster preparedness & relief
- **N** Recreation, sports, leisure, athletics
- **O** Youth development
- **P** Human services

Q International, foreign affairs, national security

R Civil rights, social action, advocacy

S Community improvement, capacity building

T Philanthropy, voluntarism and grantmaking foundations

U Science and technology research

V Social science research

W Public affairs, society benefit

X Religion, spiritual development

Y Mutual/membership benefit

Z Unknown, unclassifiable

Item 12. Here you are asked to describe your purposes and the programs you have and for which you solicit funds. You can get this information from any Form 990 or 990-EZ you've filed with the IRS. If you have none, your IRS Form 1023, *Application for Recognition for Exemption*, will have this information. Again, remember that the URS is a public document. This is the place to sell your nonprofit and its programs.

Officers, Directors, and Employees (Items 13-14)

Item 13. For this item, you need to attach a list of the officers, directors, and executives of your organization, specifying their residence addresses and telephone numbers. Note carefully that their individual residence addresses are required, not your nonprofit's office address. This means that the residence addresses of your nonprofit's officers, directors, and executives will become a public record. Many states—California, for example—don't require residence addresses in their individual registration applications. So, if you don't want to list residence addresses, don't use the URS.

You can include a daytime phone number instead of the residence phone number if the person can generally be reached at that number during normal business hours.

Item 14. The information in item 14 can be important because it can indicate that one or more officers, directors, or employees has a conflict of interest with your nonprofit. A conflict of interest arises when a person in a position of authority over a nonprofit, such as a director, officer, or manager, may benefit personally from a decision he or she could make. Because the

URS is a public document, anyone can examine it and see if such a conflict exists.

Item 14(A)(1) and **(2).** Check the appropriate box for each of these items. If you answer "yes" to any of the relationships described you will need to attach a separate sheet that specifies the relationship and provides the names, businesses, and addresses of the related parties. In addition, you will want to show that you followed IRS rules for related party transactions.

Related persons. Item 14(A)(1) asks whether any of your organizations' officers, directors, trustees, or employees is related to (1) any other officers, directors, or employees; (2) any hired fundraising professionals; or (3) any firm or member of a firm that provides goods or services to your nonprofit. If any such relationship exists, there is a conflict of interest.

Financial interests. Item 14(A(2) requires you to identify any conflicting financial interests between any officer, director, employee or anyone with a financial stake in the organization and any business transaction or organization doing business with your nonprofit. For example, a conflict of interest exists if an officer, director, or board member owns a business that wants to enter into a contract to do business with your nonprofit.

As a general rule, your nonprofit is not barred from doing business with people or firms with whom one or more of your officers, directors, or employees has a conflict of interest. Indeed, this happens all the time and is permissible as long as your nonprofit follows IRS rules for related party transactions. In responding to the questions, you should clearly describe the conflict (including the specific information requested— the transaction, and the name, businesses, and addresses of the related parties). You should also describe the specific measures you have taken to ensure that—despite the conflict—the transaction was fair and in the organization's best interest. To do this, you should show that you followed IRS rules on related party transactions. These rules should already be in place as part of your organization's governance policies—check your bylaws or other organizational documents. Generally, they require that anyone with a conflict not be involved in the review or approval of the transaction with the conflict and that the transaction is otherwise fair and in the best interests of the organization. So, for example, if you had a transaction where a director owned a company that wanted to do business with your nonprofit, in addition to describing the transaction and parties involved, you would want to describe how the transaction was approved (without that director's involvement) and that the transaction itself was fair and in the best interests of the organization. (For more guidance on conflicts and related party transactions, see *Every Nonprofit's Tax Guide*, by Stephen Fishman (Nolo).)

Who Handles the Money and Checks the Books (Items 15-16)

Item 15. This is self-explanatory. You need to provide the names and addresses of the people listed. Make sure you clearly indicate which person has which responsibility. You also need to specify the names, addresses, and phone numbers of all the banks and all accounts (with account numbers) where you have funds. The person responsible for "custody" of funds means the person with legal custody—usually the treasurer. The person responsible for "distribution" of funds means the person who has the primary day-to-day authority over the disposition of the organization's funds (usually the president or chief executive).

   Item 16. Here you provide information about your accountant or auditor. If you don't have an accountant, you should find one before you answer this item. All nonprofits should have an accountant—not just a bookkeeper. As the name implies, a bookkeeper keeps your books up to date—that is, inputs numbers. An accountant performs services that a bookkeeper does not, like creating financial statements such as your balance sheets.

Service of Process (Item 17)

Item 17. Leave this item blank unless you are registering in:
- Mississippi
- New Mexico
- South Carolina
- Virginia, or
- Utah.

   If your nonprofit is a corporation that is not incorporated in the state in which you are registered, it is a "foreign corporation." The five states listed above require foreign nonprofit corporations to appoint a registered agent within the state as part of the fundraising registration process. A registered agent (sometimes called a "resident agent") is a person legally designated by the organization to receive on its behalf legal documents generated in that state. Ordinarily, a nonprofit must file a separate application to appoint a registered agent. However, the states listed above —except for Illinois— permit you to do so by filling out item 17. Fill in this item only for each such state, and then, only with the name, address, and telephone number of the agent for that state.

You should also fill out item 17 if you are a foreign corporation registering in Illinois. However, you are still required to apply to the Illinois Secretary of State for a Certificate of Authority to Transact Business in Illinois and include a copy of the certificate with your URS. You must appoint a registered agent as part of this process. See Appendix A for more details.

See Chapter 6 for detailed guidance on appointing a registered agent.

Involvement with Other Organizations (Item 18)

This item requires you to identify your nonprofit's financial or ownership involvement with other organizations. If you answer "yes" to any question, you must attach an explanation with the name of the person or organization, the address, the relationship to your organization, and the type of organization (meaning nonprofit or profit and its business structure—nonprofit corporation, partnership, or unincorporated association).

Item 18(A). Check the "yes" box if your nonprofit receives funding from other nonprofits. This includes financial support from foundations, public charities, and combined campaigns. For example, check the "yes" box if you get funding from your local United Way.

Item 18(B). Check the "yes" box only if your nonprofit shares its revenue with another nonprofit or shares governance with another nonprofit. One example of revenue and governance sharing is where the regional or state chapters of a national organization share their revenue with the umbrella organization and members of the national organization serve on the boards of directors of the various chapters.

Item 18(C). Nonprofits are not owned by anybody. Nonprofit corporations don't issue stock and no one can own a percentage interest in them. Thus, you'd check the "yes" box here only if your nonprofit is a more than 10% owner of a for-profit business.

Do You Use Professional Fundraisers? (Items 19-22)

These items are important because they require you to disclose whether your nonprofit uses professional fundraisers to help raise money. Most states regulate professional fundraisers even more than they do the nonprofits they work for. Forty-five states require professional solicitors to register (or be licensed) with the state, pay an annual fee, and file annual financial reports on their solicitation activities. Most states also require that nonprofits enter into written contracts with any professional fundraisers they hire, and require that such contracts be filed with the state. Some states also mandate that certain provisions be included in the contract.

Item 19. This item asks whether you use volunteers or professionals to solicit directly. Volunteers are not paid for their services. Professionals are paid for their services. Check the second "yes" box only if you use outside professionals to help with fundraising. Employees who help with fundraising do not count.

A person solicits "directly" when they have actual physical or voice contact with potential donors, such as by making telephone calls or going door-to-door. Presumably, email contacts don't count as direct solicitation because there is no personal contact.

Item 20. If your nonprofit uses outside professional fundraisers, it is very important to complete this item correctly. You must provide a list of all outside professional fundraisers your nonprofit contracts with, and describe the services they provide. Although the terminology can vary from state to state, professional fundraisers come in three broad categories:

- **Professional fundraisers** (also called paid solicitors, professional solicitors, professional commercial fundraisers, professional fundraising firms, paid fundraisers, or commercial fundraisers). These are people or companies who, for compensation, solicit funds for charitable purposes—in other words, they ask people for money.

- **Fundraising counsel** (also called fundraising consultants or professional fundraisers). These aren't lawyers, rather they are people who, for compensation, plan, manage, or consult with nonprofits on charitable solicitations; however, they do not directly ask people for money. Direct marketing firms often fall into this category.
- **Commercial co-venturers.** These are organizations, whether nonprofits or for-profit entities, that help you earn money by selling goods or services, rather than soliciting charitable donations—for example, companies conducting "cause-related marketing" for your benefit.

For each such outside person or company, you must provide the following information on a separate sheet:

- name, address (street and post office box number), telephone number, and location of offices they use to perform work on your behalf
- a simple statement of the type of services they provide
- a description of how they are paid
- the date or dates you entered into your contract or contracts with them
- the date or dates of the campaigns or events they were involved with
- whether they solicit on your behalf, and
- whether they at any time have custody or control of donations.

Here is an example of how to complete this item included in the URS instructions: "Great Telemarketing, Inc., 543 First Ave, New York, NY, 10036, 212-555-1212; plans and manages telephone campaign for public support and awareness; GTI charges us $4.50 per completed call plus $1.50 per pledge; our contract with GTI is from January 1, 20xx to December 31, 20xx; the campaign will run from April 20xx to October 20xx; GTI, through another firm it employs, solicits donations on our behalf; GTI does not itself handle donations but employs a caging company that receives, logs, and deposits contributions."

There is no prescribed format to complete this item. If you need to list many professionals, you could organize the information into a chart or table if you prefer.

> **CAUTION**
>
> **Make sure it is clear which states the professionals you list perform their services in.** If you fail to do so, each state receiving the URS will assume all the professionals listed are subject to that state's laws and will proceed accordingly with enforcement. For example, if you file the URS in five states, but only use the fundraising professional in one of these states, the other four states will assume you are using the professional in their states as well if you fail to make clear that the professional only performs services for you in the one state. In this event, the other states may require you to submit copies of your fundraising contracts and contact the listed fundraisers and ask them why they haven't registered in their state. You can make clear where the services are performed by listing the states in each entry— for example, in the sample entry above, you could add: "Only conducts campaigns for us in New York, Massachusetts, New Jersey, and Pennsylvania."

Item 21. You need to provide the total amount paid in fees and attributable expenses to any outside fundraising professionals during the previous reporting year. Make sure to state the period covered by this total (for example, fiscal year from July 1, 2010 through June 30, 2011). You should be able to derive all or most of this total number from Line 16a of Part I of Form 990.

Item 22. Make sure that the numbers you provide in Item 22 are the same as the numbers you've already reported to the IRS in Form 990 or 990-EZ, if any. The URS instructions that describe which portions of Forms 990 and 990-EZ correspond with item 22 are out of date. Both 990 forms were extensively updated after the URS instructions were created. The following chart shows you which lines on the current Form 990 and 990-EZ correspond with the numbers asked for in item 22.

URS Item	Form 990	Form 990-EZ
Item 22(A): Total contributions	Part I, Line 12	Part 1, Line 1
Item 22(B): Program service expenses	Part I, Line 9	None
Item 22(C): Management & general expenses	Part IX, Line 25, Column (C)	None
Item 22(D): Fundraising expenses	Part 1, Line 16b	None
Item 22(E): Total expenses	Part 1, Line 18	Part 1, Line 17

Item 22(F). List here the total contributions for the year covered by this URS. Take the number listed on your Form 990, Part VIII, Line 1h and subtract from it the amount (if any) shown on Part VIII, Line 1b (membership dues). If you file Form 990-EZ, subtract the total listed in Part 1, line 3 from the amount listed in Part I, Line 1.

Item 22(G). To determine this number, divide the total of item 22C and item 22D by item 22A—that is: (item 22C + item 22D) ÷ item 22A

Item 22(H). To determine this number, divide the total in item 22B by item 22E.

Signatures

You need to create a separate URS for each state in which you register and have it signed by one or more of your nonprofit's officers or directors. Signatures can not be photocopied—the application must be executed with original signatures. Some states require one signature, some two. Some require that the application be signed by the president and/or chief fiscal officer. Others permit any authorized officer or other person to sign. See Appendix A for the requirements of each state.

In addition, the following states require that the signatures be notarized—that is, signed before a notary public who will stamp and sign the form:

- Alabama
- Arizona
- Arkansas
- Florida
- Georgia
- Maine
- Mississippi
- Missouri
- North Carolina
- North Dakota
- Ohio (if application made by mail)
- West Virginia, and
- Wisconsin.

Supplemental Documents Required With URS

Alabama

☐ Articles of incorporation

☐ Bylaws

☐ IRS determination letter

Alaska

☐ Form 990 or 990-EZ

☐ Audited financial statements

☐ Fundraiser contracts

Arizona

☐ Irs determination letter

Arkansas

☐ Supplemental state form

☐ Articles of incorporation

☐ IRS determination letter

☐ Form 990 or 990-EZ

☐ Audited financial statements if revenue exceeds $500,000

☐ Fundraiser contracts

California

☐ Articles of incorporation

☐ Bylaws

☐ IRS determination letter

Connecticut

☐ Form 990 or 990-EZ

☐ Audited financial statements if revenue exceeds $500,000

District of Columbia

☐ Supplemental state form

☐ Articles of incorporation

☐ Bylaws

☐ IRS determination letter

☐ Financial statements (statement need not be audited)

Georgia

☐ Supplemental state form

☐ IRS determination letter

☐ Form 990 or 990-EZ

☐ Audited financial statements if revenue is over $1 million; CPA review if revenue is $500,000–$1 million

☐ Fundraiser contracts

Illinois

☐ Supplemental state form

☐ Articles of incorporation

☐ Bylaws

☐ IRS determination letter

☐ Form 990 or 990-EZ

☐ Fundraiser contracts

Kansas

☐ Supplemental state form (if no Form 990)

☐ Form 990 or 990-EZ

☐ Audited financial statements if annual contributions over $500,000

Supplemental Documents Required With URS (continued)

Kentucky
- ☐ IRS determination letter

Louisiana
- ☐ Articles of incorporation
- ☐ Bylaws
- ☐ IRS determination letter
- ☐ Form 990 or 990-EZ
- ☐ Fundraiser contracts

Maine
- ☐ Supplemental state form
- ☐ IRS determination letter

Maryland
- ☐ Articles of incorporation
- ☐ IRS determination letter
- ☐ Form 990 or 990-EZ
- ☐ Audited financial statements if contributions over $500,000 million; CPA review if revenue $200,000–$500,000
- ☐ Fundraiser contracts

Massachusetts
- ☐ Articles of incorporation
- ☐ Bylaws
- ☐ IRS determination letter

Michigan
- ☐ Supplemental state form
- ☐ Articles of incorporation

- ☐ Bylaws
- ☐ IRS determination letter
- ☐ Form 990 or 990-EZ
- ☐ Audited financial statements if contributions over $500,000 million; CPA review if revenue $250,000–$500,000
- ☐ Fundraiser contracts

Minnesota
- ☐ Supplemental state form
- ☐ Articles of incorporation
- ☐ IRS determination letter
- ☐ Form 990 or 990-EZ

Mississippi
- ☐ Supplemental state form
- ☐ Articles of incorporation
- ☐ Bylaws
- ☐ IRS determination letter
- ☐ Form 990 or 990-EZ
- ☐ Fundraiser contracts

Missouri
- ☐ Articles of incorporation
- ☐ Form 990 or 990-EZ
- ☐ Fundraiser contracts
- ☐ Copies of solicitation materials

Supplemental Documents Required With URS (continued)

New Hampshire

- ☐ Articles of incorporation
- ☐ Bylaws
- ☐ IRS determination letter
- ☐ Audited financial statements if revenue over $1 million; CPA review if revenue $500,000–$1 million
- ☐ Current conflict-of-interest policy; dissolution provision

New Jersey

- ☐ Articles of incorporation
- ☐ Bylaws
- ☐ Irs determination letter
- ☐ Form 990 or 990-EZ
- ☐ Audited financial statements if revenue over $250,000

New York

- ☐ Articles of incorporation
- ☐ Bylaws
- ☐ IRS determination letter

North Carolina

- ☐ Optional annual financial report form
- ☐ Articles of incorporation
- ☐ Bylaws
- ☐ IRS determination letter
- ☐ Form 990 or 990-EZ
- ☐ Fundraiser contracts

North Dakota

- ☐ Supplemental state form
- ☐ IRS determination letter
- ☐ Form 990 or 990-EZ
- ☐ Fundraiser Contracts

Ohio

- ☐ Articles of incorporation
- ☐ Bylaws
- ☐ IRS determination letter
- ☐ Form 990 or 990-EZ

Oregon

- ☐ Supplemental state form
- ☐ Articles of incorporation
- ☐ Bylaws
- ☐ IRS determination letter

Pennsylvania

- ☐ Articles of incorporation
- ☐ Bylaws
- ☐ IRS determination letter
- ☐ Form 990 or 990-EZ
- ☐ Audited financial statements if revenue over $300,000; CPA review if revenue $50,000–$300,000

Supplemental Documents Required With URS (continued)

Rhode Island

- ☐ IRS determination letter
- ☐ Audited financial statements if revenue over $500,000; Form 990 or CPA review if revenue less than $500,000
- ☐ Fundraiser contracts

South Carolina

- ☐ IRS determination letter

Tennessee

- ☐ Supplemental state form
- ☐ Articles of incorporation
- ☐ Bylaws
- ☐ IRS determination letter
- ☐ Form 990 or 990-EZ
- ☐ Audited financial statements if revenue over $500,000
- ☐ Fundraiser contracts

Utah

- ☐ Supplemental state form
- ☐ Articles of incorporation
- ☐ Bylaws
- ☐ IRS determination letter
- ☐ Form 990 or 990-EZ
- ☐ Fundraiser contracts

Virginia

- ☐ Articles of incorporation
- ☐ Bylaws
- ☐ IRS determination letter
- ☐ Audited financial statements (may substitute Form 990)
- ☐ Fundraiser Contracts
- ☐ New nonprofits must submit budget

Washington

- ☐ Supplemental state form
- ☐ IRS Determination Letter
- ☐ Form 990 or 990-EZ
- ☐ Audited financial statements if revenue over $3 million
- ☐ Fundraiser contracts

West Virginia

- ☐ IRS determination letter
- ☐ Form 990 or 990-EZ
- ☐ Fundraiser contracts

Wisconsin

- ☐ Supplemental state form
- ☐ Articles of incorporation
- ☐ Bylaws
- ☐ IRS determination letter
- ☐ Out-of-state nonprofits must submit certificate of incorporation

Qualifying to Do Business Out of State

This chapter explains when a nonprofit corporation has to "qualify to do business" in a state before engaging in certain activities in that state. This requirement is separate from, but related to, state fundraising registration. First, in a handful of states, simply registering to fundraise triggers the qualifying to do business requirement in the state. In most states, however, your nonprofit must engage in more activity than merely registering to fundraise before it will have to qualify to do business there. Some of the activities related to fundraising can trigger the qualification requirement. We discuss both the rules related to qualifying to do business in a state and the type of activities that might trigger that requirement for your nonprofit.

What is "Qualifying to Do Business"?

If, like most nonprofits, your organization is legally organized as a nonprofit corporation, it will be incorporated in a particular state—usually where it has its main office. Legally speaking, your nonprofit corporation is a "domestic corporation" in its state of formation and a "foreign corporation" in all other states. For example, a nonprofit corporation formed in California is a domestic corporation in California and a foreign corporation in the other 49 states. "Foreign" in this context means a corporation formed out-of-state, not in a country other than the United States.

All 50 states have laws that require foreign corporations to register with the state before doing business there. The circumstances that trigger the requirement to register or qualify to do business differ state by state. When you qualify to do business in a state, it means you have secured approval from a state agency—usually the secretary of state—to conduct business or engage in certain activities in that state. This is a fairly simple process that involves appointing a registered agent in the state, filing an application, and paying a fee.

State foreign corporation laws apply to both nonprofit and for-profit corporations. They are totally separate from state charitable solicitations laws and are often administered by different state agencies. It might seem confusing that a nonprofit would have to qualify to "do business" in a state when it is a not-for-profit business. However, for these purposes "doing business" is not limited to commercial profit-making activities. Rather, it includes the exercise of any corporate function. In the case of a nonprofit corporation, this can include soliciting donations or other activities related to fundraising or carrying out its nonprofit purpose. Thus, your nonprofit may be required to qualify to do business in one or more states because of its fundraising or other activities outside its home state. Whether and where it must qualify will depend on the nature and extent of the activities it conducts outside of its home state and the rules of the particular state where it engages in these activities.

Fundraising Registration Can Trigger Qualification Requirement

A handful of states require all foreign nonprofit corporations to qualify to do business as part of the fundraising registration process under their charitable solicitations laws. In other words, your nonprofit won't be permitted to register in these states unless it qualifies to do business there. These states consider registering to conduct charitable solicitations in the state sufficient in and of itself to constitute "doing business" in the state.

These states are:
- Colorado
- District of Columbia
- Illinois, and
- North Dakota.

Michigan also requires qualification as part of the registration process if your nonprofit is a parent organization that controls one or more local, county, or area chapters in Michigan and you want these chapters included in your solicitation license.

You should qualify to do business in these states before you submit your fundraising registration application. You'll need to submit a copy of the certificate of authority to do business in the state or similar document issued to your nonprofit by the secretary of state as part of the registration process.

TIP

Some states require you to appoint an agent for service of process when you register to fundraise. A few states require you to appoint an agent for service of process when you register to fundraise, but don't require you to qualify to do business in the state. These are:

- Mississippi
- New Mexico
- South Carolina, and
- Utah.

If you file the Unified Registration Statement (URS), you can appoint your agent by completing item 17 of the application form. See the discussion below for more information about what an agent for service of process does and how to find one.

Intrastate Versus Interstate Business

If you are not in one of the four jurisdictions listed above that require nonprofits to qualify as part of the registration process, you may still have to qualify to do business in a state under its foreign corporation laws. Although every state's corporations law has its own variations on when a foreign corporation must qualify to do business, they all share one basic principle—foreign corporations must qualify in a state if they are engaged in intrastate business in that state. If the business in which they are engaged in a state is merely incidental to a larger interstate business operation, they do not have to qualify. Even in the eleven states that don't have charitable solicitation laws, foreign corporations, including nonprofit corporations, must qualify to do business if they engage in intrastate business in the state.

Most states define what constitutes "doing business" for purposes of qualification similarly because most states have modeled their state law rules after the Model Business Corporation Act. However, the exact requirements or wording can differ from state to state. You should always check the laws of the state where you are engaged in any activity to see if you need to qualify there. The first place to look to learn about a particular state's requirements is the website of the state's secretary of state or similar official. There is information on these offices with links later in this chapter in "The Mechanics—How You Qualify." Links to the corporation laws of all 50 states can be found at the Legal Information Institute's website at http://topics.law.cornell.edu/wex/table_corporations. If you are still uncertain after reading this chapter and looking at the state rules, check with a lawyer.

In-State Business That Requires Qualification

Most states define "intrastate business" (or business that requires qualification) broadly and somewhat ambiguously. In California, for example, doing intrastate business is defined as "entering into repeated and successive [business] transactions" in the state. (Cal. Corp. Code Sec. 191.) New York courts say that for a foreign corporation to be "doing business" in New York, it must engage in systematic, regular, and continuous activities constituting a fairly substantial part of its corporate business.

As a general rule, engaging in charitable solicitations in a state is not enough by itself to constitute the conduct of intrastate business requiring qualification. There must be something more. The following activities are often found to trigger qualification, regardless of whether or not they involve charitable solicitations.

- **Employees in the state.** If your nonprofit pays employees located in another a state, you are more likely than not transacting intrastate business there and required to qualify.

    EXAMPLE: An incorporated nonprofit college located in Massachusetts leases an office in New York City to serve as the fundraising headquarters in the state and hires clerical and development staff to help solicit funds. It must qualify to do business in New York.

- **Sales of goods or services within a state.** If your nonprofit sells goods or services from a location within a state—that is, the sale does not require approval from representatives of the nonprofit outside that state—or if the sale is made from inventory held in that state, most states will require you to qualify there.

    EXAMPLE: A Nevada nonprofit corporation owns and operates a thrift store in Los Angeles, California where it sells used donated clothing. It must qualify in California.

- **Providing services or labor.** Most states require qualification if your nonprofit provides services or labor within the state, unless the services or labor are incidental to an interstate sale.

    EXAMPLE: A Georgia educational nonprofit contracts with the State of Florida to provide job training to the unemployed in Miami, Florida. The nonprofit must qualify in Florida.

- **Real property.** Renting or owning real property in another state also usually constitutes doing intrastate business there.

    EXAMPLE: An Illinois nonprofit corporation rents part of a warehouse in Indiana to store donated items. It must qualify in Indiana.

In-State Business That Doesn't Require Qualification

If your nonprofit's activities in a state are primarily interstate business, you probably don't need to worry about qualifying there. Interstate business (more commonly called "interstate commerce") means transactions that are conducted across state lines—for example:

- national (not local) advertising campaigns
- postal or electronic mail or telephone solicitations from outside the state
- transactions conducted across state lines over the Internet, and
- purchasing goods within a state.

As long as you conduct any of these activities from your own state, the fact that they cross state lines to reach residents of another state does not mean you have to register in that state. Thus, for example, your nonprofit wouldn't have to qualify in a state if, from its home office, it makes phone solicitations there, sends email there, or accepts out-of-state donations from the state through its website. On the other hand, if you set up a branch office in another state and/or have employees who work there, you're going to have to qualify there.

Exempt Activities

All states exempt certain types of activities from their definition of intrastate business. In other words, most states specify certain types of activities that foreign corporations can engage in without having to qualify for business in the state. Common examples of the types of business activities that foreign corporations can conduct within a state without having to qualify are:

- holding meetings of the board of directors, or carrying on other activities concerning the corporation's internal affairs
- appearing in court, having settlement meetings, or mediating or arbitrating a dispute
- maintaining bank accounts (however, due to the Patriot Act, most banks will require a foreign corporation to qualify to do business in the state before opening a bank account)
- creating, securing, or collecting its own debts
- engaging in an isolated transaction completed within 30 days and not part of a course of similar repeated transactions
- selling through independent contractors, and
- soliciting or obtaining orders, whether by mail or through employees or agents or otherwise, if the orders require acceptance outside this state before they can become a contract.

Some of these exemptions have more application to nonprofits than others. The exemption for isolated transactions is particularly important to nonprofits. It means you can conduct occasional fundraising activities in another state and not have to qualify there.

> **EXAMPLE:** Save Historic Eugene (SHE), a nonprofit incorporated in Oregon, holds a fundraising dinner every year at a San Francisco hotel. SHE need not qualify in California because of the dinner. Holding one dinner a year in California is an isolated transaction (obviously completed within 30 days) and therefore exempt.

On the other hand, engaging in repeated special fundraising events in another state can give rise to the requirement to qualify in that state.

> **EXAMPLE:** Every year the nonprofit Save Historic Eugene conducts four charity auctions in various cities across Washington state. This repeated and ongoing activity likely means that the Oregon nonprofit must qualify to do business in Washington.

The Mechanics—How You Qualify

Qualification is a relatively simple registration process that involves filing paperwork and paying fees—similar to the procedures and fees required for incorporating. The qualification fees vary from state to state. Some states have lower fees for nonprofit corporations than for-profit ones.

The procedures differ from state to state, but usually you must:

- Complete and file a certificate of authority (or similarly titled document) to transact business in the state. The certificate contains general information about your corporation, such as its name and address and a certification that it is in good standing in its state of formation.
- Publish a notice in a newspaper. If a state requires publication of a notice in a newspaper when a corporation is formed, it usually requires the same when a foreign corporation qualifies in the state. Local newspapers or corporate service providers can help you make this publication for a moderate fee.
- Pay your annual report fees. These fees are due each year with the annual statement that gives the names of your directors and officers, agent for service of process, and other basic information.
- Appoint a registered agent or registered agent that will receive corporate documentation and accept service of process within the state.

To learn the exact requirements and procedures of the state in which you need to qualify, visit the website of the state's secretary of state or similar official. Links to all state secretary of state offices can be found at the National Association of Secretaries of State website at www.nass.org.

The states listed in the chart below do not have a secretary of state office. Instead, contact the agency listed in the chart.

State	Agency	Website
Alaska	Corporations, Business and Professional Licensing	www.commerce.state.ak.us/occ/home.htm
Washington, D.C.	Consumer and Regulatory Affairs	http://brc.dc.gov/index.asp
Hawaii	Dept. of Commerce & Consumer Affairs	http://hawaii.gov/dcca
Maryland	Department of Assessments and Taxation	www.dat.state.md.us/sdatweb/nonmaryland.html
New Mexico	New Mexico Public Regulation Commission	www.nmprc.state.nm.us/cb.htm
Utah	Division of Corporations and Commercial Code	http://corporations.utah.gov/business/dp.html
Virginia	State Corporations Commission	www.scc.virginia.gov/clk/index.aspx
Wisconsin	Department of Financial Institutions	www.wdfi.org/corporations/

Appointing a Registered Agent

A registered agent (also called a resident agent or statutory agent in some states) is a resident person or company in the state who agrees to accept legal papers on your nonprofit's behalf. Your nonprofit cannot serve as its own agent, nor can it appoint a state agency such as the secretary of state or attorney general. There are two mains types of registered agents.

Noncommercial registered agents. Any individual who resides in the state can serve as your registered agent. Business entities such as corporations can serve as well as long as they are qualified to do business in the state and have a physical address there. For example, you could use another nonprofit with an office in the state. The person or entity would have to complete a form agreeing to serve as your agent.

Commercial registered agents. There are many private companies in the business of serving as registered agents for corporations. Some of these companies operate nationally, and can serve as your registered agent in any state. This can be a real advantage if you're engaged in intrastate business in multiple states. Of course, these companies charge fees for their services. Many secretaries of state have lists of commercial registered agents in their states, usually available on their websites.

Getting Professional Help

There are a number of private companies, such as The Company Corporation (TCC) (www.corporate.com), that can assist you in preparing qualification papers, paying qualification fees, finding and appointing registered agents, and filing annual report forms in one or more states outside your nonprofit's state of formation. Using these professionals can be a real timesaver if your nonprofit must qualify in multiple states.

What If You Fail To Qualify to Do Business?

If your nonprofit corporation fails to qualify in a state in which it does intrastate business, it can be subject to financial penalties known as late-qualification penalties. Under California law, for example, there is a late-qualification penalty of $250 plus $20 per day for willful (a knowing, not inadvertent) failure to qualify. These penalties can add up: If the California Secretary of State determined that you willfully did business in California for two years prior to qualifying, the secretary of state could bill your nonprofit for approximately $15,000 (365 x $20 x 2 years = $14,600 + $250 = $14,850).

Other states simply authorize the assessment of a flat amount for failure to qualify. For example, the Florida Business Corporation Act imposes a $500 to $1,000 per year penalty for failure to qualify.

Most states will also prevent foreign corporations that fail to qualify from bringing a lawsuit in that state's courts. Under these laws (known as closed-door statutes), a court will delay or dismiss your lawsuit if the defendant objects because you did not qualify your business in the state. In some states, your lawsuit will be dismissed; in others it will be delayed until your company qualifies or pays any late qualification fees owed.

If you conclude that your activities might be considered intrastate business, it's best to qualify to do business in that state or states. That way you know you can use that state's courts to enforce your contracts and you will not have to pay a late qualification fee. Better to deal with the inconvenience and modest filing fees ahead of time rather than face the higher fees, penalties, and delays in getting into court that you might otherwise face.

State-by-State Rules for Registration

This Appendix summarizes the state fundraising registration laws and requirements of all 50 states. If you engage in any fundraising activities, you'll need to know these rules for the states where you fundraise. Otherwise, you may have registration and filing obligations that you are failing to meet. While most states follow the same basic format—requiring registration prior to fundraising, providing exemptions from registration, and annual filing requirements—the specifics vary greatly from state to state. So, for example, just because you are exempt from registration in one state does not mean you will be exempt in every state. The rules all differ so you'll need to check each state's requirements before you engage in any fundraising activities outside your home state.

We go through each state's rules for registration, exemptions, fees, and other filing or documentation requirements. We also provide other useful information such as the state's website for the agency that administers the charitable solicitations laws as well as each state's charitable solicitations laws so you can look up more information on your own.

Specifically, for each state, we provide the following information:

Governing law. This shows you where to find the state's charitable solicitations law. These laws are all available on the Internet where they can be viewed or downloaded for free.

State website. This section provides the Internet address for the website of the state agency that administers the state's fundraising registrations. Some of these websites are excellent, some not so good. Regardless, they are the first place you should look if you have a question about a state's registration rules or procedures.

Registration requirements. This explains when you are required to register in a particular state. All states (except California) require that you register before your organization solicits donations in the state or has donations solicited on your behalf by professional fundraisers or others.

Exemptions from registration. All states exempt certain types of organizations from registration. Each state's exemptions are different so you will need to go through this section carefully to determine if your organization is exempt in a particular state. Some states require you to apply for an exemption by filing a state exemption form or letter. Even if this is not required, you may ask the state agency to confirm that your organization is exempt. (See Chapter 2 for more information on confirming exemptions.)

Registration procedures. This section summarizes what you must do to register in a particular state. These rules vary a great deal from state to state.

Application form. This tells you whether you may file the Unified Registration Statement (URS) or whether you must file a state registration form or register online. See Chapter 5 for a detailed discussion on how to complete the URS.

Documents to be included with application. Almost every state requires you to provide certain documents with your application form. The requirements vary from state to state, but typically include the following:

- articles of incorporation
- bylaws, and
- IRS determination letter—this is the letter the IRS sends your nonprofit when it approves your application for tax-exempt status.

Most states also require you to submit copies of your nonprofit's most recently filed IRS Form 990 or 990-EZ, if any. If you do so, do not include the list of contributors that is on a schedule to the form. If you do provide this list, it will usually be made available to the public by the state—something your contributors may not appreciate.

Other states require copies of current contracts that your nonprofit has entered into with professional fundraisers. Still others may require you to provide audited or reviewed financial statements.

Signatures required. States vary as to whether one or two people must sign the application and whether the signatures must be notarized.

Fee. Registration fees vary widely; a few states charge nothing.

Filing procedure. This explains where and how to file the application. The majority of states require you to postal mail your application. Some require you to file online. In some states you have a choice.

Renewal registration. The great majority of states require you to renew your registration, usually every year. The procedure differs from state to state. Take special note of the state deadlines for filing the renewal, which can vary. Detailed information is provided on how to obtain an extension of time to file the renewal.

Annual financial report. Most states require registered nonprofits to provide an annual financial report of some kind. This is usually included with the annual renewal as a single filing, but in some states it is filed separately. Many states accept copies of your filed IRS Form 990 or 990-EZ; others may require you to fill out state financial report forms or submit audited financial statements.

Alabama

Governing Law

Alabama has a charitable solicitation statute codified in the Code of Alabama, sections 13A-9-70 through 13A-9-84. The law is administered by the Alabama attorney general, Consumer Affairs section, and can be accessed from its website.

State Website

The Alabama attorney general's website has a Consumer Affairs section with downloadable copies of the state laws, state forms, and some limited information about filing requirements for fundraising registration. The website address is www.ago.state.al.us/consumer_charities.cfm.

Registration Requirements

Unless exempt, a charitable organization must register with the Alabama attorney general if:

- it is located in the state of Alabama
- it intends to solicit charitable contributions in Alabama, or
- it intends to have charitable solicitations solicited on its behalf in Alabama by other charities, paid solicitors, or commercial co-venturers.

Exemptions

Alabama exempts more types of nonprofits from registration than most states. It is not necessary to apply for an exemption.

$25,000 exemption. Any charitable organization that does not intend to solicit and receive nationwide contributions of over $25,000 in one fiscal year is exempt, provided that all of its fundraising functions are carried on by unpaid volunteers. The nonprofit can have salaried staff and hire independent contractors as long as they don't perform fundraising-related functions. The nonprofit must register within 30 days if its gross contributions exceed $25,000 during any fiscal year. You don't include membership dues and similar payments in the annual limit. However, if your nonprofit sells merchandise or services, you must include the amounts you receive from those sales in your total gross contributions.

Alabama

Religious organizations. Any religious organization that qualifies as a 501(c)(3) nonprofit under federal tax law is exempt from registration in Alabama. This includes any religious society, sect, persuasion, mission, church, parish, congregation, temple, convention, diocese or presbytery, or other organization.

Educational institutions. Educational institutions are exempt. This includes schools, colleges, or other institutions which have a defined curriculum, student body, and faculty and which conduct classes on a regular basis. There is no requirement that the school be officially accredited. Foundations related to exempt educational institutions are also exempt.

Political organizations. Section 527 groups are exempt. These are groups organized under section 527 of the Internal Revenue Code to raise and spend money to elect candidates to office, and to engage in voter mobilization and issue advocacy.

Fraternal organizations. Alabama exempts fraternal, patriotic, benevolent, social, educational, alumni, historical, and civil rights organizations, and any auxiliaries associated with any such organization. This includes fraternities and sororities.

Civic leagues and civic organizations. Civic leagues and civic organizations which solicit solely from their own membership are exempt.

Donations for single individuals. It is not necessary to register if you are requesting contributions for the relief of any single individual, specified by name at the time of the solicitation. No more than $10,000 may be collected and it all must be turned over to the named beneficiary.

United Way and community chests. Nonprofits that receive an allocation of funds from an incorporated community chest or united fund are exempt provided:

- the chest or fund has complied with the registration and reporting rules
- the nonprofit does not actually receive, in addition to the allocation, contributions over $25,000 during the fiscal year, and
- all the nonprofit's fundraising is carried out by volunteers.

Other exemptions. Alabama also exempts:

- veterans organizations, including their local posts or chapters
- volunteer firefighters

- ambulance companies and rescue squads, and
- bona fide auxiliaries or affiliates of these organizations.

To qualify for these exemptions, all of the organization's fundraising activities must be carried on by the organization's members, their family members, volunteers, or an affiliate of the organization. The nonprofit's members cannot receive any compensation for their fundraising efforts.

Registration Procedure

Application form. Alabama accepts the URS or you can use the state's own application form, which is very similar to the URS. If you use the URS, you are not required to file any supplemental state forms. You can download the state form, called the *Charitable Organization Registration Statement*, from the state website.

Documents to be included with application. The following documents must be included with the application:

- articles of incorporation
- bylaws
- IRS determination letter
- Alabama tax-exempt letter, if any.

Signatures required. The application must contain the notarized signatures of the organization's president or other authorized officer, and the chief fiscal officer.

Fee. $25, payable to the Office of the Attorney General.

Filing procedure. The application form and supporting documents must be mailed to:

Office of the Attorney General
Consumer Protection Section
500 Dexter Avenue
Montgomery, Alabama 36130-0152.

Renewal registration. Alabama is unusual in that the initial registration stays in effect indefinitely, unless it is cancelled or withdrawn by the attorney general. However, your nonprofit is required to notify the Attorney General's office within 10 days of any change in the information in your initial application. To do this, file a new initial application form using the Alabama state form, and check the update box.

Annual Financial Report

Every registered nonprofit must file an annual financial report within 90 days after the close of its fiscal year—March 31st for nonprofits that use the calendar year as their fiscal year. You need not submit audited financial statements. You can submit a copy of IRS Form 990 for this purpose. However, note that the Alabama financial report is due before the due date for filing your annual Form 990 with the IRS—4½ months after the close of your tax year. Thus, unless you complete and file your Form 990 early, you won't have a current Form 990 to file with Alabama.

You can seek an extension of time to file the Alabama financial report until your Form 990 for the most recent year is completed. Call or email the Alabama Attorney General Consumer Affairs Section to do this. However, you are not required to file Form 990. You may produce your own report containing your nonprofit's gross income, expenses, and net income; a balance sheet as of the close of the fiscal year; and a schedule of the activities you carried on in fulfilling your mission and the amounts you spent doing so. There is no state form for financial reporting.

You must send in a $25 fee with the financial report, along with the *State of Alabama Charitable Organization Registration Statement Annual Renewal* form, which you can download from the state website. This form must be signed and notarized by your nonprofit's president or other authorized officer, and your chief fiscal officer.

Alaska

Governing Law

Alaska's charitable solicitations law is codified at Alaska Statutes sections 45.68.010 through 45.68.900. A copy of the law can be found on the state website. The law is administered by the Alaska Attorney General Consumer Protection Unit.

State Website

The Alaska attorney general maintains a website for the Consumer Protection Unit section at www.law.state.ak.us/department/civil/consumer/cpindex.html. This website contains links to charitable solicitation registration forms but does not have FAQs or much other useful information.

Registration Requirements

A charitable organization may not solicit contributions of money or other property in Alaska unless it is registered with the Alaska Department of Law.

Exemptions

The following nonprofits are exempt from registration. You do not have to apply for an exemption from registration in Alaska.

$5,000 exemption. Nonprofits that do not intend to raise contributions, excluding government grants, of over $5,000 during a fiscal year are exempt. So are nonprofits that do not receive contributions from more than ten people during the fiscal year. Both these limits apply nationwide, not just to Alaska.

However, to use this exemption, all the nonprofit's functions, including fundraising, must be performed by volunteers. If any officer or member of the nonprofit is paid, the nonprofit must register. Any nonprofit exempt on this basis must maintain financial records for five years that prove it qualifies for the exemption.

Religious institutions. Any church or other religious organization that is exempt from having to file an annual information return with the IRS is exempt from the registration requirements.

Political candidates and groups. Candidates for political office (local, state, or federal) are exempt. So are political parties, committees, or groups that file financial information with the State of Alaska or Federal Election Commission.

Registration Procedure

Application form. You can use either the URS or state of Alaska application form. If you use the URS, you are not required to file any supplemental state forms. The state form, called the *Charitable Organization Registration Form*, may be downloaded from the State of Alaska, Consumer Protection Unit website at www.law.state.ak.us/department/civil/consumer/charityreg.html.

Documents to be included with application. The following documents must be submitted with the registration application:

- fundraiser or solicitation contracts, if any
- Form 990 filed for the most recent year, if any—if none, not required
- audited financial report for most recent year, if any—if none, not required.

Alaska is one of the few states that does not require a copy of the nonprofit's IRS determination letter.

Signatures required. A single signature from someone authorized to sign for the nonprofit. Notarized signature is not required.

Fee. $40, payable to "State of Alaska"; payable by check or credit card.

Filing procedure. Mail or fax form (with credit card payment only) to:

State of Alaska
Department of Law
1031 W. 4th Avenue, Suite 200
Anchorage, AK 99501-1994
Fax: 907-276-3697

Renewal Registration

Time for renewal. All registrations expire on September 1st of each year and must be renewed by September 1st of each year, no matter when your nonprofit initially registered. Alaska does not grant extensions for charitable organization registrations. However, there is no late fee for filing late.

Procedure. File the *State of Alaska Charitable Organization Annual Registration Form*, which may be downloaded from the state website.

Fee. $40.

Annual Financial Report

You must file a financial report each year along with the renewal registration. You can submit a copy of your IRS Form 990 for the most recent fiscal year. If you do not have a completed IRS Form 990 for the most current fiscal year prepared at the time of registration, you can submit your most recently filed Form 990 with the registration form. You should explain on the registration form or cover letter why a Form 990 for the most recent fiscal year is not available. You can then update your file by submitting an IRS Form 990 for the most recent fiscal year when it becomes available.

If you do not use a Form 990, you can submit an audited financial report prepared for the most recent fiscal year. If you don't have a Form 990 or audited financial report, you must provide financial information on the registration form, but audited statements are not required.

Alaska

Arizona

Governing Law

Arizona has a charitable solicitations law codified at Arizona Revised Statutes section 44-6551 through 44-6561. A copy of the law is available on the state website. The law is administered by the Arizona Attorney General, Charitable Organizations section.

State Website

The Arizona secretary of state maintains a Charitable Organizations section on its website at www.azsos.gov/business_services/charities. It contains links to the state forms for fundraising registration but doesn't have any FAQs or other useful information.

Registration Requirements

Any charitable organization must register with the Arizona secretary of state before soliciting donations in the state, whether by itself or through a professional solicitor.

Exemptions

Arizona has the fewest exemptions from registration of any state. The only entities exempt from registration are:

- Arizona cities, counties, and state agencies, and
- political parties, candidates for office, and campaign committees required to file financial information with federal, state, or local election agencies.

Unique among the states, Arizona requires churches and other religious organizations to register. However, a tax-exempt religious organization is not required to provide any financial information with its registration provided that:

- it only solicits donations from the organization's membership, congregation, or previous donors
- it does not file Form 990 with the IRS, and
- the organization's conduct and fees charged for services are primarily supported and paid through government grants or contracts.

Presumably, this means that if a church charges fees for services that are not primarily supported by the government—a religious school, for example—it would have to provide financial information in the same manner as any other nonprofit.

Registration Procedure

Application form. You can file either the URS or the state form. The state form requires less information than the URS.

Documents to be included with application. The only document that must be included with the application is the nonprofit's IRS determination letter. You do not need to provide a financial report with your initial registration.

Signatures required. You must have a notarized signature of the president of the organization or an equivalent officer.

Fee. None.

Filing procedure. Mail registration to:

Ken Bennett, Secretary of State
Charities Division
1700 W. Washington, 7th Floor
Phoenix, AZ 85007

Renewal Registration

Time for renewal. Every state registration expires on September 1st of each year. You must renew your registration during the period from September 1st through September 30th.

Procedure. You must file the state *Charitable Organization Registration Form* (available on the state website). No supplemental documents are required.

Fee. None, if you file your renewal by September 30th. You will be charged a $25 late fee if you file after September 30th.

Annual Financial Report

You must include a financial report with your renewal registration. An audited report is not required. You may submit:

- IRS Form 990 filed for the previous fiscal year
- a website address where financial records are available, or

- a completed state financial report form, *Charitable Organization Financial Statement*, which may be downloaded from the state website.

Arkansas

Governing Law

Arkansas has a charitable solicitations law codified at Arkansas Code Annotated sections 4-28-401 through 4-28-416. The law can be found at the Arkansas State Legislature's website at: www.arkleg.state.ar.us/assembly/2009/2010F/Pages/Home.aspx.

State Website

The Arkansas attorney general has links to state forms for registration on its website at www.ag.arkansas.gov/pdfs/charitables/Charity_Registration.pdf. It has summaries of the state laws but not much other useful information about registration.

Registration Requirements

A charitable organization must register with the Arkansas attorney general before soliciting contributions within the state.

Exemptions

Arkansas exempts from registration the organizations listed below. However, you must apply for an exemption by filing the state *Verification of Exemption From Registration* form with the Attorney General's office. You must include a copy of your nonprofit's articles of incorporation with the form, along with an IRS determination letter or other applicable supporting document.

$25,000 exemption. Any charitable organization that does not intend to solicit, and does not actually receive, contributions over $25,000 during the calendar year is exempt, provided all of the organization's functions, including fundraising, are carried on by volunteers.

Religious organizations. Any bona fide tax-exempt religious entity is exempt.

Educational institutions. Any accredited educational institution or parent-teacher association is exempt.

Political candidates and organizations. Any candidate for national, state, or local elective office is exempt. Any political party or other committee required to file information with the Federal Election Commission or any state election commission is also exempt.

Governmental organizations. All governmental organizations are exempt, including any department, branch, or other instrumentality of the federal, state, or local government.

Nonprofit hospitals. This includes any nonprofit hospital licensed by Arkansas or any other state.

Individuals. Any person who solicits solely for the benefit of an exempt organization is exempt.

Chapters and affiliates. A chapter, branch, or affiliate of a registered parent organization is not required to register, provided the parent organization files a consolidated financial report or tax information form for itself and the chapter, branch, or affiliate. You don't need to file an exemption application under these circumstances.

Registration Procedure

Application form. You may file the URS or the state form. If you use the URS, you must file the state's *Consent for Service Charitable Organization* form with it (available on the state website).

Documents to be included with application.

- IRS determination letter of tax-exempt status or the completed IRS Form 1023, Application for Recognition of Exemption
- articles of incorporation
- most recent IRS Form 990, or IRS Form 990-EZ and the Arkansas Attachment to IRS Form 990-EZ, or the state *Annual Report of Charitable Organization* form
- audit report prepared by a CPA if your total revenue exceeds $500,000
- an executed *Consent for Service* form (available on the state website) if your nonprofit is located outside of Arkansas
- all contracts with paid solicitors, commercial co-venturers, and fundraising counsel.

Signatures required. You must provide the notarized signature of any person authorized to sign for your nonprofit.

Fee. None

Filing procedure. Mail your application to:

Office of the Attorney General—Consumer Protection Division
Attn: Charitable Registration
323 Center Street, Suite 200
Little Rock, Arkansas 72201-2610.

Renewal Registration

Time for renewal. All registrations last for one year and must be renewed by the anniversary date of your initial registration.

Procedure. You must file the state *Charitable Organization Application for Registration* form, available on the state website. Include the following documents:

- all contracts with paid solicitors, commercial co-venturers, and fundraising counsel
- an executed *Consent for Service* form, if your nonprofit is located outside of Arkansas
- your most recently filed IRS Form 990 or 990-EZ, if not previously submitted with financial report, and
- an audit report prepared by a CPA if your nonprofit's total revenue exceeds $500,000.

Fee. None.

Annual Financial Report

By May 15th of each year, each registered nonprofit must file a copy of the organization's most recently filed IRS Form 990 or 990-EZ with the Arkansas attorney general. You must include copies of all the schedules filed with the form, except any schedules of contributors to the organization. If you file Form 990-EZ, you must complete and file the Arkansas Attachment to IRS Form 990-EZ (available on the state website). This form contains a functional expense statement and a schedule of contributions showing total direct public support and government grants as separate figures.

If your nonprofit is not required to file IRS Form 990 or 990-EZ, it must complete and file the state *Charitable Organization Annual Report* form (available on the state website).

If your nonprofit has gross revenue over $500,000 in any fiscal year it is registered, you must include with your annual financial report an audit report prepared by a certified public accountant. For these purposes, "gross revenue" does not include grants or fees from government agencies.

You can obtain an extension of up to six months to file your renewal by applying in writing to the attorney general and explaining why you need the extension—for example, the necessary financial documents aren't ready.

California

Governing Law

California's state charitable solicitations law is codified at California Government Code sections 12580-12599.7 and California Code of Regulations, Title 11 sections 300-307, 311, and 999.1. Links to the law may be found on the state website. The law is administered by the California attorney general through its Registry of Charitable Trusts (despite the name, the registry handles registrations for all types of nonprofits, not just trusts).

State Website

The California attorney general has a section on its website dealing with nonprofit registration at http://ag.ca.gov/charities. This is one of the most extensive and helpful state nonprofit registration websites with forms, FAQs, links to state publications, and other information.

Registration Requirements

California's charitable solicitations law is different from other states. It provides that a nonprofit must register with the attorney general's Registry of Charitable Trusts within 30 days after it initially receives any money or property for charitable purposes. Thus, as far as nonprofits based in California are concerned, the registration requirement is triggered by the *receipt* of money or property in California, as opposed to *making a charitable solicitation* within the state. All other states require nonprofits to register before making a charitable solicitation.

Out-of-state charitable corporations must register in California if they hold property in California for charitable purposes or do business in California. Doing business in California includes soliciting donations in California by mail, advertisements in publications, or any other means from outside of California. Other examples of doing business in California include:

- holding meetings of the board of directors or corporate members in California
- maintaining an office in California
- having officers or employees who perform work in California, or

- conducting charitable programs in California.

If an out-of-state nonprofit's sole contact with California is limited to (1) making grants to people, programs, or charitable organizations located in California, or (2) maintaining financial accounts or investments at an office of a financial institution located in California, it is not considered to be doing business in California and need not register.

Exemptions

California's exemptions from registration are quite limited. Unlike most states, California does not have an exemption for very small charities—thus, even charities that raise little or no money must register. California only exempts:

- nonprofit religious organizations
- nonprofit educational institutions
- nonprofit hospitals
- licensed health care service plans
- federal or state or agencies
- religious corporations holding property for religious purposes
- political committees reporting to the California Secretary of State, and
- cemetery corporations.

It is not necessary to apply for an exemption.

Registration Procedure

Application form. If you are a nonprofit based in California, you must use the state Form CT-1, *Initial Registration Form*. You cannot use the URS. Out-of-state charitable corporations can register by filing either the URS or the state Form CT-1. Form CT-1 is a bit simpler than the URS, and should take less time to complete.

Documents included with application. Copies of the following documents must be included with your application:

- articles of incorporation and all amendments
- bylaws
- IRS Form1023, if submitted to IRS
- IRS determination letter, if received from IRS

Signatures required. The application may be signed by any single officer, director, or trustee. Notarized signatures are not required.

Fee. $25, payable to "Department of Justice."

Filing procedure. Mail your application to:

California Attorney General's Office
Registry of Charitable Trusts
P.O. Box 903447
Sacramento, CA 94203-4470

Renewal Registration

Time for renewal. All registrations must be renewed annually, even those for small nonprofits. The renewal is due 4½ months after the close of the nonprofit's tax year. If you use a calendar year, the due date is April 15th. This is the same date that IRS Form 990 and 990-EZ must be filed with the IRS.

If your nonprofit obtains an extension of time to file its annual IRS Form 990, 990-EZ, or 990-PF, that extension will be honored by the Registry of Charitable Trusts for purposes of filing the renewal registration and accompanying IRS forms. All nonprofits may obtain an automatic three-month extension of time to file the 990 forms by filing IRS Form 8868, *Application for Extension of Time to File an Exempt Organization Return*, with the IRS. By doing so, the due date for your state renewal will be extended by three months as well—7½ months after the end of your tax year (July 15th for calendar year nonprofits). File a copy of Form 8868 when you file the renewal with the state. It is not necessary to send the state a copy of Form 8868 before filing the renewal.

Procedure. File the state *Annual Registration Renewal Fee Report* (RRF-1), available on the state website. Charities with total gross revenue or assets of $25,000 or more must file with the RRF-1, a copy of their most recent IRS Form 990, 990-EZ, or 990- PF and attachments. These IRS forms may be filed electronically. See the state website for details.

Fee. Sliding scale based on nonprofit's gross income.

California

California

Gross Annual Revenue	Fee
Less than $25,000	0
$25,000–$100,000	$25
$100,001–$250,000	$50
$250,001–$1 million	$75
$1,000,001–$10 million	$150
$10,000,001–$50 million	$225
Over $50 million	$300

CAUTION

There can be harsh consequences if your nonprofit fails to file the annual renewal after being requested to do so by the attorney general. Namely:

- the California Franchise Tax Board will be notified to disallow your nonprofit's state tax exemption
- your nonprofit will be billed $800 plus interest by the Franchise Tax Board, which represents the minimum tax penalty, and
- late fees of $25 will be imposed by the Registry of Charitable Trusts for each month or partial month for which the reports are delinquent.

Moreover, your nonprofit's directors, trustees, officers, and return preparers responsible for the failure to timely file these reports will be personally liable for payment of all late fees and penalties. Charitable assets cannot be used to pay them. In other words, they must pay them out of their own pockets!

Annual Financial Report

All registered nonprofits with gross annual revenues of $2 million or more must prepare annual financial statements audited by an independent certified public accountant (CPA). The $2 million threshold excludes grants received from governmental entities if, as part of the grant, the nonprofit must provide an accounting of how it uses the grant funds.

The financial statements must follow generally accepted accounting principles and the CPA must use generally accepted auditing standards. If the accounting firm and CPA performing the audit also provide nonaudit services to the nonprofit, the accounting firm and CPA must follow the independence standards in the Yellow Book issued by the U.S. Controller General.

You do not have to file your audited financial statements with the Registry of Charitable Trusts. Instead, you must make sure they are available for inspection and copying by the California attorney general and the public no later than nine months after the close of the fiscal year they cover. For these purposes, you will be in compliance if you follow the IRS rules that apply to public inspection of Form 990 returns filed by nonprofits.

Specifically, if your nonprofit has a principal office with regular business hours, you must permit members of the public to come to your office to inspect the financial statements at regular working hours. In-person requests for inspections must be allowed on the same day the request is made. Inspections must also be allowed at any regional or district offices with at least three employees. If you don't have a permanent office, you can mail copies of the statements or arrange for personal inspection.

In addition to making the statements available for public inspection, you must furnish copies to any person who asks for them. The copying requirement is automatically deemed satisfied if the statements are "made widely available" to the public—for example, by posting them on your nonprofit's website. These rules are explained in detail in Appendix D of the *Instructions for IRS Form 990*, available from the IRS website at www.irs.gov.

Other Requirements

Applying for state tax exemption. Under California law, an out-of-state nonprofit corporation (called a "foreign corporation") is a taxable entity and must pay a $800 minimum California franchise tax each year, unless the corporation applies for and obtains tax-exempt status from the California Franchise Tax Board. After filing its *Statement and Designation By Foreign Corporation* with the California Secretary of State, a foreign nonprofit corporation may apply for tax-exempt status in California by mailing an *Exemption Application* (FTB Form 3500), along with an endorsed copy of the *Statement and Designation By Foreign Corporation* and all other required supporting documentation to the Franchise Tax Board, P.O. Box 942857, Sacramento, California 94257-4041. You can download a copy of Form 3500 from the Franchise Tax Board's website at www.ftb.ca.gov and the

Statement and Designation By Foreign Corporation from the California Secretary of State's website at www.sos.ca.gov. For further information regarding franchise tax exemption, refer to the Franchise Tax Board's website or call the Franchise Tax Board at 916-845-4171.

Colorado

Governing Law

Colorado has a charitable solicitations law codified at Colorado Revised Statutes sections 6-16-101 through 6-16-104. The law may be accessed from the state website. It is administered by the Colorado Secretary of State, Licensing Division.

State Website

The Secretary of State's Licensing Division has a website at www.sos.state. co.us/pubs/charities/charitable.htm. This is an outstanding website with extensive FAQs, tutorials on how to register online, and other information for nonprofit registration. You must register to fundraise online through this website.

Registration Requirements

Every charitable organization that solicits contributions in Colorado by any means, or that has contributions solicited in Colorado on its behalf by any other person or entity, or that participates in a charitable sales promotion, must register. You must complete the registration process before you do any solicitations in the state.

Impact of websites on registration. Colorado has adopted the Charleston Principles to help out-of-state nonprofits determine whether they must register in Colorado solely because they have a website. Of course, an out-of-state nonprofit that directly solicits Colorado residents by other means— for example, sending fundraising materials to residents—would have to register on that basis, whether or not it has a website.

The Charleston Principles are discussed in detail in Chapter 2. Under these principles and Colorado law, nonprofit websites are divided into two categories: interactive and noninteractive. A website is interactive if donors can make contributions or purchase products by electronically completing the transaction through the website, even if completion requires the use of a linked or redirected site. Noninteractive websites do not have this capacity.

A foreign (non-Colorado) nonprofit must register if it maintains an interactive website and either (1) targets people in Colorado, or (2) receives contributions on a repeated and ongoing basis or a substantial basis through its website. "Repeated and ongoing basis" means 50 or more online contributions in any fiscal year, and "substantial basis" means $25,000 or 1% of total contributions, whichever is less, in online contributions in a fiscal year.

If a nonprofit solicits contributions through a website that is not interactive, it must register if:

- it satisfies the same requirements as an interactive website above, and
- it specifically invites further offline activity to complete a contribution —for example, by including an address to send contributions or establishing other contacts with Colorado, such as sending email messages or other communications that promote the website.

Exemptions

Colorado exempts the following types of nonprofits from registration. It is not necessary to apply for an exemption.

$25,000 exemption. Charitable organizations that do not intend to, and do not actually have gross revenue over $25,000 during a fiscal year are exempt. To determine gross revenue, exclude:

- government grants
- grants from tax-exempt section 501(c)(3) organizations, and
- bona fide membership fees, dues, and similar payments.

Include all other revenue from all sources without reduction for any costs or expenses. This calculation is based on your nonprofit's nationwide income, not the income it receives just from Colorado residents.

Organizations that do not receive contributions from more than ten people nationwide during a fiscal year are also exempt.

Religious organizations. Colorado exempts tax-exempt religious organizations including:

- churches and their integrated auxiliaries
- interchurch organizations of local units of churches
- associations or conventions of churches
- exclusively religious activities of religious orders
- mission societies sponsored by or affiliated with one or more churches or denominations that spend over half of their resources to help people in foreign countries, and

- schools below college level affiliated with a church or operated by a tax-exempt religious order.

Religious organizations that file a Form 990 with the IRS are not exempt and must register.

Political groups. Political parties, candidates for federal or state office, and political action committees required to file financial information with federal or state elections commissions are exempt.

Appeals for a single person. Charitable appeals on behalf of a specific individual or family in need are not covered by the Colorado charitable solicitations law and are exempt from registration.

Registration Procedure

Registration is accomplished entirely online through the secretary of state's website. When your initial registration is approved, you will be issued a registration number and you will receive an electronic "certificate of registration" from the secretary of state in the form of a printable electronic certificate.

If your nonprofit has been in existence prior to the initial registration, you must file for every year you have been soliciting in Colorado, or three years, whichever is less.

Application form. You must use the Colorado Secretary of State's online application. You cannot use the URS. You will be guided step-by-step through the following forms:

- Registration Statement or Consolidated Registration Statement
- Annual Financial Report
- Solicitation Notice (if your nonprofit has contracted with an external paid solicitor)
- Solicitation Campaign Financial Report (if your nonprofit has contracted with an external paid solicitor)

Documents included with application. None.

Signatures required. When you initially set up the user signature account, your nonprofit will be issued a password and an authorized officer's identity is established with the web application. Whenever this authorized officer logs in with his or her password and selects the button labeled "Sign Report" near the end of the form, the system automatically

Colorado

enters the person's name on the signature line of the electronic form that is being worked on.

Fee. $10. Paid by credit card.

Filing procedure. All documents are filed online. Your nonprofit must create an account and obtain a unique user ID number.

Renewal Registration

The initial registration lasts for one year. All registered nonprofits must file a renewal registration each year thereafter.

Time for renewal. All renewals must be filed by the 15th day of the fifth month after the close of a nonprofit's fiscal year. If you use a calendar year, the due date is May 15th. This is the same date the IRS Form 990 must be filed with the IRS. If you are late with your renewal filing, you will be subject to late fees. You can extend the time to file the renewal by filing an extension on or before the filing deadline. All requests for an extension must be filed electronically on the secretary of state's website by logging in and e-filing the necessary document. Neither filing for an extension with the IRS nor submitting a copy of such a request (IRS Form 8868) to the secretary of state is sufficient to extend a state filing deadline.

Early renewal registrations. If you were unable to provide financial information covering your nonprofit's most recent fiscal year at the time of initial registration, you must update your financial information as soon as it is available by filing a renewal registration. In most cases, newly-formed charitable organizations will file an initial registration statement consisting of estimated financial information, and then file a renewal containing actual financial information by the 15th day of the fifth month after the close of the first fiscal year. Be sure to file the renewal because an initial registration consisting of estimated financial information is valid only until the 15th day of the fifth month following the close of the fiscal year for which estimated financial information was filed.

Procedure. The renewal is filed online through the secretary of state's website.

Fee. $10.

Annual Financial Report

All registered nonprofits must electronically file an annual financial report with the secretary of state by the 15th day of the fifth calendar month after the close of each fiscal year—the same time as the annual renewal. The report is filed online through the secretary of state's website by completing an online financial report form. The information on this form corresponds to certain line items on Form 990 or Form 990-EZ. You can refer to the IRS instructions for Form 990 or Form 990-EZ for more information on how to complete this form.

Requests for extensions of time to file the financial form are granted under the same terms and procedures that apply to obtaining an extension for filing a Form 990 return from the IRS. Under IRS rules, all nonprofits may obtain an automatic three-month extension of time to file the 990 forms. To obtain an extension, fill out the *File Extension* form on the state website.

Other Requirements

Colorado requires out-of-state ("foreign") nonprofits that register under its charitable solicitations law to obtain authorization to transact business in Colorado by filing a Statement of Foreign Entity Authority with the Colorado Secretary of State. This form is found on the Colorado Secretary of State's website by selecting "Business" from the homepage. An out-of-state nonprofit must select an agent for service of process in Colorado to obtain authorization to do business in the state. See Chapter 6 for a detailed discussion of appointing an agent for service of process.

All nonprofits in Colorado must include the following disclosure statement on every printed solicitation and every written confirmation, receipt, or reminder of a contribution:

> Colorado residents may obtain copies of registration and financial documents from the office of the Secretary of State, 303-894-2860, www.sos.stae.co.us/ re: Reg. No. _____ .

Connecticut

Governing Law

Connecticut has a charitable solicitations law that is administered by the Connecticut Department of Consumer Protection ("DCP"). The law is codified at General Statutes of Connecticut sections 21a-175 through 21a-1901. You can find these laws on the state website.

State Website

The Connecticut Department of Consumer Protection has a website at www.ct.gov/ag/site/default.asp with information on nonprofit registration. You can download state forms and access the state law from this website. It contains little other information.

Registration Requirements

Any organization that solicits contributions for charitable purposes in Connecticut must register with the Department of Consumer Protection prior to the commencement of solicitation and must remain registered while it solicits funds in the state.

Exemptions

Connecticut exempts the following groups and individuals from registration. It has a particularly high exemption ceiling for small nonprofits—$50,000 per year. Here are the groups exempt from registration:

- any religious corporation, religious institution, or religious society
- any parent-teacher association
- any accredited educational institution
- any nonprofit hospital licensed by Connecticut or another state
- any government agency
- any person who solicits solely on behalf of an organization described above, and
- any organization that normally receives less than $50,000 in contributions annually, provided that it does not compensate any person primarily to conduct solicitations (membership dues and similar payments need not be counted). The nonprofit can have salaried staff and hire independent contractors as long as their primary function is not to perform fundraising-related activities.

An organization falling within one of these exempt categories is not automatically exempt. The exemption must be claimed by filing Form CPC-54, *Claim of Exemption From Registration*, which may be obtained from the state website. There is no filing fee. You only have to claim an exemption once and it does not have to be renewed, although the DCP may from time to time require you to verify your continued eligibility for the exemption.

A chapter, branch, or affiliate of a registered parent organization need not file its own exemption document, provided the parent organization files a consolidated annual registration for itself and its chapter, branch, or affiliate.

Registration Procedure

Application form. You may use the URS or file the state *Charitable Organization Registration Application*, available from the state website.

Documents to be included with application. The following documents must be included with the application:

- A completed IRS Form 990, 990-EZ, or 990-PF for your nonprofit's most recently completed year. You may attach the prior year's IRS form if your most recently completed year-end IRS form is not done yet. Don't include the list of contributors contained on your Form 990 schedules. If you do, it will become a public record which your contributors may not like.

- If the Form 990 filed with the application shows that your nonprofit received more than $500,000 in gross revenue (before any deductions), you must also file an audit report prepared by an independent public accountant. This requirement may be satisfied in either of two ways: (1) the audit opinion may refer directly to the IRS Form 990 filed with the application, or (2) the opinion may refer to a set of financial statements. If the latter is chosen, the financial statements to which the audit opinion refers must be filed in addition to the Form 990. All audit reports must be on the accountant's letterhead and signed. Compiled or reviewed financial statements do not fulfill the audit requirement. If your nonprofit is newly organized and has not yet completed its initial fiscal year, you will not need to file a financial report. Your nonprofit will have to include a financial report when it renews its registration.

Signatures required. The application must be signed by two authorized representatives. Notarized signatures are not required.

Fee. $50, payable to "Department of Consumer Protection."

Filing procedure. Mail the application and accompanying documents to:

Public Charities Unit c/o Office of the Attorney General
P.O. Box 120
55 Elm Street
Hartford, CT 06141-0120

Renewal Registration

All registrations last for one year and expire on the last day of the fifth month after the nonprofit's fiscal year ends. To renew, file the state *Charitable Organization Registration Application* along with copies of the completed IRS Form 990, 990-EZ, or 990-PF for your most recently completed year. You will have to pay a $50 fee.

If you need an extension of time to file your renewal, send a request for one by email to charity.extensions@po.state.ct.us before the expiration date of your current registration. The Public Charities Unit will grant an extension of up to six months. All extension requests must include the Connecticut Charities Registration Number, the federal ID number, the name and current address of the registered organization, and the fiscal year end date for which you are requesting an extension.

Annual Financial Report

You must file an audit report prepared by a CPA with your renewal if your nonprofit had gross income over $500,000. You can obtain an extension of time of up to six months to file the report. Use the email procedure described above.

Delaware

Delaware has no charitable solicitations law and does not require nonprofits to register before soliciting contributions in the state. However, and out-of-state nonprofit corporation may have to register to do business in the state if it conducts intrastate business there. See Chapter 6 for detailed information.

Delaware

District of Columbia

Governing Law

Although not a state, the District of Columbia has its own laws that apply within its borders. It has a charitable solicitations law that is administered by the Department of Consumer and Regulatory Affairs. The law is codified at District of Columbia Code sections 44-1701 through 44-1714 and is available through the D.C. website.

D.C. Website

The D.C. Department of Consumer and Regulatory Affairs has a website at http://dcra.dc.gov/dcra/site/default.asp with some information on charitable solicitation. (Click on "Business Licensing" and then on "Nonprofit Information Center" then on "BBL Charitable Information.") This is a confusing and poorly organized website.

Registration Requirements

No organization or person may solicit funds for charitable purposes in the District of Columbia unless it obtains a valid certificate of registration that authorizes the solicitation. Under D.C. law, solicitation includes applying for government grants or other funding for charitable purposes. Thus, if your nonprofit applies for funding from the federal government in Washington, D.C., it will be required to register unless it is exempt.

Exemptions

D.C. has very few exemptions. The exemption ceiling for small nonprofits is the lowest in the nation—$1,500.

$1,500 exemption. Organizations that receive less than $1,500 in gross revenues in a calendar year are exempt from registration, as long as all their fundraising is carried on by volunteers.

Religious organizations. Tax-exempt churches, religious corporations, and corporations or unincorporated associations under the supervision and control of a church or religious corporation are exempt from registration. Indeed, these organizations are exempt from all the provisions of the District's charitable solicitations law.

However, registration may be required a church or other religious organization conducts nonreligious activities such as when running schools, day care centers, soup kitchens, thrift shops, or other activities that must be inspected or investigated.

Educational institutions. Solicitations for educational purposes are exempt.

Membership organizations. Membership organizations that raise funds only from their members, and not the public, are exempt.

American Red Cross. This organization is exempt.

Registration Procedure

Unfortunately, D.C. has some of the most onerous registration procedures in the country. Applicants must not only file a completed URS, but must also apply for a basic business license. The license requirement applies even to nonprofits not located in D.C. (See Chapter 6 for information on applying for a business license.)

Application forms. The URS must be submitted along with the D.C. basic business license application form (BBL-EZ Form). You can download the BBL form from the D.C. website.

Documents to be included with application. An extensive list of documents must be included with the application:

- a copy of your nonprofit's charter (articles of incorporation for corporations)
- your bylaws
- a separate written statement fully explaining the character and extent of the charitable work being done by your nonprofit
- a copy of your nonprofit's IRS determination letter; or if a determination letter has not yet been issued, a certified copy of IRS Form 1023 filed by your nonprofit with the IRS
- if your nonprofit is a corporation, a certified resolution authorizing a corporate officer to do the registration application in the District of Columbia
- a tax certificate from the District of Columbia Office of Tax and Revenue (see below), and
- an itemized financial statement for the last preceding calendar or fiscal year—this need not be an audited financial statement by a CPA.

Signatures required. The BBL application must be signed by any person authorized to sign for your nonprofit. If your nonprofit is a corporation, a corporate officer must sign.

Fee. $303, payble to "DC Treasury."

Filing procedure. Mail the signed BBL-EZ application, URS, accompanying documents, and a check or money order for all fees, payable to "DC Treasurer," to:

Bank of America
Attention: DC Government Wholesale Lockbox #91360
11333 McCormick Road
Hunt Valley, MD 21031

Renewal Registration

The D.C. basic business license is valid for two years. The expiration date is listed on the license. To even out the workload of the Department of Consumer and Regulatory Affairs, the expiration dates are issued on a staggered basis. The renewal date is the date of your nonprofit's incorporation, or the date of organization if your nonprofit is unincorporated.

To renew, follow the same procedure as for initial registration described above.

Other Requirements

Before applying for a charitable solicitation license, nonprofits must register with the local D.C. tax agency. In addition, out-of-state nonprofit corporations must obtain a certificate of authority to do business in D.C.

D.C. Office of Tax and Revenue. Federally tax-exempt 501(c)(3) organizations ordinarily qualify for an exemption from the D.C. franchise, sales, use, and personal property taxes. However, under District law, obtaining tax-exempt status from the IRS does not mean you are automatically exempt from these other taxes. You must apply for an exemption from the D.C. Office of Tax and Revenue ("OTR").

To obtain the exemption, you must complete and file Form FR-500, *Combined Business Tax Registration Application*, the general tax registration form, with Form FR-164, *Application for Exemption*, which allows your nonprofit to become a tax-exempt entity in the District. Both forms are available from the OTR website at http://otr.cfo.dc.gov/otr/site/default.asp. For more information, call the Tax Customer Center at 202-727-4829.

You should apply for your tax exemption before applying for your basic business license because you must submit a copy of your tax registration certificate with your license application.

D.C. Corporations Division. If your nonprofit corporation is not located in D.C., you must obtain a certificate of authority to do business in the District from the Corporations Divisions of the Department of Regulatory and Consumer Affairs. You must file an *Application for Certificate of Authority for Foreign Nonprofit Corporation* with the Corporations Division. As part of this process, your nonprofit must appoint a resident agent or an attorney-in-fact who lives or works in an office in the District who will be the official recipient of any financial, process, or legal notices that need to be sent to you. You must include Form RA-1, *Registered Agent Written Consent*, with your application. You can obtain the application and Form RA-1 from the DCRA's website at http://dcra.dc.gov/dcra. Click on "Corporate Registration."

The Corporations Division maintains a list of registered agents. For more information, contact the Corporations Division at 202-442-4400.

You must submit a photocopy of a Certificate of Authority issued by the Corporation Division to the Office of Tax and Revenue with the *Application for Exemption*. So you should apply for this first.

Florida

Governing Law

Florida has a charitable solicitations law codified at Florida Statutes section 406.401 through 496.426. The law is administered by the Florida Department of Agriculture and Consumer Services and may be accessed through that Department's website.

State Website

The Florida Department of Agriculture and Consumer Services has a website at www.doacs.state.fl.us/onestop/cs/solicit.html. It contains the state forms and links to state laws on charitable solicitation.

Registration Requirements

Any charitable organization that intends to solicit contributions in Florida by any means must register with the Florida Department of Agriculture and Consumer Services. The initial registration must be completed before any solicitation is made.

Under Florida law, a solicitation does not occur when a person applies for a grant or award from the government or a tax-exempt nonprofit. Thus, an out-of-state nonprofit whose sole contact with Florida is applying for a grant from a nonprofit located in Florida would not have to register.

Exemptions

Florida exempts the following types of nonprofits from registration. Unlike most states, there is no exemption for very small nonprofits.

Religious institutions. "Religious institution" means any church, ecclesiastical or denominational organization, or established physical place for worship at which nonprofit religious services and activities are regularly conducted. It also includes bona fide religious groups which do not maintain specific places of worship. "Religious institution" also includes any separate group or corporation which forms an integral part of a tax-exempt religious institution, and which is not primarily supported by funds solicited outside its own membership or congregation. These religious organizations are exempt from all the provisions of Florida's charitable solicitations law.

Religious organizations that file a Form 990 with the IRS are not exempt and must register.

Educational institutions. "Educational institution" includes all accredited state tax-supported, parochial, church, and nonprofit private schools, colleges, and universities. It also includes:

- private nonprofits such as the PTA or alumni groups that raise funds for schools teaching grades kindergarten through 12, colleges, or universities
- museums open to the public
- nonprofit libraries
- art galleries
- performing arts centers that provide educational programs for school children involving performances or other educational activities at the center, provided that a minimum of 50,000 school children are served each year
- tax-exempt college and university newspapers, and
- tax-exempt educational television and radio stations.

Membership organizations. Membership organizations that solicit contributions from their membership only are exempt.

Government entities. Government agencies and other government entities need not register.

Solicitations for a single person. A person who solicits contributions for a single named individual does not need to register as long as all the contributions collected are placed in a trust account and are turned over to that individual.

Political groups. Political groups who solicit contributions in accordance with the Florida election laws need not register.

Registration Procedure

Application form. You must use the *Florida Charitable Organizations/ Sponsors Registration Application*, which can be downloaded from the state website. The URS is not allowed as an alternative.

Documents to be included with application. Include the following documents with your application:

- IRS determination letter

Florida

- copies of all current contracts with any solicitors hired by your nonprofit, and
- a financial report—this may consist of a copy of the Form 990 or 990-EZ that your nonprofit filed with the IRS for the immediately preceding fiscal year, or you may complete the financial statement on the application form; if your nonprofit is brand new and has no financial history, you may submit a budget for the current year using the financial statement on the application form or your own form.

Audited financial statements are not required.

Signatures required. The application must contain the notarized signature of your nonprofit's treasurer or chief financial officer.

Fee. The filing fee is on a sliding scale, based on your nonprofit's contributions for the proceeding fiscal year. Your check should be made payable to ""Florida Department of Agriculture and Consumer Services."

Contributions Received During Prior Fiscal Year	Fee
Less than $5,000	$10
$25,000 or less and nonprofit has no paid officers or professional solicitors or consultants	$10
$5,000–$100,000	$75
$100,000–$200,000	$125
$200,000–$500,000	$200
$500,000–$1,000,000	$300
$1,000,000–$10,000,000	$350
$10,000,000 or more	$400

Filing procedure. Mail the completed application and check to:

Florida Department of Agriculture and Consumer Services
Solicitation of Contributions
P.O. Box 6700
Tallahassee, FL 32399-6700

Renewal Registration

All Florida nonprofit registrations expire after one year and must be renewed each year. The expiration date is one year from the date you completed your initial registration. The Florida Department of Agriculture and Consumer Services will mail your nonprofit a renewal statement at least 60 days before the renewal date.

Annual Financial Report

Filed with renewal. You may submit a copy of your Form 990 or 990-EZ filed with the IRS for the preceding fiscal year. Alternatively, you may submit a separate report consisting of:

- a balance sheet
- a statement of support, revenue and expenses, and any change in the fund balance
- the names and addresses of the charitable organizations or sponsors, professional fundraising consultant, professional solicitors, and commercial co-venturers used, if any, and the amounts received from each of them, if any, and
- a statement of functional expenses that must include, but not be limited to, expenses in the following categories: program, management and general, and fundraising.

Other Requirements

All nonprofits in Florida must include the following disclosure statement on every printed solicitation and every written confirmation, receipt, or reminder of a contribution:

A COPY OF THE OFFICIAL REGISTRATION AND FINANCIAL INFORMATION MAY BE OBTAINED FROM THE DIVISION OF CONSUMER SERVICES BY CALLING TOLL-FREE, 1-800-435-7352 WITHIN THE STATE. REGISTRATION DOES NOT IMPLY ENDORSEMENT, APPROVAL, OR RECOMMENDATION BY THE STATE.

Georgia

Governing Law

Georgia has a charitable solicitations law codified at Georgia State Code section 43-17-1 through 43-17-23. The law is administered by the Georgia secretary of state and may be accessed from its website.

State Website

The Georgia Secretary of State's website at http://sos.georgia.gov/securities contains state forms for nonprofit registration, links to state laws, and other information on nonprofit registration.

Registration Requirement

All charitable organizations, wherever located, that intend to solicit charitable contributions in Georgia must register with the Georgia Secretary of State.

Exemptions

The following organizations are exempt from Georgia's registration requirement.

$25,000 exemption. Any charitable organization is exempt if:

- its total nationwide revenue from contributions has been less than $25,000 for the immediately preceding and current calendar years, and
- it does not have any agreement with a paid solicitor, although paid employees or salaried staff can perform fundraising work.

Membership dues, government grants and contracts, and grants or subsidies from 501(c)(3) organizations need not be counted toward the annual ceiling.

Religious organizations. This includes any entity:

- that conducts regular worship services, or
- is recognized as a tax-exempt religious organization by the IRS and is not required to file IRS Form 990.

These religious organizations are excluded from Georgia's definition of a "charitable organization." Thus, the state's charitable solicitations law does not apply to them at all. Religious organizations that file a Form 990 with the IRS are not exempt and must register.

Educational institutions. This includes any entity organized and operated exclusively for educational purposes and which normally maintains a regular faculty, curriculum, and regularly enrolled student body. It also includes any organization accredited by a nationally recognized, independent higher education accreditation body. It also includes tax-exempt organizations, foundations, associations, corporations, charities, and agencies operated, supervised, or controlled by a nonprofit educational institution.

Professional associations. Professional, business, and trade associations that do not solicit members or funds from the general public are exempt.

Fraternal and social organizations. Fraternal, civic, benevolent, patriotic, and social organizations who solicit only from their membership and whose fundraising is carried on by volunteers are exempt.

Appeals for named individuals. Any person soliciting contributions for a named individual is exempt, provided all of the contributions collected are turned over to the named beneficiary. If contributions exceed $5,000, you may need a written accounting of funds.

Volunteer firefighters. Any volunteer fire department or rescue service operating in conjunction with a Georgia city or county government is exempt, provided it received less than $25,000 in both the immediately preceding and current calendar years.

Hunters, fishermen, and target shooters. Any tax-exempt local or state organization of hunters, fishermen, or target shooters is exempt.

Political organizations. Political parties, political action committees, and candidates for federal or state office who file financial information with federal or state election commissions are exempt.

Local affiliates. Any local Georgia affiliate of a registered or exempt state-wide or national parent organization does not have to register separately with the Georgia Secretary of State.

Registration Procedure

Application form. You may use the URS or the Georgia state form—*Georgia Charitable Solicitations Act Charitable Organization Registration* (Form C-100)—which you can download from the state website. If you use the URS, you must also submit the state *Control Persons* form, which is the last page of the Georgia application form.

Georgia

Documents included with application. You must submit the following documents with your application:

- Include a copy of your IRS determination letter, if any. If you haven't received it yet, you must send it to the secretary of state within 30 days after it is issued.
- If your nonprofit has received any contributions, you must include copies of the IRS Form 990 or 990-EZ your nonprofit filed for the previous two taxable years.
- Your nonprofit must also submit a financial statement dated within one year of filing the application. The type of statement required depends on how much income your nonprofit received in the preceding fiscal year:

Income received during either of two preceding fiscal years:	Financial reports to be filed:
more than $1 million	financial statements for two preceding fiscal years certified by an independent CPA
$500,000 to $1 million	financial statements for two preceding fiscal years reviewed by an independent CPA (certification not required)
less than $500,000	financial statements for two preceding fiscal years that do not need to be reviewed or certified by a CPA

If your nonprofit has received less than the amount required by the IRS to file Form 990 or Form 990-EZ, you must provide financial statements that disclose your income and expenses for the prior two fiscal years.

If your nonprofit received no funds prior to filing your application, attach a signed statement from an officer to that effect.

You must also complete and file with your application the Georgia *Control Persons* form. This is the last page of the Georgia application form. You must submit this form even if you file the URS.

Signatures required. The application must be signed by an authorized executive officer and the signature must be notarized.

Fee. $35, payable to "Secretary of State."

Filing procedure. Mail the application and fee to:

Securities and Business Regulation
2 Martin Luther King, Jr. Drive S.E.
Suite 802 West Tower
Atlanta, Georgia 30334

Renewal Registration

Your Georgia registration is valid for 24 months from its effective date. You must renew it by the expiration date. The secretary of state will mail a renewal notice to you during the month prior to the expiration date. This notice should be signed and returned with the requested attachments, including financial statements, and the renewal fee of $20. If you received any contributions during the preceding two fiscal years, you must provide copies of the IRS Form 990 or Form 990-EZ filed with the IRS for those two preceding years.

Financial Report

If your nonprofit received more than $500,000 during either of its two preceding fiscal years, you must provide financial statements with your renewal.

If your nonprofit received more than $1 million during either of its two preceding fiscal years, the financial statements for those years must be certified financial statements prepared by a CPA. If your nonprofit received more than $500,000 during either of its two preceding fiscal years, the financial report for those years must be reviewed by a CPA, but need not be certified.

If additional time is needed to file the financial statements, you must submit a written request for an extension accompanied by the $20 renewal fee and the renewal form. Your request must specify the reason the financial statements cannot be filed and a date when they will be completed and filed. Your request for extension must be received by the secretary of state before the expiration date of your registration.

Other Requirements

All nonprofits in Georgia must include the following disclosure statement on every printed solicitation and every written confirmation, receipt, or reminder of a contribution:

Georgia

Georgia

> A full and fair description of [*name of charity*] and its financial statements are available upon request at the address indicated above.

Hawaii

Governing Law

Hawaii has a charitable solicitations law codified at Hawaii Revised Statutes sections 467B-1 through 467B-15. The law is administered by the Hawaii attorney general and can be accessed from the attorney general's website.

State Website

The Hawaii attorney general has a website with detailed information on registration at http://hawaii.gov/ag/charities. This is an outstanding website with detailed guidance on how to register using the state's online registration procedure.

Registration Requirements

Every charitable organization must register with the Hawaii attorney general before soliciting any charitable contributions in the state or prior to having any solicitation conducted on its behalf by others.

Money or property received from the government or from a section 501(c)(3) nonprofit is not covered by the registration requirement. Thus, an out-of-state nonprofit need not register if its sole contact with Hawaii is receiving a grant from the government or a Hawaii-based 501(c)(3) charity or foundation.

Exemptions

The following types of charitable organizations are exempt from Hawaii's registration requirement:

$25,000 exemption. Hawaii exempts any charitable organization that normally receives less than $25,000 in contributions annually, provided it does not use professional solicitors. The nonprofit can have salaried staff perform some fundraising activities as long as the person is not paid primarily for fundraising work. You need not count toward the annual limit:

- money or property received from any governmental authority
- grants or subsidies from tax-exempt organizations, or
- membership dues, fees, and similar payments.

Religious organizations. Any duly organized religious corporation, institution, or society is exempt.

Educational institutions. This includes any accredited educational institution and any parent-teacher association. But this does not include a supporting organization or foundation of an educational institution.

Membership organizations. Organizations that obtain all of their income from membership dues and assessments are exempt.

Nonprofit hospitals. Any licensed nonprofit hospital is exempt. But this does not include a supporting organization or foundation of a nonprofit hospital.

Government agencies. Any state or federal government agency or entity is exempt.

Fundraisers. Any person who solicits solely for the benefit of any of the exempt organizations described above is also exempt. This includes an officer or employee of an exempt charity, but not a paid solicitor.

Registration Procedure

Hawaii uses an Internet-based registration system through the state website. Users must obtain a log on identification and password from this site and then complete and submit the registration data.

Application form. You must use the state online application. The URS may not be used.

Documents to be included with application. None.

Fee. The filing fee is based on a sliding scale, depending on your nonprofit's annual gross revenue (this amount can be found on Form 990, Line 12, or Form 990-EZ, Line 9).

Annual Gross Revenue	Annual Fee
Less than $25,000	$10
$25,000 but less than $50,000	$25
$50,000 but less than $100,000	$50
$100,000 but less than $250,000	$100
$250,000 but less than $500,000	$150
$500,000 but less than $1 million	$200
$1 million but less than $2 million	$300
$2 million but less than $5 million	$500
$5 million and over	$750

You can pay by credit card or check through the state of Hawaii payment processing site at http://ag.ehawaii.gov/charity/fein.html. Your check should be made payable to "Hawaii Attorney General."

Signatures required. Two authorized directors or officers must electronically sign the application. They must each obtain their own login IDs to sign.

Filing procedure. You must file all documents online.

Renewal Registration

Hawaii does not require nonprofits to renew their registration. However, they must update the registration each year by submitting IRS Form 990 or 990-EZ, and annual financial reports.

Annual Financial Report

All registered nonprofits must submit their IRS Form 990 or 990-EZ each year when it is due with the IRS. If you file your Form 990 or 990-EZ electronically, then it can be filed online with the Hawaii attorney general. If you file a hard copy of the Form 990 or 990-EZ with the IRS, you can convert it to a PDF and upload it to the Hawaii registration site. You must pay an annual filing fee that is the same as the initial registration fee.

The deadline for the annual filing is the same as the IRS deadline for the forms (including authorized extensions). The deadline for Form 990 or 990-EZ is 4½ months after the end of your nonprofit's tax year. Thus, if your nonprofit's tax year ends on December 31, your Form 990 will be due on May 15 the following year. You can get an automatic three-month extension for filing your Form 990 or 990-EZ by submitting Form 8868 to the IRS. Thus, you can legitimately file your Form 990 or 990-EZ with the IRS (and the Hawaii attorney general) 7½ months after your fiscal year ends.

In addition, any nonprofit with gross revenues over $500,000 (which includes all income except government grants) must submit an audited financial statement. You also are required to file an audited statement if you were required to prepare one by another governmental authority or third party. Like the Form 990 or 990-EZ, the audited financial report must be submitted online to the Hawaii registration website. You can fill out an online form or create a PDF of the report and upload it to the website.

Idaho

Idaho has a charitable solicitations law, but it does not require nonprofits to register or obtain a license before soliciting contributions in the state.

Although Idaho does not require registration, its solicitations law bars the use of unfair or deceptive practices while soliciting charitable contributions. The law is codified at Idaho Statutes sections 48-1201 through 48-1206. You can access the laws from the Idaho state legislature's website at http://legislature.idaho.gov/statutesrules.htm.

Illinois

Governing Law

Illinois has a charitable solicitations law codified at 225 Illinois Compiled Statutes sections 460/0.01 to 460/23 (Solicitation for Charity Act). The law is enforced by the Illinois attorney general, and may be accessed from the attorney general's website.

State Website

The Illinois attorney general's website has information on charities and registration requirements at www.illinoisattorneygeneral.gov/charities/index.htm. It contains all the state forms, links to state laws and rules, and FAQs.

Registration Requirements

Any charitable organization that solicits charitable contributions in Illinois must first register with the Illinois attorney general unless it is exempt.

Exemptions

Illinois exempts the following organizations from registration. The state is unusual in that it requires religious organizations to apply for their exemption, but does not extend this requirement to other exempt organizations. Small nonprofits must register, but those with an annual income of less than $15,000 need not file annual financial reports.

   Religious organizations. All religious organizations and their affiliates are exempt. However, to obtain an exemption, the organization must file two forms with the attorney general: Illinois Form CO-3, *Religious Organization Exemption Form* and Form CO-1, *Charitable Organization Registration Statement*, both of which can be downloaded from the state website. A religious organization with multiple affiliates or subdivisions may obtain a blanket exemption covering all of them. Thus, for example, the central body of a church or denomination can obtain a blanket exemption that covers the church and all of the affiliated agencies controlled by the church and listed in the exemption request.

   Educational institutions. All accredited educational institutions are exempt, as are any charitable foundations they establish. Any other educational institution that solicits contributions only from its student body, alumni, faculty, trustees, and their families is also exempt.

Illinois libraries that file annual financial reports with a state agency are also exempt.

Membership organizations. Fraternal, patriotic, social, educational, alumni organizations, and historical societies are exempt, provided solicitation of contributions is confined to their membership. This exemption applies to any subsidiary of a parent or superior organization.

Appeals for single individuals. Volunteers who solicit charitable contributions for a named individual need not register provided the contributions collected are turned over to the named beneficiary.

Political organizations. Any bona fide union, political organization, or political action committee which does not solicit funds for a charitable purpose is exempt.

United Way. Any charitable organization receiving an allocation from a duly registered incorporated community chest or united fund is exempt, provided it does not receive contributions of $4,000 or more from other sources during any 12 month period ending June 30th.

Veterans' organizations. All veterans' organizations chartered or incorporated under federal law and their affiliates are exempt, provided they file all required financial reports.

Other exemptions. The following organizations are also exempt, as long as all of their fundraising is carried on by volunteers:

- volunteer firefighters and their affiliates and auxiliaries
- any nonprofit operating a nursery for infants awaiting adoption
- local parent teacher organizations, and
- any boys' club affiliated with the Boys' Club of America.

Registration Procedure

Application form. You can use the URS or the Illinois state Form CO-1, *Charitable Organization Registration Statement*, which you can download from the state website.

Documents included with application. You must include the following documents with your application:

- articles of incorporation
- bylaws

- copies of IRS Form 990, 990-EZ, or 990-PF for the last three years, if any
- a copy of the IRS Determination Letter or, if the IRS tax-exempt determination is pending, a copy of IRS Form 1023 or 1024
- copies of all contracts with professional fundraisers
- a certificate of authority to do business from the Illinois secretary of state (see "Other Requirements," below).

Signatures required. The president and the chief financial officer or other authorized officer are both required to sign. They must be two different individuals. Notarized signatures are not required.

Fee. $15, payable to "Illinois Charity Bureau Fund." You will have to pay a late fee of $200 if your nonprofit solicits contributions in Illinois before you are registered.

Filing procedure. Mail the completed application, accompanying documents, and application fee to:

Office of the Illinois Attorney General
Charitable Trust and Solicitations Bureau
100 West Randolph Street, 11th Floor
Chicago, Illinois 60601-3175

Renewal Registration

The initial registration lasts indefinitely. Thus, there are no renewal requirements.

Annual Financial Report

Subject to the exceptions noted below, registered nonprofits must file a financial report with the Charitable Trust and Solicitations Bureau each year. Larger nonprofits must file audited financial statements.

Time to file. The annual financial report is due within six months after the end of your nonprofit's tax year—whether it's a calendar or other fiscal year. You may obtain a 60-day extension by filing a request in writing before the due date.

Contents. You must include the following documents with your report:
- the IRS Form 990, 990-EZ, or 990-PF your nonprofit filed one for the preceding year

- a completed Illinois Form AG990-IL, *Illinois Charitable Organization Supplement*
- an audited financial statement if your nonprofit's gross contributions for the year exceeded $300,000 or if you used a paid professional fundraiser who raised contributions in excess of $25,000 (contributions include the total amounts paid by the public for merchandise and services, as well as cash donations)
- a completed Illinois Form IFC, *Attorney General Report of Individual Fundraising Campaign*, if your nonprofit used a paid professional fundraiser; a separate campaign report form is required for each campaign, and each report must be signed by both the professional fundraiser and an officer or director of your nonprofit.

Fee. $15. If a proper and complete annual report along with all fees and attachments is not received prior to the due date, you will have to pay a $100 late report filing fee. The report will not be accepted and will not be considered filed if it is late and the late fee is not paid.

Small organizations (simplified filing). If your nonprofit had gross revenue and assets of $25,000 or less during the fiscal year, you may file a simplified Form AG990-IL, disclosing only total revenue, total expenditures, and assets at the fiscal year end (Lines A, G, and O of Form AG990-IL).

$15,000 exemption. Nonprofits that do not receive contributions over $15,000 during the calendar year need not file a financial report.

Other Requirements

If your nonprofit is a corporation that is incorporated in a state other than Illinois, you must include with your registration application a Certificate of Authority to do business from the Illinois Secretary of State. You can obtain the certificate by filing the secretary of state Form NFP-113.15, *Application for Authority to Conduct Affairs in Illinois,* and paying a $50 fee. You must appoint a registered agent for service of process in Illinois to obtain the certificate. The form and instructions are available from the secretary of state's website at: www.cyberdriveillinois.com/publications/pdf_publications/nfp11315.pdf.

In addition, all nonprofits in Illinois must include the following disclosure statement on every printed solicitation and every written confirmation, receipt, or reminder of a contribution:

> Contracts and reports regarding [*name of charity*] are on file with the Illinois Attorney General.

Illinois

Indiana

Indiana

Indiana does not have a charitable solicitations law and does not require nonprofits to register with a state agency before soliciting contributions in the state. However, an out-of-state nonprofit corporation may have to register to do business in the state if it conducts intrastate business there. See Chapter 6 for detailed information on qualifying to do business.

Iowa

Iowa does not have a charitable solicitations law and does not require nonprofits to register with a state agency before soliciting contributions in the state. However, an out-of-state nonprofit corporation may have to register to do business in the state if it conducts intrastate business there. See Chapter 6 for detailed information.

Iowa

Kansas

Governing Law

Kansas has a charitable solicitations law codified at Kansas Statutes Annotated sections 17-1760 through 17-1776. The law is administered by the Kansas secretary of state and may be accessed from its website.

State Website

The Kansas secretary of state has information for charitable organization registrations on its website at www.kssos.org/business/business_charitable. html. You can download the state registration form from the website; otherwise the website has little information.

Registration Requirements

All nonprofits must register with the Kansas secretary of state before soliciting charitable contributions in Kansas, or having such solicitations made on their behalf by professional fundraisers or others.

Exemptions

Kansas has an extensive list of exemptions from registration. It is not necessary to apply for an exemption.

$10,000 exemption. Any charitable organization that does not intend to solicit and receive, and does not actually receive, nationwide contributions over $10,000 during its tax year is exempt, provided all of its fundraising functions are carried on by unpaid volunteers. The nonprofit can have salaried staff and hire independent contractors as long as they don't perform fundraising-related functions. You don't have to count unsolicited contributions toward the $10,000, unless they are received in conjunction with a solicitation drive.

100 person exemption. You need not register if your nonprofit does not solicit or receive contributions from more than 100 people during the year. This limit applies to nationwide contributions, not just from Kansas.

Religious organizations. All religious organizations and their affiliates are exempt. This includes any "religious agency or organization which serves religion by the preservation of religious rights and freedom from persecution or prejudice or by fostering religion, including the moral and ethical aspects of a particular religious faith."

Educational institutions. All accredited educational institutions are exempt, as are any nonprofit foundations they establish. Any other educational institution is exempt if it solicits contributions only from its student body, alumni, faculty, trustees, and their families.

Kansas libraries that file annual financial reports with a state agency are also exempt.

Health organizations. All nonprofit licensed medical care facilities are exempt. So are:

- licensed community mental health centers and mental health clinics
- licensed community mental retardation centers and their affiliates, and
- any charity operating a nursery for infants awaiting adoption if all fundraising is carried on by volunteers.

Membership organizations. Fraternal, patriotic, social, educational, and alumni organizations, and historical societies are exempt, provided they solicit contributions only from their membership. This exemption applies to any subsidiary of a parent or superior organization.

Appeals for single individuals. Volunteers who solicit charitable contributions for a named individual do not need to register as long as they turn over the contributions they collect to the named beneficiary (reasonable expenses may be deducted).

United Way. Incorporated community chests, united funds, and united way are exempt, as are nonprofits whose sole support comes from them.

Public foundations. Any publicly supported community foundation or community trust to which deductible contributions can be made by individuals, corporations, public charities, and private foundations is exempt.

Other exemptions. The following organizations are also exempt:

- any charitable organization whose funds are used to support any activity by a Kansas municipality
- volunteer firefighters and their affiliates (no paid fundraisers)
- the junior league, including local community organization affiliated with it
- the Boy Scouts of America and the Girl Scouts of America, including regional or local organizations affiliated with either one

Kansas

- the Young Men's Christian Association and the Young Women's Christian Association, including regional or local organizations affiliated with either one
- any girls' club affiliated with the Girls' Club of America, provided the affiliate properly files the reports required by the national organization
- any boys' club affiliated with the Boys' Club of America, provided the affiliate properly files the reports required by the national organization, and
- any corporation established by Congress that is required by federal law to submit annual itemized financial reports after being audited by the department of defense or other federal department.

Registration Procedure

Application form. You can use the URS or the state form SC 53-10, *Registration Statement for Solicitations.* The state form can be downloaded from the state website at www.kssos.org/forms/business_services/SC.pdf.

Documents to be included with application. You must include the following documents with your registration:

- a copy of your IRS Form 990, 990-EZ, or 990-PF from the preceding year (not including schedules listing individual contributors)
- if your nonprofit has no Form 990 to file—for example, because it's new—you must complete and attach the state financial statement form (Form FS) which may be downloaded from the state website
- if your nonprofit received contributions exceeding $500,000 during its fiscal year, you must attach audited financial statements and an opinion letter prepared by an independent CPA in accordance with generally accepted accounting principles.

Signatures required. This application must be signed by two separate authorized officers, one of whom must be the chief fiscal officer. Notarized signatures are not required.

Fee. $35, payable to "Secretary of State."

Filing procedure. Mail application, accompanying documents, and fee to:

Kansas Secretary of State
Ron Thornburgh Memorial Hall, 1st Floor
120 S.W. 10th Avenue
Topeka, KS 66612-1594

Renewal Registration

The annual registration expires on the last day of the sixth month following the month in which your nonprofit's tax year ends. For example, if you use the calendar year, it expires on June 30th each year. You must file a renewal before the expiration date each year.

Complete and file state Form SC 53-10, *Registration Statement for Solicitation*, before the expiration date. This is the same form that is used for your initial registration. Check the renewal/update box on the form. Include with the application the same documents that are required for your initial registration (see "Registration Requirements," above). You must pay a $35 fee.

Annual Financial Report

You must provide an audited financial statement with your renewal registration if your nonprofit received contributions exceeding $500,000 during its fiscal year.

Kentucky

Governing Law

Kentucky has a charitable solicitations law codified at Kentucky Revised Statutes sections 367.650 through 367.670. The law is administered by the Kentucky attorney general and can be accessed from its website.

State Website

The Kentucky attorney general has a website at http://ag.ky.gov/civil/consumerprotection/charity with links to forms and the state's charitable solicitations law.

Registration Requirements

Every tax-exempt nonprofit must register with the Kentucky attorney general before soliciting charitable contributions in the state.

Exemptions

The following organizations are exempt from registration in Kentucky. It is not necessary to apply for an exemption.

Religious organizations. Religious organizations are exempt if they solicit funds for religious purposes, such as to maintain a house of worship, conduct services, or propagate faith and tenets. "Religious organization" is broadly defined to include any organization whose activities are protected by the First Amendment, or the Kentucky state constitution's similar provision. These religious organizations are exempt from all provisions of Kentucky's charitable solicitations law.

Educational institutions. Publicly-owned or nonprofit privately-endowed educational institutions are exempt if they only solicit contributions from their alumni, faculty members, student body and their families, and corporations.

Membership organizations. Membership organizations that solicit contributions only from members and their families are exempt.

PTAs and student groups. PTAs and student groups are exempt if they only solicit contributions locally for an educational institution, provided they do so with the approval of the administration of the educational institution.

Registration Procedure

Application form. If your nonprofit has already filed an IRS Form 990, 990-EZ, 990-PF, or 990-N, you can file a copy of that form to register.

If your nonprofit is newly formed and you have not yet filed a Form 990 with the IRS, then you can file the URS. There is no state registration form.

Documents included with application. If you file the URS, include your IRS determination letter, if any.

Signatures required. See instructions for the URS application in Chapter 5.

Fee. None

Filing procedure. Mail the Form 990 or completed URS to:

Office of the Attorney General
Consumer Protection Division
Attn: Charity Registration
1024 Capital Center Drive
Frankfort, Kentucky 40601-8204

Renewal Registration

All registrations expire on December 31 of each year. Each year, your nonprofit must file with the Kentucky attorney general one of the following forms at the same time you file the form with the IRS:

- Form 990
- Form 990-EZ
- Form 990-PF
- Form 8868, or
- Form 990-N (electronic postcard filed by small nonprofits).

If your nonprofit does not have an IRS form to file, you must file a new URS.

Louisiana

Governing Law

Louisiana has a charitable solicitations law codified at Louisiana Revised Statutes sections 51:1901 through 51:1909, and Louisiana Administrative Code, Title 16, Part III, section 515. The law is administered by the Louisiana attorney general and can be accessed from its website.

State Website

The Louisiana attorney general has a website at http://ladoj.ag.state.la.us/Article.aspx?articleID=3&catID=18 with links to the state law and forms for nonprofit registration.

Registration Requirements

Louisiana's registration requirement is very unusual. Under its solicitations law, only charitable organizations that use a professional solicitor to help receive donations are required to register with the Louisiana Attorney General's office. All other nonprofits are exempt.

A "professional solicitor" means any person or entity that is paid to solicit contributions on behalf of a charitable organization. Under Louisiana law, solicitors must register with the attorney general before soliciting contributions in the state. The solicitor's office does not need to be located in Louisiana. A person who solicits Louisiana residents from out of state is deemed to be a professional solicitor.

Salaried officers or employees of your nonprofit are not professional solicitors. However, anyone employed or paid by a nonprofit who also solicits contributions on behalf of other charitable organizations is deemed a professional solicitor if the other organization pays a fee for that person's services.

Exemptions

As explained above, all nonprofits that don't use professional solicitors in Louisiana are exempt from registration. The following organizations are also exempt, even if they employ solicitors:

- religious organizations, if they are not primarily supported from funds solicited outside their membership or congregations

- educational institutions approved by the Louisiana Department of Education, and
- Louisiana hospitals and voluntary health organizations.

Registration Procedure

Application form. There is no state form—you must use the URS.

Documents included with application. The following documents must be included with the application:

- articles of incorporation
- bylaws
- IRS determination letter
- most recently filed IRS Form 990
- all contracts with professional solicitors, and
- a list of other states in which your organization is registered.

Signatures required. See instructions to URS application in Chapter 5.

Fee. $25, payable to "Louisiana Department of Justice."

Filing procedure. Mail the application, accompanying documents, and fee to:

Public Protection Division
1885 N. 3rd Street, 4th Floor
Baton Rouge, LA 70802

Renewal Registration

All nonprofits required to register in Louisiana must do so annually. The renewal must be completed by the anniversary date of the initial registration. To renew, you must file:

- a completed URS application
- a copy of your most recent Form 990
- copies of all contracts with professional solicitors, and
- a list of other states in which your organization is registered.

Send these and a $25 fee to:

Public Protection Division
1885 N. 3rd Street, 4th Floor
Baton Rouge, LA 70802

Louisiana

Maine

Governing Law

Maine has a charitable solicitations law codified at Maine Revised Statutes Annotated, Title 9, Chapter 385, sections 5001 through 5007. The law is administered by the State of Maine Department of Professional and Financial Regulation and can be accessed from its website.

State Website

The Maine Department of Professional and Financial Regulation has information on charitable solicitations on its website at www.maine.gov/pfr/professionallicensing/professions/charitable/index.htm.

Registration Requirements

All charitable organizations must obtain a state license at least 30 days before soliciting contributions in Maine, or having contributions solicited there on their behalf. Money or property received from any governmental agency or from a charitable or educational foundation is not considered a contribution and does not by itself trigger a registration requirement.

Exemptions

The only charitable organizations that Maine completely exempts from registration are bona fide religious organizations. These religious organizations are exempt from all the provisions of Maine's charitable solicitations law.

The other type of nonprofits listed below, while technically exempt, are still required to register and obtain a charitable exemption license and renew it each year as described below. However, the license fee is lower than for nonexempt nonprofits.

$10,000 exemption. Nonprofits that do not solicit or receive nationwide contributions over $10,000 in the calendar year are exempt, provided all their fundraising is conducted by volunteers. The nonprofit can have salaried staff and hire independent contractors as long as they don't perform fundraising-related functions.

Money or property received from any governmental agency or charitable or educational foundation or membership dues, or any similar payments need not be counted toward the $10,000 ceiling.

Ten-person exemption. Nonprofits that do not receive contributions from more than ten people nationwide are exempt if all fundraising is done by volunteers.

Membership organizations. Organizations that solicit primarily within their membership are exempt, provided the solicitations are conducted by their members.

Named individuals. Solicitations for named individuals are exempt if all the contributions collected, without any deductions, are turned over to the named beneficiary.

Educational institutions. Accredited educational institutions and organizations operated by their student bodies are exempt.

Nonprofit hospitals. Hospitals that are nonprofit and charitable are exempt.

Registration Procedure—Nonexempt Nonprofits

If your nonprofit does not come within of the exempt categories listed above, you must register to obtain a charitable solicitations license.

Application form. Charitable organizations can submit either the Maine-specific application or the Unified Registration Statement ("URS"). If you choose the URS, you should attach the first page of the Maine-specific application to the front and you should note the information contained in the second page.

Documents to be included with application. Include a copy of your IRS determination letter with your application.

Signatures required. The application must be signed by your nonprofit's principal officer and the signature must be notarized.

Fee. $50, payable to "Maine State Treasurer."

Filing procedure. Mail the application, accompanying documents, and fee to:

> State of Maine Department of Professional and Financial Regulation
> Charitable Solicitations Program
> 35 State House Station
> Augusta, Maine 04333-0035
> Registration Procedure—Exempt Nonprofits

Renewal Registration—Exempt Nonprofits

If your nonprofit falls within one of the exempt categories listed above, you must still register and obtain an exempt organization license. The procedure differs somewhat from that for nonexempt nonprofits.

Application form. You must use the Maine application form, *Application for Licensure as an Exempt Charitable Organization*, also called an *Affidavit for Exemption*. You can download the form from the state website. You may not use the URS.

Documents included with application. Include the following documents with your affidavit:

- your IRS determination letter, if any
- a copy of any financial statement, report, or return filed with the IRS
- a statement of your organization's purpose (this can be stated in the affidavit or you may attach a copy of your articles of incorporation or similar document)
- a current list of your nonprofit's officers, directors, and trustees, including your principal officer—this list should include mailing addresses, contact phone numbers, and email addresses.

Signatures required. The affidavit must be signed by your nonprofit's principal officer. The signature must be notarized.

Fee. $10, payable to "Maine State Treasurer."

Filing procedure. Mail the affidavit, accompanying documents, and fee to:

> State of Maine Department of Professional and Financial Regulation
> Charitable Solicitations Program
> 35 State House Station
> Augusta, Maine 04333-0035

Renewal Registration—Nonexempt Nonprofits

Renewal procedures differ depending on whether your nonprofit falls within one of the exempt categories listed above.

Time for renewal. All licenses expire on November 30 of each year and must be renewed each year before that date. You will need to submit a renewal application by the next November 30th, even if that date falls within the same calendar year as the effective date of your initial license.

Procedure. You mail file the URS or complete the state of Maine *Charitable Organization Renewal Application*, which you can download from the state website. If you use the URS, attach the first page of the Maine-specific application to the front and note the information contained in the second page. As with the Maine-specific application, the signature on the URS should be notarized.

Include the following documents with your application:

- a copy of your most recent IRS Form 990 and Schedule A or Form 990-EZ, and
- a copy of your nonprofit's audited financial statements for your most recently audited fiscal year.

If you don't have audited financial statements, contact the Maine Office of Licensing and Regulation.

You should have already filed your *Annual Fundraising Activity Report* (AFAR) for the previous calendar year by September 30th of the current year. If you have not filed it by November 30, you will not be able to renew your registration and you may be subject to penalties. You may submit the AFAR and the renewal application together if you file them by the earlier due date of September 30. See "Annual Financial Report," below.

Fee. $25.

Renewal Registration—Exempt Nonprofits

If your nonprofit falls within one of the exempt categories listed above, your renewal process is simpler.

Time for renewal. Exempt organization licenses expire on November 30 of each year, the same as for nonexempt nonprofits.

Procedure. You must use the state of Maine form, *Exempt Charitable Organizations Renewal Application*, which you can download from the state website.

You should include a copy of your organization's most recent audited financial statements and your most recent IRS Form 990 or Form 990-EZ with the application. Submit both, if available. If you have neither a Form 990 nor audited financial statements, submit a copy of your budget.

Fee. $10.

Annual Financial Report

Nonprofits must file two different financial reports with Maine each year. These requirements do not apply to exempt nonprofits, only those that are nonexempt.

Annual fundraising activity report (AFAR). You must file an annual fundraising activity report for the previous calendar year by September 30 of each year. The AFAR should reflect your nonprofit's 50-state fundraising activity for the previous calendar year. The Maine Office of Licensing and Regulation may compare the figures on this form with those on your Form 990 or 990-EZ, so they should be consistent.

To complete this report, use the state of Maine *Annual Fundraising Activity Report*, which you can download from the state website. You may submit the AFAR and the renewal application together, if you file them by September 30.

Audited financial statements. Maine also requires that a financial statement covering your most recently audited fiscal year be included as part of your annual renewal application. If you don't have audited financial statements, contact the State of Maine Department of Professional and Financial Regulation, Charitable Solicitations Program.

Maryland

Governing Law

Maryland has a charitable solicitations law codified at Maryland Annotated Code, Business Regulation Article, sections 6-101 through 6-205. The law is administered by the Maryland secretary of state and may be accessed from its website.

State Website

The Maryland Secretary of State's website has information on charitable solicitations at www.sos.state.md.us/Charity/CharityHome.aspx, including forms, links to the state law, and instructions.

Registration Requirements

A charitable organization must register with the Maryland secretary of state and obtain a certification letter before soliciting donations in Maryland.

Exemptions

The following organizations are exempt from the registration requirement. Exemption is not automatic. Except in the case of the $25,000 exemption, you must submit a letter to the Maryland Secretary of State, Charitable Organizations Division that contains proof that your nonprofit qualifies for the exemption. In the letter you should cite the applicable exemption statute (this will be the application portion of section 6-101 of the Maryland Solicitation Act), and include articles of incorporation, bylaws, your IRS determination letter (if any), and your most recently filed IRS Form 990 or 990-EZ (if any).

$25,000 exemption. Nonprofits whose annual charitable contributions from the public are less than $25,000 are exempt, provided they do not employ professional solicitors. Contributions include all donations from individuals, corporations, foundations, and other entities, and the gross revenue from special fundraising events. It does not include government grants or membership dues. To determine the level of charitable contributions received, add Lines 1(a), 1(b), and 9(a) on IRS Form 990 for the most recently completed fiscal year or Lines 1 and 6(a) on the IRS Form 990-EZ for the most recently completed fiscal year. Nonprofits that come within this exemption need not register or pay a filing fee. However, they must complete and file the Maryland *Exempt Organization Fundraising Notice* each year. You can get this form from the state website. You are not required to submit a letter to the secretary of state showing you qualify for this exemption.

Religious organizations. Religious organizations, parent organizations of religious organizations, and schools affiliated with religious organization are exempt, provided they have a determination letter from the IRS confirming that they are tax-exempt. To request an exemption on religious grounds, submit a copy of your IRS tax determination letter, articles of incorporation, and other information explaining your organization's mission.

Membership organizations. Organizations that solicit contributions only from their members are exempt. To qualify for this exemption, members must receive some benefit and have the right to hold office or vote for office in the organization. To request a membership exemption, submit a copy of your organization's bylaws showing the rights of the members and a statement explaining from whom solicitations for contributions are made.

Educational organizations. An accredited school, college, or university that solicits contributions only from students, former students, parents of students or former students, present or former board members, and staff members is exempt.

Appeals for named individuals. People who solicit contributions for a named individual are exempt, provided they don't use a professional solicitor and all contributions are delivered to the individual.

Grants. Nonprofits that only receive contributions from for-profit corporations and/or tax-exempt private foundations are exempt.

Volunteer firefighters. The registration requirement does not apply to fundraising by a volunteer firefighter organization or rescue or ambulance personnel for its ambulance, firefighting, or rescue operations.

Registration Procedure

Application form. You may use the URS or the Maryland state form, *Registration Statement for Charitable Organizations*, which you can download from the state website.

Documents included with application. Include the following documents with your completed application:

- a copy of your nonprofit's articles of incorporation or other governing instruments (bylaws or charter)
- a copy of your IRS tax determination letter
- copies of all contracts and sub-contracts with professional solicitors or fundraising counsel used in Maryland, and
- a copy of a completed and signed IRS Form 990 or 990-EZ (it is not necessary that this form already have been filed with the IRS).

If you don't have a signed Form 990 or 990-EZ because you are exempt from filing them or only file Form the 990-N, you must complete and submit the secretary of state's Form COF-85, *Financial Form to be Filled Out by Organizations Not Filing Form 990*, which can found on the state website. If your IRS Form 990 is incomplete, submit an approved IRS Form 8868, the IRS request for an extension of the Form 990 filing deadline.

In addition, if your nonprofit's charitable contributions are over $200,000, but less than $500,000, you must submit a financial review performed by an independent certified public accountant. If your organization's charitable contributions are $500,000 or more, you must submit a copy of an audit performed by an independent certified public accountant.

Signatures required. The application must be signed by your nonprofit's president, chairman, or principal officer. The signature need not be notarized.

Fee. The fee is on a sliding scale based on your nonprofit's level of contributions. Your check should be made payable to "Secretary of State."

Charitable Contributions	Fee
Less than $25,000	0
$25,001 to $50,000	$50
$50,001 to $75,000	$75
$75,001 to $100,000	$100
$100,001 and over	$200

Filing procedure. Mail completed application, accompanying documents, and fee to:

Office of the Secretary of State
Charitable Organizations Division
State House
Annapolis, Maryland 21401-1547

Renewal Registration

Time for renewal. Every registered nonprofit must file a renewal registration within six months after the end of its fiscal year. If you use the calendar year as your fiscal year, the deadline is June 30th.

Procedure. Complete and postal mail to the Maryland secretary of state the *Maryland Annual Update of Registration* form and include the following documents:

- a copy of a completed and signed IRS Form 990 or 990-EZ (it is not necessary that this form already have been filed wit the IRS). If you don't have a signed Form 990 or 990-EZ because you are exempt from filing or only file Form 990-N, you must complete and submit the secretary of state's Form COF-85, *Financial Form to be Filled Out by Organizations Not Filing Form 990,* which you can find on the state's website. If your IRS Form 990 is incomplete, submit a copy of a filed IRS Form 8868, the IRS request for an extension of the Form 990 filing deadline.
- copies of all contracts and sub-contracts with professional solicitors or fundraising counsel used in Maryland
- an updated list of the names and home or alternative business addresses of the board of directors
- any changes to your previous registration or documents submitted with it (for example, updated articles of incorporation), and
- financial report (see below)

Fee. The same sliding scale as for initial registration.

Annual Financial Report

If your annual contributions exceed $200,000, you must submit a financial statement with your annual update. If your nonprofit's charitable contributions are over $200,000 but less than $500,000, you must submit a financial review performed by an independent certified public accountant.

If your charitable contributions are $500,000 or more, you must submit a copy of an audit performed by an independent certified public accountant.

Other Requirements

All nonprofits in Maryland must include the following disclosure statement on every printed solicitation and every written confirmation, receipt, or reminder of a contribution:

> For the cost of postage and copying, documents and information filed under the Maryland charitable organizations laws can be obtained from the Secretary of State, Charitable Division, State House, Annapolis, MD 21401, 800-825-4510

Maryland

Massachusetts

Governing Law

Massachusetts has a charitable solicitations law codified at Massachusetts General Law Chapter 12, sections 8e and 8f; Chapter 68, sections 18 through 35. The law is enforced by the Massachusetts attorney general, Division of Public Charities, and may be accessed from its website.

State Website

The Massachusetts attorney general website has information on charitable solicitations at www.mass.gov. Go to "Attorney General," then "Non-Profits & Charities." The website contains all the state forms, links to state laws, and instructions.

Registration Requirements

Any charity that wishes to solicit funds in Massachusetts must obtain a Certificate for Solicitation before engaging in fundraising activities.

Exemptions

Massachusetts exempts the following types of nonprofits from registration:

$5,000 exemption. Any nonprofit that raises $5,000 or less during the calendar year is exempt as long as all of its fundraising is conducted by unpaid volunteers. Membership dues, fees, and similar payments need not be counted toward the annual limit.

Ten-person exemption. A nonprofit that receives contributions from ten people or less during the calendar year is exempt if all of its fundraising is done by volunteers.

Religious organizations. Religious organizations and their affiliates are exempt.

Fundraising for an individual. Fundraising for a specific individual is not considered to be charitable fundraising in Massachusetts because the public at large does not benefit. Thus, this type of fundraising is not subject to the registration or financial reporting requirements.

Fraternal organizations. Fraternal groups, such as police and fire associations and unions, are generally not public charities and thus do not have to register. However, if a fundraising appeal by a police or fire group states that a charitable purpose (for example, a scholarship fund or assistance to the police or fire department) will benefit in any way by the donations, the group must register.

Named organizations. The following organizations are exempt: American National Red Cross; the Grand Army of the Republic; American Veterans of World War II; Korea and Vietnam; Vietnam Veterans of America; AMVETS; the United Spanish War Veterans; the American Legion; the disabled American Veterans of the World War; Military Order of the Purple Heart; the Paralyzed Veterans of America; the Veterans of World War I of the U.S.A.; and the Veterans of Foreign Wars of the United States

Registration Procedure

Application form. Out-of-state nonprofits have the option of using the URS or the state application form, Short Form PC. In-state nonprofits (nonprofits based in Massachusetts) cannot use the URS. They must use Massachusetts state Form PC or Short Form PC. If your nonprofit has been in existence for at least one fiscal year, use Form PC. If your nonprofit is less than one year old, use Short Form PC. You may obtain these forms from the state website.

Documents included with application. Include the following documents with your application:

- a copy of your nonprofit's articles of organization, charter, or similar document establishing your organization
- a copy of your nonprofit's bylaws
- a list of the current officers and directors and their addresses, and
- a copy of your IRS determination letter, if any (if you have applied for 501(c)(3) status but have not yet received it, it is not necessary to send a copy of IRS Form 1023; instead, note that the application is pending in a cover letter and submit the determination letter when it is received).

It is not necessary to send a copy of your most recent Form 990 or 990-EZ or financial statements.

Signatures required. Two signatures are required—from your nonprofit's president and another authorized officer or trustee. The signatures need not be notarized.

Fee. If the URS or Short Form PC is filed, the fee is $50. If a Form PC is filed, there is a sliding scale (see table). Your check should be made payable to "Commonwealth of Massachusetts."

Gross support and revenue	Fee
Less than $100,001	$35
$100,001 to $250,000	$75
$250,001 to $500,000	$125
$500,001 or more	$250

Filing procedure. Mail the completed application, accompanying documents, and fee to:

Non-Profit Organizations/Public Charities Division
Office of the Attorney General
One Ashburton Place
Boston, MA 02108

Renewal Registration

The initial registration lasts for one year and must be renewed each year.

Time to renew. Your renewal registration must be filed no later than 4½ months after the end of each fiscal year. If your nonprofit uses the calendar year, it is due by May 15th. This is the same as the filing deadline for the Form 990. You may request up to two six-month extensions to file the report. You can make the request by email to CharitiesExtensions@state. ma.us. Either attach a copy of the IRS Form 8868, *Application for Extension of Time to File an Exempt Organization Return*, to the email, or explain why you need an extension in the body of the email.

Procedure. File the Massachusetts Form PC, which is available from the state website. Include a copy of your filed Form 990 or 990-EZ for the prior year, with all required IRS schedules except Schedule B. If your nonprofit is not required to file a IRS Form 990, 990-EZ, or 990-PF with the IRS, you must attach a completed IRS Form 990 or 990-EZ to the Form PC. This applies to small nonprofits that file Form 990-N with the IRS.

Fee. Sliding scale based on income (see table above).

Financial Report

If your nonprofit's annual contributions exceed $200,000 for the fiscal year, you must submit a financial statement along with your renewal (Form PC). If your nonprofit's charitable contributions are over $200,000 but less than $500,000, you may submit a financial review performed by an independent certified public accountant or an audited financial statement. If your charitable contributions are $500,000 or more, you must submit a copy of audited financial statements performed by an independent certified public accountant. Private foundations that file Form 990-PF with the IRS are exempt from this requirement.

Michigan

Governing Law

Michigan has a charitable solicitations law codified at Michigan Code of Laws sections 400.271 through 400.292. The law is enforced by the Michigan attorney general and can be accessed from its website.

State Website

The Michigan attorney general has a website at www.michigan.gov/ag (click on the "Charities" link) with links to forms for charitable solicitation registration.

Registration Requirements

Any charitable organization that solicits or intends to solicit contributions from Michigan residents by any means must first obtain a license from the Michigan attorney general.

Exemptions

The following types of organizations are exempt from the registration requirement. However, exemptions must be approved by the Attorney General Charitable Trust Section. To receive approval, you must file the state *Request for Exemption* form available from the state website. You must provide documentation or other evidence showing your nonprofit qualifies for the claimed exemption.

$8,000 exemption. Nonprofits that receive less than $8,000 in a 12-month period are exempt, provided they don't pay any individuals (even employees) for fundraising services of any kind. A nonprofit must make available to its members and the public a financial statement of its activities for the most recent fiscal year. In determining whether your nonprofit comes within the $8,000 limit, do not include grants or other money received from government agencies or foundations that are restricted as to use, or dues, fees, or similar payments by members of your organization.

Religious organizations. Also exempt is any duly constituted religious organization or group affiliated with and forming an integral part of a religious organization. These religious organizations are excluded from Michigan's definition of a "charitable organization." Thus, the state's charitable solicitations laws do not apply to them.

Educational institutions. Any educational institution certified by the Michigan State Board of Education is exempt.

Appeals for named individuals. Unpaid volunteers who solicit charitable contributions for named individuals need not register as long as all the money collected is turned over to the individual, less reasonable expenses.

Governmental entities. All local, state, and federal government agencies and units are exempt.

Veterans organizations. Veterans' organizations that are chartered by the U. S. Congress are exempt.

Hospitals. Hospitals licensed in the state of Michigan and their foundations and auxiliaries are exempt. A hospital-based foundation or auxiliary that solicits contributions solely for one or more licensed hospitals is also exempt.

PTAs. A school booster organization or parent-teacher organization operating with the knowledge and approval of a school for the support or promotion of educational, artistic, musical, or athletic programs or events is exempt.

Advocacy groups. An advocacy or lobbying organization, or an organization associated with an advocacy organization, political party, candidate, or committee is exempt.

Private foundations. Private foundations that receive contributions only from the members, directors, incorporators, or members of the families of those individuals are exempt. These organizations can conduct solicitations no more than once every calendar quarter.

Child-care providers. Organizations that are licensed by the State of Michigan to serve children and families, such as day care facilities, are exempt.

Sole support. Organizations whose sole source of funding is another charitable organization that holds a current Michigan charitable solicitation license are exempt.

Service clubs. A nonprofit service club or organization (1) that is tax-exempt with the IRS under a section other than section 501(c)(3), and (2) whose principal purpose is not charitable but solicits from time to time for a charitable purpose is exempt. In addition, all its fundraising must be performed by unpaid volunteers who are members of the organization to qualify for this exemption.

Registration Procedure

Application form. You may use the URS or the state application form, *Initial Solicitation Application/Registration*, which you can obtain from the state website. However, if you use the URS, you must complete and file a supplemental *Michigan Statement of Functional Expenses* form if your nonprofit (1) has gross receipts of $100,000 or more, and (2) files IRS Form 990-EZ. You can obtain the supplemental form from the state website.

Documents to be included with application. Include the following documents with your application:

- articles of incorporation
- bylaws
- a list of all chapters to be included in the solicitation license
- for out-of-state corporations, a copy of a Certificate of Authority to Transact Business in Michigan if you are incorporated in another state and have chapters in Michigan
- a copy of your IRS determination letter
- copies of your current contracts with professional fundraisers, consultants, or commercial co-venturers, if any
- samples of all solicitation materials
- a copy of your filed IRS Form 990-T if your nonprofit had unrelated business income, and
- a copy of your most recently filed IRS Form 990, 900-EZ, or 990-PF—but this is not required if your nonprofit is newly formed or you file Form 990-N. (If you file Form 990 or 990-EZ, do not provide a copy of Schedule B, Schedule of Contributors).

In addition, larger nonprofits must provide financial statements with their application. If your nonprofit received $500,000 or more in contributions in its immediately preceding tax year (as reported on your filed Form 990), you must provide audited financial statements prepared by an independent CPA. If your nonprofit received $250,000 to $500,000 in contributions, you may submit either audited financial statements or statements that have been reviewed by a CPA. These limits will be increased by $25,000 starting in 2015.

If the required financial statements are in the process of being prepared or you have already hired an auditor to perform the review or audit, attach a letter to your application requesting a conditional license. In your letter, state when you expect the financial statements to be available. Also, attach a copy of the engagement letter agreement with the audit firm. Your solicitation license will include the condition that the required financial statements be provided by a specified date.

If you have not engaged an auditor for the necessary financial statements, you may attach a request for a one-time waiver of the requirement. In your request, specify the fiscal year for which the waiver is requested and state that the necessary financial statements will be provided in all future years in which reviewed or audited financial statements are required.

Signatures required. One signature from a principal officer or director is required. It need not be notarized.

Fee. None.

Filing procedure. The application may be submitted by mail or e-filing. To submit the application by mail, send the application and accompanying documents to:

> Department of Attorney General, Charitable Trust Section
> P.O. Box 30214
> Lansing, MI 48909

To e-file your application, go to the Michigan attorney general's website at www.michigan.gov/ag. Click on "Charities" and scroll down to the link for "How to E-File or Mail Your Forms."

Renewal Registration

Time for renewal. Your solicitation license expires approximately six months after the close of your fiscal year. Renewal applications are due 30 days before the expiration of the solicitation license. If you need an extension of time to file the renewal application, you must request one in writing before the license expires. Extensions and second extensions will generally be for 90 days unless otherwise requested. However, they will not extend beyond IRS allowable extensions.

Procedure. You may use the URS or the state *Renewal Solicitation Application* form, which may be obtained from the state website. If you use the URS, you must complete and file a supplemental *Michigan Statement of Functional Expenses* form if your nonprofit (1) has gross receipts of $100,000 or more, and (2) files IRS Form 990-EZ. The supplemental form may be obtained from the state website.

Include the following documents with your renewal application:

- copies of current contracts with professional fundraisers, consultants, or commercial co-venturers, if any
- samples of all solicitation materials
- a copy of your filed IRS Form 990-T if your nonprofit had unrelated business income
- a copy of your most recently filed IRS Form 990, 990-EZ, or 990-PF—but these are not required if your nonprofit files Form 990-N; (if you file Form 990 or 990-EZ, do not provide a copy of Schedule B, *Schedule of Contributors*), and
- if your nonprofit received $500,000 or more in contributions, you must provide audited financial statements prepared by an independent CPA; if it received $250,000 to $500,000 in contributions, submit financial statements that are either audited or reviewed by a CPA.

The application may be submitted by mail or e-filed as described above.

Fee. None.

Annual Financial Report

This is included with the renewal application as described above.

Minnesota

Governing Law

Minnesota has a charitable solicitations law codified at Minnesota Statutes, sections 309.50; 309.515; 309.52; and 309.53. The law is enforced by the Minnesota attorney general and can be accessed from its website.

State Website

The Minnesota attorney general has a website with charitable solicitation information at www.ag.state.mn.us/Charities. This website contains all the state forms, registration instructions, and links to state laws.

Registration Requirements

All nonexempt nonprofits must register with the Minnesota attorney general before soliciting charitable donations in the state.

Exemptions

Minnesota exempts the following types of nonprofits from registration. To qualify for an exemption, you must submit the state *Verification Of Exemption From Registration* form, which can be downloaded from the state website.

$25,000 exemption. Nonprofits that do not receive, and do not plan to receive, more than $25,000 in total nationwide contributions during their fiscal year are exempt. To qualify for this exemption, the nonprofit must be an entirely volunteer organization with no paid staff and it must not hire any professional fundraisers. Grants received from government entities are not counted toward the $25,000 limit. If your nonprofit sells goods or services to the public, you need only count the difference between the cost of the goods or services and the price they were sold for.

Religious organizations. Religious organizations or societies that are exempt from filing an IRS Form 990 are exempt from Minnesota registration as well.

Educational institutions. Accredited educational institutions are exempt.

Private foundations. Private foundations that do not solicit contributions from more than 100 people during their accounting year are exempt.

Membership organizations. Organizations such as alumni, trade, or professional organizations that limit their solicitations to voting members are exempt.

Appeals for single individuals. Organizations that solicit contributions for a single specific individual are exempt as long as all the contributions collected are transferred to the person (no deductions for expenses or other costs are allowed).

Registration Procedure

Application form. You may use the URS or the *Minnesota Initial Registration/Annual Report* form, which may be obtained from the state website. If you use the URS, you must submit the *State of Minnesota Supplement to Unified Registration Statement* form.

Documents to be included with application. Include the following documents with your application:

- a copy of your articles of incorporation (or other corporate formation document such as a corporate charter)
- your IRS determination letter, if any, and
- a copy of your most recently filed IRS Form 990 or a financial statement for your most recent 12-month period (this may be an audited statement or any other statement which contains financial information about your nonprofit).

Signatures required. Two signatures from any two officers are required. They need not be notarized. Before signing, your board of directors must adopt a resolution approving and certifying the contents of the application and the date of the resolution.

Fee. $25, payable to "State of Minnesota."

Filing procedure. Mail the completed application, accompanying documents, and fee to:

Office of the Attorney General
1200 Bremer Tower
445 Minnesota Street
St. Paul, MN 55101-2130

Renewal Registration

No renewal is required, but all registered nonprofits must file an annual financial report with the Minnesota attorney general (see below).

Annual Financial Report

Each year following initial registration, your nonprofit must file an annual financial report with the Minnesota attorney general. If you fail to file the report on time, your registration is not continued, and your nonprofit may not solicit contributions in Minnesota.

Time for filing. Your annual report must be filed no later than the 15th day of the seventh month following the close of your nonprofit's fiscal year. If your nonprofit uses a calendar year, the due date is July 15.

You may request up to a four-month extension from the attorney general to file the annual report. You should make your request for an extension electronically at www.ag.state.mn.us/Charities/ExtensionRequest.asp. You must make the request before the due date for your annual report or you will be fined $50.

Procedure. You must complete and file either the URS or the *State of Minnesota Charitable Organization Initial Registration & Annual Report* form, which is available at the state website. However, if you use the URS, you must also submit the *State of Minnesota Supplement to Unified Registration Statement* form.

You must also submit a financial statement containing a balance sheet, statement of income and expense, and statement of functional expenses. The financial statement must be prepared in accordance with generally accepted accounting principles (GAAP), and must fully disclose financial information such as total receipts and total income from all sources, costs of management and general operating expenses, costs of fundraising, and costs of public education.

If your nonprofit's total revenue exceeds $750,000, you must provide a copy of audited financial statements prepared by a CPA in accordance GAAP.

You must also include your most recently filed IRS Form 990, 990-EZ, or 990-PF, if any.

Fee. $25.

Mississippi

Governing Law

Mississippi has a charitable solicitations law codified at Mississippi Code Annotated sections 79-11-501 through 79-11-511. The law is administered by the Mississippi secretary of state and can be accessed from its website.

State Website

The Mississippi secretary of state has a website at www.sos.state.ms.us/regenf/charities/charities.asp. The website contains the state form, instructions, and links to the state charitable solicitations law.

Registration Requirements

Prior to soliciting any charitable contributions in Mississippi, a charitable organization must register with the Mississippi Secretary of State.

Exemptions

Mississippi exempts the following types of nonprofits from its registration requirements:

Religious institutions. Religious institutions are not considered charitable organizations in Mississippi, and are not subject to the state's charitable solicitations law. Not only do they not need to register, they need not comply with any other provisions of this law. Religious institutions include:

- organizations with a regular place for religious services, including ecclesiastical or denominational organizations, churches, diocese, or presbytery
- religious groups that don't have a specific place of worship
- tax-exempt groups or corporations that form an integral part of a religious organization, and
- organizations that solicit contributions to construct and maintain a house of worship or clergyman's residence.

Unlike the other exemptions listed below, religious organizations need not file an application with the secretary of state to receive their exemption. These organizations are excluded from Mississippi's definition of a "charitable organization." Thus, the state's charitable solicitations law does not apply to them at all.

However, religious organizations that file a Form 990 with the IRS are not exempt and must register.

$25,000 exemption. Nonprofits that do not intend to solicit or receive more than $25,000 per year in contributions during the 12-month period ending on June 30 of the year are exempt, provided all fundraising is done by unpaid volunteers. The nonprofit can have salaried staff and hire independent contractors as long as they don't perform fundraising-related functions.

For these purposes, contributions do not include government grants or membership dues.

Educational institutions. All accredited educational institutions and their associated foundations are exempt. Also exempt are educational institutions that solicit donations only from their student body, alumni, faculty, trustees, and their families. Mississippi libraries are also exempt.

Membership organizations. Historical societies and fraternal, patriotic, social, educational, and alumni organizations that only solicit contributions from their membership are exempt.

Appeals for individuals. Unpaid volunteers who solicit contributions for a named individual in need are exempt, provided all contributions are turned over to the individual (deductions may be made for the cost of banquets or social gatherings).

United Way. Organizations that receive allocations from registered united funds or community chests and receive less than $4,000 from other sources during the 12-month period ending on June 30 of the year are exempt.

Volunteer firefighters. All volunteer fire departments and rescue units that are chartered as nonprofit organizations by the State of Mississippi are exempt.

Humane societies. Any humane society which contracts with counties or municipalities for the care and keeping of stray animals is exempt.

To obtain their exemptions, nonprofits other than religious organizations must file the state *Notice of Exemption* form with the secretary of state. The form may be obtained from the state website. A Statement of Exemption will be issued by the Charities Division upon receipt of the *Notice of Exemption*. You need file this form only once, since the registration remains in effect until you notify the Charities Division that you no longer qualify for the exemption or have stopped soliciting contributions in the state.

Registration Procedure

Application form. You must use the URS and also complete the state *Annual Financial Statement Report Form* (Form FS), which may be obtained from the state website.

Documents included with application. Include the following documents with your application:

- a copy of your nonprofit's articles of incorporation (or similar founding document)
- a copy of your bylaws
- a copy of your IRS determination letter, if any
- copies of all your contracts with professional fundraisers or fundraising counsel, and
- a copy of your last IRS Form 990 or 990-EZ.

You must also submit a financial statement. You must submit an audited financial statement prepared by a CPA if:

- your nonprofit had contributions over $500,000, or
- you used professional fundraisers or fundraising counsel.

You must submit a statement reviewed by a CPA if your nonprofit received contributions of $250,000 to $500,000.

If your nonprofit received contributions of less than $250,000, you can submit a financial statement that has not been audited or reviewed by a CPA.

Signatures required. The application must be signed by your nonprofit's president or other authorized officer and your chief fiscal officer. The signatures must be notarized.

Fee. $50, payable to "Mississippi Secretary of State."

Filing procedure. Mail the application, accompany documents, and fee to:

Mississippi Secretary of State's Office
Charities Registration
P.O. Box 136
Jackson, MS 39205-0136

Renewal Registration

Each registration expires one year after its date of issuance and must be renewed annually.

Time for renewal. The registration must be renewed by the date on the Certificate of Registration issued by the Charities Division. No extensions of time to renew are granted.

Procedure. Complete and file a URS along with the state *Supplement to Unified Registration Statement—Annual Financial Statement Report Form* (FORM FS). You must also include a copy of your most recent Form 990 or 990-EZ and a financial statement. Depending on the amount of your annual contributions, the financial statement may have to be audited or renewed by a CPA. See the rules listed in "Documents to be submitted with registration," above.

Fee. $50.

Annual Financial Report

This is submitted when your registration is renewed.

Other Requirements

All nonprofits in Mississippi must include the following disclosure statement on every printed solicitation and every written confirmation, receipt, or reminder of a contribution:

> The official registration and financial information of [name of charity] may be obtained from the Mississippi Secretary of State's office by calling 1-888-236-6167. Registration by the secretary of state does not imply endorsement.

Missouri

Governing Law

Missouri has a charitable solicitations law codified at Missouri Revised Statutes, Title XXVI, sections 407.450 through 407.462. The law is enforced by the Missouri Attorney General's office, Consumer Protection Division. You can find a link to the state law on the Missouri General Assembly's website at www.moga.mo.gov.

State Website

The Missouri Attorney General's office maintains a website at http://ago. mo.gov/checkacharity/charityregistration.htm. The website contains all the state forms and instructions for nonprofit registration.

Registration Requirements

Subject to the broad exemptions noted below, charitable organizations must register with the Missouri Attorney General's office before soliciting for donations in Missouri.

Exemptions

Missouri exempts most types of nonprofits from its registration requirements. Most significantly, it exempts all organizations that the IRS has recognized as tax exempt under Internal Revenue Code sections 501(c)(3), 501(c)(7), or 501(c)(8). To be recognized as tax exempt by the IRS and thereby qualify for the Missouri exemption, you must have obtained a determination letter from the IRS.

Section 501(c)(3) covers most types of nonprofits, including all those formed for charitable, educational, scientific, religious, or literary purposes; or for testing for public safety, to foster national or international amateur sports competition, or for prevention of cruelty to children or animals. Section 501(c)(7) covers social and recreational clubs, and section 501(c)(8) covers fraternal and benevolent organizations.

Also exempt, even if they lack an IRS determination letter, are:

- religious organizations
- educational institutions and their authorized and related foundations

- fraternal, benevolent, social, educational, alumni, and historical organizations and their auxiliaries, provided their solicitations of contributions is confined to their membership
- hospitals and auxiliaries of hospitals, provided all fundraising activities are carried on by hospital employees and not by any professional fundraiser employed as an independent contractor, and
- political organizations subject to Missouri's campaign finance laws (Missouri Rev. Stat., Title IX, Ch. 130).

If your organization falls within any of these exemptions, you must submit a written request for exemption to the Missouri attorney general. In the request you should state the reason you are claiming the exemption and submit supporting documents. Your articles of incorporation (or similar document) and IRS determination letter should be sufficient.

Registration Procedure

Application form. You can use the URS or the Missouri state form, *Charitable Organization Initial Registration Statement*, which can be obtained from the state website.

Documents to be included with application. Include the following documents with your application:

- articles of incorporation
- IRS Form 990, if any
- fundraiser contracts, if any, and
- copies of all written sales presentations, ads, phone scripts, or other solicitations.

Signatures required. One notarized signature of an officer, director, or other person authorized to sign for your nonprofit.

Fee. $15, payable to "Merchandising Practices Revolving Fund."

Filing procedure. Mail the application, accompanying documents, and fee to:

Missouri Attorney General's Office
Attention: Rhonda Johnson
P.O. Box 899
Jefferson City, MO 65102

Renewal Registration

No renewal is required, but you must file an annual financial report.

Annual Financial Report

Registered nonprofits must file a brief annual financial report using the state *Charitable Organization Annual Report Form* and pay a $15 fee. The report is due within 5 months after the end of your fiscal year. If you use the calendar year, it is due by March 15.

However, the following types of organizations are exempt from filing an annual report:

- any charitable organization that receives an allocation of money from an incorporated community chest or united fund
- any charitable organization that does not actually raise or receive contributions over $10,000 during the 12-month period immediately preceding the date on which its annual report would otherwise be due, and
- any charitable organization that is a local affiliate of a statewide or national charitable organization, if all local fundraising expenses are paid by the statewide or national organization and the statewide or national organization files an annual report.

Montana

Montana has no charitable solicitations law and does not require nonprofits to register before soliciting contributions in the state.

Nebraska

Nebraska has no charitable solicitations law and does not require nonprofits to register before soliciting contributions in the state. However, and out-of-state nonprofit corporation may have to register to do business in the state if it conducts intrastate business there. See Chapter 6 for detailed information.

Nevada

Nevada has no charitable solicitations law and does not require nonprofits to register before soliciting contributions in the state. However, and out-of-state nonprofit corporation may have to register to do business in the state if it conducts intrastate business there. See Chapter 6 for detailed information.

New Hampshire

Governing Law

New Hampshire has a charitable solicitations law codified at New Hampshire Revised Statutes, Title 1, sections 7:21 through 7:32b. The law is administered by the New Hampshire Department of Justice, Charitable Trust Division. The law can be accessed from the website of the New Hampshire State Legislature at http://gencourt.state.nh.us.

State Website

The New Hampshire Department of Justice has a website at http://doj.nh.gov/charitable. This website has a lot of helpful information on charitable solicitations, including all the state forms, FAQs, instructions, and even a video explaining how to register to fundraise in New Hampshire.

Registration Requirements

All charitable organizations must register with the New Hampshire attorney general before soliciting charitable donations in the state.

Exemptions

Only religious organizations are exempt from the state's registration requirements. This includes any religious organization which holds property for charitable or religious purposes and its integrated auxiliaries, and conventions or associations of churches. Religious organizations that file Form 990 with the IRS are not exempt and must register. Qualifying religious organizations are exempt from all the provisions of New Hampshire's charitable solicitations law.

Registration Procedure

Application form. You may use the URS or the state application form, *Application for Registration* (NHCT-1), which you can find on the state website.

    Documents to be included with application. Include copies of the following documents with your application:

- articles of incorporation (or similar founding document)
- bylaws

- IRS determination letter
- a financial statement
- your current conflict-of-interest policy (if you don't have one, your board must adopt one; a sample is provided in the state application form)
- your current provision for dissolution of your organization (this should be in your articles or bylaws); if your organization was organized in a state that does not require a dissolution provision, you must submit a copy of IRS Form 1023
- if your nonprofit has annual revenue, gains, and other support of $500,000 to $1,000,000, you must provide your latest financial statements prepared in accordance with GAAP—this need not be an audited statement; if your revenue was $1,000,000 or more, you must provide an audited financial statement prepared in accordance with GAAP (if providing such financial statements would be a financial burden, you can apply to the director of charitable trusts for an exemption from the requirement for up to three years).

Signatures required. The application must be signed by your organization's president and treasurer. Notarized signatures are not required.

Fee. $25, payable to "State of New Hampshire."

Filing procedure. Mail the completed application, accompanying documents, and fee to:

> Office of the New Hampshire Attorney General
> Charitable Trust Unit
> 33 Capitol Street
> Concord, N.H. 03301

Once you are registered, you will receive a Certificate of Registration signed by the New Hampshire Assistant Director of Charitable Trusts, together with a cover letter stating when your first annual financial report must be filed.

Renewal Registration.

No renewal required, but you must file an annual financial report.

New Hampshire

Annual Financial Report

All registered organizations are required to file an annual financial report with the attorney general and pay a $75 fee. You can satisfy this requirement by filing:

- the state Annual Report form, Form NHCT-2A, which will be mailed to you at the end of your fiscal year (if your nonprofit is not required to file IRS Form 990 or 990-EZ because of its income, you must complete the state financial disclosure statement on the form), or
- a copy of your most recently filed IRS Form 990, 990-EZ, or 990-PF.

In addition, if your nonprofit had annual revenue, gains, and other support of $500,000 to $1,000,000, you must provide your latest financial statements prepared in accordance with GAAP—this need not be an audited statement. If your nonprofit had annual revenue, gains, and other support of $1,000,000 or more, you must provide an audited financial statement prepared in accordance with GAAP. However, if providing such financial statements would be a financial burden, you can apply to the director of charitable trusts for an exemption from the requirement for up to three years.

The financial report is due four months and 15 days from the close of your organization's fiscal year. If you use the calendar year, it is due by May 15. This is the same date that the IRS Form 990 is due.

If you need an extension of time, complete and file Form NHCT-4, *Application For Extension of Time to File Annual Report with Charitable Trusts Unit*, which will be mailed to you along with Form NHCT-2A. If you do not hear from this division within 21 days, you may assume that your request has been granted.

New Jersey

Governing Law

New Jersey has a charitable solicitations law codified at New Jersey Statutes Annotated, sections 45:17A-18 through 45:17A-40. The law is administered by the New Jersey Department of Law & Public Safety, Department of Consumer Affairs and may be accessed from its website.

State Website

The Department of Consumer Affairs has a website at www.njconsumeraffairs.com/charity/charfrm.htm. The website contains all the state forms and instructions for charitable registration.

Registration Requirements

Charitable organizations must register with the New Jersey attorney general before soliciting contributions or having them solicited on their behalf.

Exemptions

The following organizations are exempt from New Jersey's registration requirements:

Religious organizations. Organizations established for religious purposes are exempt. So are organizations established for any charitable purposes that are affiliated, supervised, or controlled by a religious organization—for example, a religious school.

Educational institutions. Accredited educational institutions are exempt, as are institutions that confine their solicitations to their student body, alumni, faculty, trustees, and their families. Libraries registered by the New Jersey Department of Education are also exempt.

$10,000 exemption. Your nonprofit is exempt if your gross contributions during your fiscal year do not exceed $10,000 and you are a totally volunteer organization with no paid staff and you don't hire any professional fundraisers. Membership dues and similar payments and government grants or contracts are not counted toward the $10,000 limit.

Local organizations. An organization that is a local unit of a parent organization is exempt if:

- the parent organization is registered and provided all required information about the local unit

- all solicitations are made by members of the local unit or volunteers, and
- the local unit does not receive contributions over $10,000 during its fiscal year (this requirement does not apply to law enforcement organizations).

Registration Procedure

Application form. You may use the URS or one of two state forms. Use the state *Short Form Registration/Verification Statement* (Form CRI-200) if your nonprofit's gross contributions did not exceed $25,000 and you don't use professional fundraisers. Use the state *Long Form Initial Registration/Verification Statement* (Form CRI-150-1), if your contributions exceeded $25,000 or you used a paid professional fundraiser.

Documents to be included with application. Include copies of the following documents with your application (whether you use the URS or one of the state forms):

- articles of incorporation (or similar founding document)
- bylaws
- IRS determination letter or copy of filed IRS Form 1023
- IRS Form 990 for the most recent year, if any, and
- an audited financial statement if your nonprofit had over $250,000 in gross revenue.

Signatures required. You must have signatures of two authorized officers and one of the signers must be the chief fiscal officer. Notarized signatures are not required.

Fee. The fee is on a sliding scale based on gross contributions. Your check should be made payable to "Public Records Filing for a New Business Entity."

Gross contributions	Fee
less than $25,000	$30
$25,001 to $100,000	$60
$100,001 to $500,000	$150
more than $500,000	$250

Filing procedure. Mail the completed application, accompanying documents, and fee to:

New Jersey Division of Consumer Affairs
Charities Registration & Investigation Section
P.O. Box 45021
Newark, NJ 07101

Renewal Registration

All registered charities must renew their registration each year.

Time for renewal. You must file the renewal within six months after the end of your nonprofit's fiscal year. If you use the calendar year, it is due by June 30. You may request an extension of time to file of up to six months by mailing *Extension Form* CRI-400 or by submitting a letter to the N.J. Charities Registration section of the Attorney General's office. The Form CRI-400 is available on the state website. The request must be postmarked by the original due date of the registration renewal and must be accompanied by the registration fee due.

Procedure. If your organization raised less than $25,000 in gross contributions or is a bona fide veterans' organization, you can use state Form CRI-200. Include a copy of your IRS Form 990 for the fiscal year being reported if you are required to file a Form 990 with the IRS.

If your organization raised more than $25,000 in gross contributions or if it had contracts with a professional fundraiser, you will need to complete and submit CRI-300R *Long Form Renewal Registration*. Include a copy of your IRS Form 990 for the fiscal year being reported.

If your organization received over $250,000 in total gross revenue during the fiscal year being reported, you will need to submit a certified audit with your renewal registration.

Fee. The same as for initial registration, above.

Annual Financial Report

An annual financial report is required with the annual renewal.

New Jersey

Other Requirements

All nonprofits in New Jersey must include the following disclosure statement on every printed solicitation and every written confirmation, receipt, or reminder of a contribution:

> INFORMATION FILED WITH THE ATTORNEY GENERAL CONCERNING THIS CHARITABLE SOLICITATION AND THE PERCENTAGE OF CONTRIBUTIONS RECEIVED BY THE CHARITY DURING THE LAST REPORTING PERIOD THAT WERE DEDICATED TO THE CHARITABLE PURPOSE MAY BE OBTAINED FROM THE ATTORNEY GENERAL OF THE STATE OF NEW JERSEY BY CALLING 973-504-6215 AND IS AVAILABLE ON THE INTERNET AT http://www.njconsumeraffairs.gov/charity/chardir.htm. REGISTRATION WITH THE ATTORNEY GENERAL DOES NOT IMPLY ENDORSEMENT.

New Mexico

Governing Law

New Mexico has a charitable solicitations law codified at New Mexico Statutes sections 57-22-1 through 57-22-.11. The law is administered by the New Mexico attorney general and may be accessed from its website.

State Website

The state website with information on charitable solicitations is located at www.nmag.gov/office/Divisions/civ/charity/Default.aspx.

Registration Requirements

Any charitable organization existing, operating, or soliciting in New Mexico must register with the New Mexico attorney general.

Exemptions

The following organizations are exempt from New Mexico's registration requirements:

Religious organizations. Religious organizations are exempt from the New Mexico charitable solicitations law. Thus, they don't have to comply with any of its provisions, including the registration requirements. Religious organizations mean:

- a church
- any organization or group organized for divine worship, religious teaching, or other specific religious activity, or
- any other organization formed in association with or to primarily encourage or support the work, worship, fellowship, or teaching of any such church, organization, or group.

Educational institutions. Educational institutions are exempt. This includes any entity organized and operated primarily as a school, college, or other instructional institution with a defined curriculum, student body, and faculty, and conducting classes on a regular basis. It also includes "auxiliary entities," such as parent-teacher organizations, and booster and support clubs for a school, college, or other instructional institution.

Appeals for named individuals. People or organizations who solicit donations for an individual or group that has suffered a medical or other catastrophe are exempt, provided that:

- the individual or group is identified by name at the time of the solicitation
- the purpose for the solicited contribution is clearly stated, and
- all contributions collected, without any deductions, are deposited directly to an account in the name of the individual or group in a local federally insured financial institution.

Registration Procedure

New Mexico is one of the few states that requires applicants to register online.

Application form. You may not use the URS. Instead, you must use New Mexico's electronic registration system, called NM-COROS, at https://secure.nmag.gov/coros. The electronic filing system allows you to complete all registration and filing requirements online, including filling out the electronic registration form, uploading documents, and getting immediate confirmation of receipt.

Documents to be included with application. You must electronically submit all the following documents with your online registration application:

- a complete electronic copy of IRS Form 1023 or IRS Form 1024
- an electronic copy of your nonprofit's articles of incorporation and bylaws
- an electronic copy of your most recently filed IRS Form 990 or 990-EZ, Schedule A, and all attachments, except for copies of the schedule of contributors attached to IRS Form 990 or IRS Form 990-EZ. If your nonprofit has not completed its first year and has not yet filed a Form 990, you need not file one.
- If your nonprofit has more than $500,000 in total revenue, an electronic copy of an audit performed by an independent certified public accountant.

Signatures required. Online signature of chief financial officer or other authorized officer.

Fee. None.

Filing procedure. You must create an account and file online at https://secure.nmag.gov/coros.

Renewal Registration

No renewal is required, but you must file an annual financial report.

Annual Financial Report

You must file an annual report with the New Mexico attorney general's Charities unit within six months following the close of your fiscal year. If your nonprofit uses the calendar year, you must file the report by June 30. You can obtain an extension of up to 5½ months by filing IRS Form 8868 with the IRS and then providing the attorney general with a copy of the IRS form. You can upload electronically a copy of IRS Form 8868 from the attorney general's electronic registration system. You must request an extension no later than six months after the end of your fiscal year.

You must complete and file the annual report electronically using NM-COROS at https://secure.nmag.gov/coros. You will need to electronically upload with your report an electronic copy of your most recently filed IRS Form 990 or 990-EZ, Schedule A, and all attachments (except copies of the schedule of contributors attached to IRS Form 990 or IRS Form 990-EZ). You need not file a Form 990 or 990-EZ if your nonprofit had less than $25,000 in total revenue and was not required to file a Form 990 or 990-EZ with the IRS. However, even if your revenue was below $25,000, you must upload an electronic copy of your completed IRS Form 990 if your nonprofit contracted with a professional solicitor.

If your nonprofit has more than $500,000 in total revenue, you will also need to provide an electronic copy of an audit performed by an independent certified public accountant.

There is no fee to file the annual report.

New York

Governing Law

New York has a charitable solicitations law codified at New York Executive Law, Article 7a, sections 171-a through 177. The law is administered by the New York State attorney general, Charities Bureau, and can be accessed from its website.

State Website

The New York attorney general has a website with charitable solicitation information at www.CharitiesNYS.com. This is an extremely informative website, with all the state forms, instructions, FAQs, and videos.

Registration Requirements

Charitable organizations must register with the New York attorney general before soliciting contributions in New York state. This includes soliciting contributions from individuals, foundations, corporations, and government agencies located in the state.

In addition, organizations that own money or property in New York may have to register under the Estate Powers and Trusts Law. This can be done at the same time you register under the charitable solicitations law.

The New York State attorney general's Charities Bureau takes the view that any nonprofit that has a website that (1) can be accessed by New York residents, and (2) can directly accept contributions through a "donate now" button or other means is engaged in publicly soliciting in New York state. Thus, it must register in New York.

Exemptions

New York has a lengthy list of organizations that are exempt from its registration requirements. If you believe that your organization is exempt, complete the state *Registration Statement for Charitable Organizations* form and include Schedule E, *Request for Registration Exemption*. You can get the forms from the state website. The charities bureau staff will determine whether you are entitled to an exemption.

$25,000 exemption. Your nonprofit is exempt if your gross contributions from New York state are less than $25,000 per year. You cannot use professional fundraisers if you want to qualify for this exemption, although you can have employees or other salaried staff perform fundraising work. Note carefully that only contributions from New York state count toward the $25,000 limit. In addition, grants or other financial assistance from government agencies must be included toward the limit. This differs from most states. Membership dues and similar payments need not be counted toward the limit.

Your nonprofit may also claim this exemption if:

- you received an allocation from a federated fund, United Way, or incorporated community appeal; contributions from all other sources did not exceed $25,000; and you did not use a professional fundraiser, or
- you received all or substantially all of your contributions from a single government agency which required you to submit an annual financial report similar to the one required here, and you did not use a professional fundraiser.

Religious organizations. Any religious corporation or other organization with a religious purpose is exempt. Organizations operated, supervised, or controlled by a religious organization are also exempt—for example, religious schools. Such religious organizations are exempt from all provisions of New York's charitable solicitations law.

Educational institutions. Any educational institution that solicits contributions only from its student body, alumni, faculty, trustees, and their families is exempt. Any educational institution or museum that files annual reports with the Board of Regents of the State University of New York or a similar agency in another state is also exempt. Libraries that file annual reports with the New York Education Department are exempt as well.

PTAs. Any New York state parent-teachers' association, or any PTA affiliated with an exempt New York educational institution, is exempt.

Membership organizations. A membership organization (fraternal, patriotic, social, or alumni) that confines its solicitation of contributions to its membership is exempt.

Appeals for single individuals. People or organizations that solicit contributions for a single named individual are exempt, provided all the contributions are paid to the person for whom the money was collected.

New York

Government agencies. All government agencies and any organizations they control are exempt.

Other exemptions. The following types of organizations are also exempt, provided they solicit contributions only from their members:

- law enforcement support groups
- a historical society chartered by the Board of Regents of the State University of New York
- veterans organizations
- volunteer firefighters organizations, and
- volunteer ambulance service organizations.

Registration Procedure

Application form. You may use the URS or the state form CHAR410, *Registration Statement for Charitable Organizations*, which may be obtained from the state website.

Documents to be included with application. Include copies of the following documents with your application:

- your certificate of incorporation or other organizational document
- your bylaws or other internal rules
- if you have applied to the IRS for a tax exemption, your application for exemption (IRS Form 1023 or 1024), and
- your IRS determination letter, if any.

Signatures required. The application must be signed by both the president or another authorized officer, and the chief financial officer or treasurer. Notarized signatures are not required.

Fee. $25, payable to "NYS Department of Law."

Filing procedure. Mail the application, accompanying documents, and fee to:

New York State Department of Law (Office of the Attorney General)
Charities Bureau—Registration Section
120 Broadway
New York, NY 10271

Renewal Registration

No renewal registration is required, but you must file an annual financial report.

Annual Financial Report

Registered organizations must submit an annual financial report.

Time to file. The report must be filed 4½ months after your fiscal year ends. If you use the calendar year, the report is due May 15th. This is the same due date as the filing deadline for the IRS Form 990.

You can receive up to a three month extension of time to file the report. Send an email request to charities.extensions@oag.state.ny.us. The subject line of the email should contain the name of your organization, your Charities Bureau registration number, and your Federal Employer Identification Number (EIN). For example, the subject line should read: Re: ABC Charity, NYS Reg No. 01-23-45, EIN 12-3456789. State the reason for the request in the body of the email or include IRS Form 8868, *Application for Extension of Time to File an Exempt Organization Return*, as an attachment. You need not pay a fee when you ask for the extension.

Procedure. You must complete the state form CHAR500, *Annual Filing for Charitable Organizations*, which may be obtained from the state website. Include copies of the following documents:

- a copy of your IRS Form 990, 990-EZ or 990PF, with schedules
- an accountant's review if your nonprofit's annual revenue is between $100,000 and $250,000
- an accountant's audit if your revenue is over $250,000.

Fee. The filing fee is $10 if your nonprofit's total support and revenue was less than $250,000. If it was more than $250,000, the fee is $25.

Other Requirements

All nonprofits in New York must include the following disclosure statement on every printed solicitation and every written confirmation, receipt, or reminder of a contribution:

> Upon request, a copy of the latest annual report can be obtained from the organization or from the Office of the Attorney General, by writing the Charities Bureau, 120 Broadway, New York, NY 10271.

North Carolina

Governing Law

North Carolina has a charitable solicitations law codified at North Carolina General Statutes, sections 131F-1 through 131F-33. The law is enforced by the North Carolina secretary of state and may be accessed from its website.

State Website

The North Carolina secretary of state has a website with charitable solicitation information at www.secretary.state.nc.us/csl.

Registration Requirements

All nonprofits must obtain a license from the North Carolina secretary of state before soliciting charitable contributions in the state.

Exemptions

The following types of nonprofits are exempt from North Carolina's registration requirements.

$25,000 exemption. Any nonprofit that receives less than $25,000 in contributions in the calendar year is exempt, provided it does not pay any officer, trustee, organizer, incorporator, fundraiser, or solicitor. Government grants and membership dues and similar payments need not be counted toward the $25,000 limit.

Religious institutions. "Religious institution" means any church, ecclesiastical, or denominational organization, or any established physical place for worship at which nonprofit religious services and activities are regularly conducted. It also includes bona fide religious groups that do not maintain specific places of worship.

"Religious institution" also includes any separate group or corporation that forms an integral part of a tax-exempt religious institution that is primarily supported by funds solicited inside its own membership or congregation. These religious organizations are exempt from all the provisions of North Carolina's charitable solicitations law.

Educational institutions. All accredited educational institutions are exempt, as are their affiliated foundations.

Other exemptions. Other exemptions include:

- licensed hospitals and affiliated foundations

- all government agencies
- noncommercial radio or television stations
- volunteer fire departments, REACT (Radio Emergency Associated Communications Teams), rescue squads, or emergency medical services
- Young Men's Christian Associations or Young Women's Christian Associations
- nonprofit continuing care facilities licensed under North Carolina law
- any tax-exempt nonprofit fire or emergency medical service organizations not involved in the sale of goods or services that does not ask for donations
- bona fide volunteers, employees, or salaried officers of charitable organizations or sponsors
- attorneys, investment counselors, or bankers who advise people to make charitable contributions.

Registration Procedure

Application form. You may use the URS or the state application form, *Initial License Application Form for Charitable or Sponsor Organizations.* The state form can be downloaded from the state website.

   Documents to be included with application. Include copies of the following documents with your application:

- articles of incorporation
- bylaws and amendments to bylaws
- contracts with solicitors or fundraising consultants, and
- IRS determination letter, if any.

You must also provide financial information about your nonprofit's preceding fiscal year. This may consist of:

- a signed and completed IRS Form 990 or Form 990-EZ, Schedule A, and attachments (except Schedule B) for the preceding fiscal year
- a completed *North Carolina Annual Financial Report Form* covering the preceding fiscal year, or
- an audit prepared by, or with an opinion by, an independent certified public accountant.

If your nonprofit is new and has not completed a fiscal year, submit a budget for the current fiscal year.

Signatures required. One notarized signature from your treasurer or chief financial officer is required.

Fee. The fee is on a sliding scale based on contributions received during the preceding fiscal year. Your check should be made payable to "North Carolina Department of the Secretary of State."

Contributions	Fee
Less than $5,000	none
$5,000 to $99,999	$50
$100,000 to $199,999	$100
$200,000 or more	$200

Filing procedure. Mail the application, accompanying documents, and fee to:

North Carolina Department of the Secretary of State
Charitable Solicitation Licensing Section
P.O. Box 29622
Raleigh, NC 27626-0622

Renewal Registration

Your charitable solicitation license is good for one year and must be renewed each year.

Time for renewal. The renewal must be filed no later than 4½ months after the end of your nonprofit's fiscal year. If you use the calendar year, it must be renewed by May 15.

Procedure. Complete the state *Renewal License Application Form for Charitable or Sponsor Organizations*. It may be obtained from the state website. You must also provide financial information about your nonprofit's preceding fiscal year. This may consist of:

- a signed and completed IRS Form 990 or Form 990-EZ, Schedule A, and attachments (except Schedule B) for the preceding fiscal year, or

- a completed North Carolina Annual Financial Report Form covering the preceding fiscal year, or
- an audit prepared by or with an opinion by an independent certified public accountant.

Fee. The same as for initial registration.

Annual Financial Report

You must include an annual financial report with your annual renewal.

Other Requirements

All nonprofits in North Carolina must include the following disclosure statement at every point of solicitation and on every printed solicitation and every written confirmation, receipt, or reminder of a contribution:

> Financial information about this organization and a copy of its license are available from the State Solicitation Licensing Branch at 888-830-4989. The license is not an endorsement by the state.

North Dakota

Governing Law

North Dakota has a charitable solicitations law codified at North Dakota Century Code, Chapter 50-22. The law is administered by the North Dakota secretary of state and may be accessed from its website.

State Website

The state has a website with limited information on charitable solicitations at www.nd.gov/sos/nonprofit/registration. This sparse website has links to relevant laws and forms.

Registration Requirements

A charitable organization may not solicit by any means in North Dakota unless it registers with the North Dakota Secretary of State.

Exemptions

The following types of nonprofits are exempt from the registration requirement:

- tax-exempt religious organizations or societies that don't file Form 990 with the IRS (such organizations are not subject to the state's solicitations law at all)
- institutions of higher learning and private and public elementary and secondary schools
- people or organizations who solicit contributions for a single named individual, provided all the money collected is turned over to the person
- a volunteer organization that solicits funds for a government entity, or for a civic or community project in which the contributions received are used solely for the project
- political organizations regulated by state or federal election commissions, and candidates for office.

Registration Procedure

Application form. You may use the URS, but you must also submit the *North Dakota Charitable Organization Registration Statement*, available from the state website.

If your nonprofit is incorporated outside of North Dakota, you must also provide a completed *Certificate of Authority—Foreign Corporation Application*, Form SFN 13100. The form is available from the state website.

Documents to be included with application. Include copies of the following documents with your application:

- IRS determination letter (if your application is pending, attach the first page of your IRS Form 1023)
- Form 990 or financial statements (if none, complete Item 12 on state application form), and
- contracts with professional fundraisers.

Signatures required. One notarized signature of an officer.

Fee. $25, payable to "Secretary of State." Out-of-state nonprofits must also pay a $50 fee for the Certificate of Authority, and a $10 fee to appoint a registered agent.

Filing procedure. Mail the application, accompanying documents, and fee to:

Secretary of State
State of North Dakota
600 E. Boulevard Ave., Dept. 108
Bismarck, ND 58505

Renewal Registration

No renewal is required, but you must file an annual financial report each year.

Annual Financial Report

Every registered nonprofit must file an annual report with the secretary of state by September 1 of every year. If you filed your initial registration in July or August, you need not file your first report until September 1 of the following year. The secretary of state may extend the filing date for the annual report if you send a written application for extension before the filing deadline.

The report should be filed using the state *Charitable Organization Annual Report*, Form SFN 11302, available from the state website. You must also include your most recently filed Form 990 or 990-EZ and a financial statement. This need not be a certified or audited statement.

Fee. The filing fee is $10.

Ohio

Governing Law

Ohio has a charitable solicitations law codified at Ohio Revised Code sections 1716.01 through 1716.99. The law is administered by the Ohio attorney general, and can be accessed from its website.

State Website

The Ohio attorney general, Charitable Law section, has a website with charitable solicitation information at www.ohioattorneygeneral.gov/Services/Non-Profits. This informative website has all state forms, FAQs, and instructions for registering to fundraise.

Registration Requirements

All charitable organizations must register with the Ohio attorney general before soliciting charitable donations in the state by any means.

Nonprofits that own property or other assets located in Ohio may also have to register under the Ohio Charitable Trust Act. See the state website for details.

Exemptions

The following types of organizations are exempt from the registration requirement. Although not required, you have the option of asking the Ohio Attorney General's office to determine whether your organization qualifies for an exemption. This way, you'll know for sure that you fall within an exemption. To make such a request, send an email or letter citing the specific exemption provision you think you qualify for (these are listed below). Also, include with your letter materials that show you qualify for the exemption, such as your articles of incorporation, IRS determination letter, proof your contributions were less than $25,000, and so on. The attorney's general office will send a letter granting or refusing the exemption, and the letter will be entered into your nonprofit's file. Send your request to:

Determination Request
Ohio Attorney General's Office
Charitable Law Section
150 E. Gay St., 23rd floor
Columbus, OH 43215

Or you can email your request to CharitableLaw@OhioAttorneyGeneral.gov.

$25,000 exemption. Any tax-exempt nonprofit whose nationwide gross revenue is $25,000 or less during the preceding fiscal year is exempt, provided it does not pay anyone primarily to solicit contributions. Salaried staff can perform some fundraising-related work as long as they are not paid primarily for that work. Grants or awards from the government or a tax-exempt organization are not counted toward the $25,000 limit. Neither are membership dues or similar payments.

Religious organizations. All religious agencies and organizations are exempt, as are charities, agencies, and organizations operated, supervised, or controlled by a religious organization.

Educational institutions. This includes:

- any educational institution that solicits contributions only from alumni, faculty, trustees, or the student membership and their families
- any public primary or secondary school that solicits contributions only from alumni, faculty, or the general population of the local school district, and
- public primary and secondary school booster clubs.

Membership organizations. Organizations that solicit charitable contributions only from their existing membership, present or former employees, or present or former trustees are exempt.

Registration Procedure

Application form. You may register online through the Ohio attorney general's Charitable Organization Information Network (COIN). The website is at https://coin.ag.state.oh.us/DesktopDefault.aspx.

Alternatively, you may use the URS or the state *Charitable Organization Registration Statement* form, available from the state website.

Ohio

Documents to be included with application. Include copies of the following documents with your application:

- articles of incorporation (or similar founding document)
- bylaws
- IRS determination letter, if any,
- most recently filed IRS Form 990, 990-EZ, or 990-PF; if none, complete the state Annual Financial Report of Charitable Organization form.

Signatures required. One signature of either your treasurer or chief financial officer is required. A notarized signature is required if the application is filed by mail.

Fee. Sliding scale based on contributions received from Ohio during the preceding fiscal year (do not count membership dues or similar payments). Your check should be made payable to "Treasurer of the State of Ohio."

Contributions Received from Ohio Residents	Fee
Less than $5,000	none
$5,000 to $25,000	$50
$25,000 to $50,000	$100
$50,000 or more	$200

Filing procedure. File online, or mail the application, accompanying documents, and fee to:

Ohio Attorney General
Charitable Law Section
150 E. Gay St., 23rd Fl.
Columbus, OH 43215

Renewal Registration

All registrations expire after one year and must be renewed each year.

Time for renewal. The annual registration must be filed with the attorney general no later than 4½ months after the end of your tax year. If you use the calendar year, it is due on May 15—the same due date as IRS Form 990. The attorney general does not grant extensions of time to file the renewal. However, it abides by extensions granted by the IRS. So, if you requested and received an IRS extension, the Ohio registration filing will be due on the same date as the IRS deadline. You can obtain an automatic three-month extension from the IRS by filing IRS Form 8868, *Application for Extension of Time To File an Exempt Organization Return*.

Procedure. You can file either by postal mail or online using the Ohio attorney general's Charitable Organization Information Network (COIN). You can use the URS or the state *Charitable Organization Registration Statement*, available from the state website. You must include your annual financial report with whichever form you choose. You must also file a copy of your IRS Form 990, 990-EZ, or 990-PF for the preceding fiscal year. All required attachments to the 990 must be included, excluding the list of donors. If your organization does not file a Form 990, 990-EZ or 990-PF with the IRS, you may use the state *Annual Financial Report of Charitable Organization*, available from the state website.

Fee. The same as for the initial registration.

Annual Financial Report

Your annual financial report is included with the annual renewal.

Oklahoma

Governing Law

Oklahoma has a charitable solicitations law codified at Oklahoma Statutes, sections 18-552.1 through 18-552.16. The law is administered by the Oklahoma Secretary of State; it can be accessed through the Oklahoma State Legislature website at www.lsb.state.ok.us/osStatuesTitle.html

State Website

The Oklahoma secretary of state has a website at www.sos.state.ok.us. Click on the forms link, which will take you to a page with a link to download a Charitable Organization Packet.

Registration Requirements

All charitable organizations must register with the Oklahoma secretary of state before soliciting charitable contributions in the state.

Exemptions

The following types of organizations are exempt from Oklahoma's registration requirements. Unlike most states, Oklahoma will not advise you as to whether or not your nonprofit qualifies for an exemption. However, you may send a letter to the secretary of state stating that your nonprofit is exempt and citing the applicable exemption. The advantage of doing so appears to be that the secretary of state will know you are exempt and won't try to make you register.

$10,000 exemption. Any organization which collects less than $10,000 per year in charitable exemptions is exempt. Under Oklahoma law, you must count any donated money or property toward the annual limit. Unlike most states, there is no exclusion for government grants. However, you can exclude membership dues and similar payments because they are not donations.

Religious organizations. Organizations incorporated for religious purposes and actually engaged in bona fide religious programs are exempt, as are any other organizations directly operated, supervised, or controlled by a religious organization.

Educational institutions. Educational institutions are exempt if they:

- Oregon child-care agencies
- all federal and state government agencies
- trustees of a charitable remainder trust where the trustee is also the sole charitable beneficiary of the trust estate, and
- cemetery corporations.

Registration Procedure

Application form. You may use the URS if you are registering in more than one state. If you only register in Oregon, you should use the state application form, Form RF-C, *Registration for Corporation*.

Documents to be included with application. Include copies of the following documents with your application:

- articles of incorporation
- bylaws, and
- IRS determination letter.

Signatures required. One signature of any officer or other authorized representative. Notarized signatures not required.

Fee. None.

Filing procedure. Mail the application, accompanying documents, and fee to:

Charitable Activities Section
Oregon Department of Justice
1515 SW 5th Avenue, Suite 410
Portland, OR 97201-5451

Renewal Registration

No renewal is required, but annual financial reports must be filed.

Annual Financial Report

All registered nonprofits must submit an annual financial report to the Charitable Activities section and pay a fee.

Time for filing. The report is supposed to be filed no later than 4½ months after the end of your fiscal year. If you use a calendar year, you must file by May 15. This is the same deadline as for filing IRS Form 990 or 990-EZ.

- have a faculty, regularly enrolled students, and offer courses of study leading to recognized degrees, and
- only solicit contributions from their student body and their families, alumni, faculty, and trustees.

Membership organizations. Fraternal, patriotic, and civic organizations are exempt if they only solicit contributions from their membership. They may not use paid fundraisers.

Appeals for individuals. People and organizations who solicit contributions for a named individual are exempt, provided all the money collected is deposited in an account established for the person at a local bank.

Registration Procedure

Application form. You must use the state *Registration Statement of Charitable Organization* form. You may not use the URS.

Documents to be included with application. Include of following documents with your application:

- a copy of IRS Form 990 filed for your most recently completed fiscal year; if your nonprofit is new and doesn't have a Form 990, submit your IRS determination letter
- a complete list of the names, street addresses, and title or position of each officer, including each principal executive staff officer, director, and trustee of the charitable organization
- copies of all fundraiser contracts
- if you use professional fundraisers, a completed Professional Fundraiser Information Attachment (available on the state website) for each fundraiser, and
- a completed and signed state financial statement form.

Signatures required. One signature from your organization's president, chairman, or principal officer. The signature need not be notarized.

Fee. $15, payable to "Secretary of State."

Filing procedure. Mail the application, accompanying documents, and fee to:

Secretary of State
Corporate Filing Department
2300 N. Lincoln Blvd, Suite 101
Oklahoma City, OK 73102-4897

Oklahoma

Renewal Registration

Your registration is valid for one year from the date of your initial registration with the secretary of state. You must renew it annually on or before the anniversary of your initial registration. You will not be sent a renewal notice. The procedure for renewal is exactly the same as the procedure for initial registration described above.

Annual Financial Report

This is filed with your annual renewal registration.

Oregon

Governing Law

Oregon has a charitable solicitations law codified at Oregon Revised Statutes, Volume 3, sections 128.610 through 128.891. The law is administered by the Oregon attorney general, Charitable Activities section, and may be accessed from its website.

State Website

The Oregon attorney general has a website at www.doj.state.or.us/charigroup/howto.shtml.

Registration Requirements

All charitable corporations organized in Oregon must register with the Charitable Activities section of the Department of Justice. Out-of-state charitable corporations must register before soliciting charitable contributions in Oregon or doing business or holding assets in Oregon.

Exemptions

Oregon exempts the following types of organizations from its registration requirements. Unlike most states, there is no exemption for very small nonprofits.

Religious corporations. Any religious corporation with a religious purpose is exempt.

Educational institutions. Educational institutions are exempt if:

- they hold no property in Oregon, and
- they solicit no Oregon residents other than their alumni.

Unincorporated organizations. Organizations that are not incorpo and are not a trust are exempt. This includes all unincorporated associations.

Mutual benefit corporations. Any corporation organized in Ore as a nonprofit mutual benefit corporation is exempt. Mutual benef corporations are nonprofit corporations formed to further the con goals of their membership, rather than the entire public—for exa homeowners' associations, social clubs, fraternal organizations, v organizations, business leagues, and labor unions.

Other exemptions. Oregon also exempts:

You may obtain up to an 180 day extension of time to file the report. You can request an extension through the Department of Justice website at www.doj.state.or.us/charigroup/howtoextend.shtml. Alternatively, you may send the Charitable Activities section a copy of your filed IRS Form 8868, extending the time to file your Form 990 or 990-EZ by three months.

Procedure. Complete and file the Oregon state Form CT-12 if your nonprofit is incorporated in Oregon. File Form CT-12F if your nonprofit is incorporated outside of Oregon. Financial report forms will be mailed to you shortly following the end of your fiscal year.

You must include the following documents with your report:
- a copy of IRS Form 990 or 990-EZ filed for the preceding fiscal year (Schedule B need not be included)
- if your nonprofit filed Form 990-N with the IRS, attach a copy of the IRS confirmation that it was filed, and
- if your nonprofit had an independent audit of its financial records performed by a certified public accountant, attach a copy of the auditor's report.

If your nonprofit did not file IRS Form 990 or 990-EZ, but had total revenue of $25,000 or more, or net assets or fund balances of $50,000 or more, you must complete and file a Form 990 or 990-EZ for Oregon purposes only.

Fee. The fee is based on a sliding scale determined by your nonprofit's Oregon revenue and fund balance held in Oregon at the end of the reporting period. Your check should be made payable to "Oregon Department of Justice."

Total Oregon Revenue	Fee
0 to $24,999	$10
$25,000 to $49,999	$25
$50,000 to $99,999	$45
$100,000 to $249,999	$75
$250,000 to $499,999	$100
$500,000 to $749,999	$135
$750,000 to $999,999	$170
$1,000,000 or more	$200

Pennsylvania

Governing Law

Pennsylvania has a charitable solicitations law codified at Pennsylvania Statutes, Title 10, Chapter 4B, sections 162.1 through 162.18. The law is administered by the Pennsylvania Secretary of State, Bureau of Charitable Organizations, and can be accessed from its website.

State Website

The Pennsylvania secretary of state Bureau of Charitable Organizations has a website with charity registration information at www.dos.state.pa.us/portal/server.pt/community/charities/12444.

Registration Requirements

Unless exempt, all organizations soliciting charitable contributions from Pennsylvania residents must register with the Bureau of Charitable Organizations.

The state website has a link to the Charleston Principles, which suggests that the Bureau of Charitable Organizations follows these rules in determining whether the existence of a website requires out-of-state nonprofits to register in Pennsylvania. (See the discussion of the Charleston Principles in Chapter 2).

Exemptions

The following types of organizations are exempt from Pennsylvania's registration requirements under its charitable solicitations law. You are not required to apply for an exemption. However, if you believe your nonprofit is exempt, you may complete section B of Form BCO-2, *Non-Renewal Notice Form* (available on the state website) and postal mail it to the Bureau of Charitable Organizations. That way the Bureau would have a record that your organization is exempt.

> CAUTION
>
> **Even if your nonprofit is exempt, you may still have to file a report with the Bureau of Charitable Organizations.** See "Additional Requirements," below.

$25,000 exemption. Any charitable organization that receives gross national contributions of $25,000 or less annually is exempt as long as it does not pay anyone to conduct solicitations. The nonprofit can have salaried staff and hire independent contractors as long as they don't perform fundraising-related functions.

When calculating your $25,000 limit, you don't need to count government grants or contracts or membership dues or similar payments.

Religious institutions. Any religious institution, and any separate group or corporation that forms an integral part of a religious institution, is exempt provided it is primarily supported by government grants or contracts, funds solicited from its own membership, congregation, or previous donors, or fees charged for services. Such religious organizations are excluded from Pennsylvania's definition of a "charitable organization." Thus, the state's charitable solicitations law does not apply to them at all.

Educational institutions. Accredited educational institutions and auxiliary associations, foundations, and support groups that are directly responsible to educational institutions, are exempt. Publicly supported nonprofit libraries are also exempt if they file annual reports with the Pennsylvania State Library System.

PTAs. Local parent-teacher organizations are exempt if they are recognized in a notarized letter from a school district.

Hospitals. Hospitals and hospital foundations are exempt if they are regulated by the Pennsylvania Department of Health or the Department of Public Welfare.

Other exemptions. The following organizations and their auxiliaries or affiliates are exempt if no one is paid to do fundraising:

- veterans' organizations chartered under federal law
- volunteer firemen
- ambulance associations
- rescue squad associations, and
- nonprofit, tax-exempt senior citizen centers and nursing homes.

Registration Procedure

Application form. You may register online from the state website or by visiting http://efile.form990.org. Alternatively, you may use the URS or state application Form BCO-10, *Charitable Organization Registration Statement,* available from the state website.

Documents to be included with application. Include copies of the following documents with your application:

- articles of incorporation (or other founding document)
- bylaws
- IRS determination letter, and
- IRS Form 990 (including Schedule A) filed with the IRS for the immediately preceding fiscal year.

If your nonprofit doesn't file IRS Form 990 with the IRS—for example, because it files Form 990-EZ, 900-N, or 990-PF—you must file the state BCO-23 Form, *Pennsylvania Public Disclosure Form*, which is available from the state website. You will also need to provide a financial statement for the immediately preceding fiscal year. The type of statement required will depend on your nonprofit's nationwide gross contributions for the previous fiscal year. To determine your gross contributions, add Part VIII Lines 1a, 1b, 1c, 1d, 1f, 8a, and 9a from your IRS Form 990, or see Line 6 from your state BCO-23 Form if you do not file a Form 990. If you filed a Form 990-EZ, add Lines 1 and 6a and subtract any government grants.

Gross Contributions	Type of Financial Statement Required
Less than $50,000	Internally prepared, compiled, reviewed, or audited financial statements
$50,001 to $99,999	Compiled, reviewed, or audited financial statements
$100,000 to $299,999	Reviewed or audited financial statements
$300,000 or more	Audited financial statements

Internally prepared financial statements must contain a balance sheet and statement of revenue, expenses, and changes in fund balances. Compiled financial statements must be prepared by a licensed CPA or licensed public accountant in accordance with Statements on Standards for Accounting and Review Services issued by the American Institute of Certified Public Accountants. Reviews and audits must be performed by an independent, licensed public accountant or an independent, licensed CPA. Reviews must be performed in accordance with the American

- have a faculty, regularly enrolled students, and offer courses of study leading to recognized degrees, and
- only solicit contributions from their student body and their families, alumni, faculty, and trustees.

Membership organizations. Fraternal, patriotic, and civic organizations are exempt if they only solicit contributions from their membership. They may not use paid fundraisers.

Appeals for individuals. People and organizations who solicit contributions for a named individual are exempt, provided all the money collected is deposited in an account established for the person at a local bank.

Registration Procedure

Application form. You must use the state *Registration Statement of Charitable Organization* form. You may not use the URS.

Documents to be included with application. Include of following documents with your application:

- a copy of IRS Form 990 filed for your most recently completed fiscal year; if your nonprofit is new and doesn't have a Form 990, submit your IRS determination letter
- a complete list of the names, street addresses, and title or position of each officer, including each principal executive staff officer, director, and trustee of the charitable organization
- copies of all fundraiser contracts
- if you use professional fundraisers, a completed Professional Fundraiser Information Attachment (available on the state website) for each fundraiser, and
- a completed and signed state financial statement form.

Signatures required. One signature from your organization's president, chairman, or principal officer. The signature need not be notarized.

Fee. $15, payable to "Secretary of State."

Filing procedure. Mail the application, accompanying documents, and fee to:

Secretary of State
Corporate Filing Department
2300 N. Lincoln Blvd, Suite 101
Oklahoma City, OK 73102-4897

Renewal Registration

Your registration is valid for one year from the date of your initial registration with the secretary of state. You must renew it annually on or before the anniversary of your initial registration. You will not be sent a renewal notice. The procedure for renewal is exactly the same as the procedure for initial registration described above.

Annual Financial Report

This is filed with your annual renewal registration.

Oregon

Governing Law

Oregon has a charitable solicitations law codified at Oregon Revised Statutes, Volume 3, sections 128.610 through 128.891. The law is administered by the Oregon attorney general, Charitable Activities section, and may be accessed from its website.

State Website

The Oregon attorney general has a website at www.doj.state.or.us/charigroup/howto.shtml.

Registration Requirements

All charitable corporations organized in Oregon must register with the Charitable Activities section of the Department of Justice. Out-of-state charitable corporations must register before soliciting charitable contributions in Oregon or doing business or holding assets in Oregon.

Exemptions

Oregon exempts the following types of organizations from its registration requirements. Unlike most states, there is no exemption for very small nonprofits.

Religious corporations. Any religious corporation with a religious purpose is exempt.

Educational institutions. Educational institutions are exempt if:

- they hold no property in Oregon, and
- they solicit no Oregon residents other than their alumni.

Unincorporated organizations. Organizations that are not incorporated and are not a trust are exempt. This includes all unincorporated associations.

Mutual benefit corporations. Any corporation organized in Oregon as a nonprofit mutual benefit corporation is exempt. Mutual benefit corporations are nonprofit corporations formed to further the common goals of their membership, rather than the entire public—for example, homeowners' associations, social clubs, fraternal organizations, veterans organizations, business leagues, and labor unions.

Other exemptions. Oregon also exempts:

Oregon

- Oregon child-care agencies
- all federal and state government agencies
- trustees of a charitable remainder trust where the trustee is also the sole charitable beneficiary of the trust estate, and
- cemetery corporations.

Registration Procedure

Application form. You may use the URS if you are registering in more than one state. If you only register in Oregon, you should use the state application form, Form RF-C, *Registration for Corporation*.

Documents to be included with application. Include copies of the following documents with your application:

- articles of incorporation
- bylaws, and
- IRS determination letter.

Signatures required. One signature of any officer or other authorized representative. Notarized signatures not required.

Fee. None.

Filing procedure. Mail the application, accompanying documents, and fee to:

Charitable Activities Section
Oregon Department of Justice
1515 SW 5th Avenue, Suite 410
Portland, OR 97201-5451

Renewal Registration

No renewal is required, but annual financial reports must be filed.

Annual Financial Report

All registered nonprofits must submit an annual financial report to the Charitable Activities section and pay a fee.

Time for filing. The report is supposed to be filed no later than 4½ months after the end of your fiscal year. If you use a calendar year, you must file by May 15. This is the same deadline as for filing IRS Form 990 or 990-EZ.

You may obtain up to an 180 day extension of time to file the report. You can request an extension through the Department of Justice website at www.doj.state.or.us/charigroup/howtoextend.shtml. Alternatively, you may send the Charitable Activities section a copy of your filed IRS Form 8868, extending the time to file your Form 990 or 990-EZ by three months.

Procedure. Complete and file the Oregon state Form CT-12 if your nonprofit is incorporated in Oregon. File Form CT-12F if your nonprofit is incorporated outside of Oregon. Financial report forms will be mailed to you shortly following the end of your fiscal year.

You must include the following documents with your report:

- a copy of IRS Form 990 or 990-EZ filed for the preceding fiscal year (Schedule B need not be included)
- if your nonprofit filed Form 990-N with the IRS, attach a copy of the IRS confirmation that it was filed, and
- if your nonprofit had an independent audit of its financial records performed by a certified public accountant, attach a copy of the auditor's report.

If your nonprofit did not file IRS Form 990 or 990-EZ, but had total revenue of $25,000 or more, or net assets or fund balances of $50,000 or more, you must complete and file a Form 990 or 990-EZ for Oregon purposes only.

Fee. The fee is based on a sliding scale determined by your nonprofit's Oregon revenue and fund balance held in Oregon at the end of the reporting period. Your check should be made payable to "Oregon Department of Justice."

Total Oregon Revenue	Fee
0 to $24,999	$10
$25,000 to $49,999	$25
$50,000 to $99,999	$45
$100,000 to $249,999	$75
$250,000 to $499,999	$100
$500,000 to $749,999	$135
$750,000 to $999,999	$170
$1,000,000 or more	$200

Oregon

Pennsylvania

Governing Law

Pennsylvania has a charitable solicitations law codified at Pennsylvania Statutes, Title 10, Chapter 4B, sections 162.1 through 162.18. The law is administered by the Pennsylvania Secretary of State, Bureau of Charitable Organizations, and can be accessed from its website.

State Website

The Pennsylvania secretary of state Bureau of Charitable Organizations has a website with charity registration information at www.dos.state.pa.us/portal/server.pt/community/charities/12444.

Registration Requirements

Unless exempt, all organizations soliciting charitable contributions from Pennsylvania residents must register with the Bureau of Charitable Organizations.

The state website has a link to the Charleston Principles, which suggests that the Bureau of Charitable Organizations follows these rules in determining whether the existence of a website requires out-of-state nonprofits to register in Pennsylvania. (See the discussion of the Charleston Principles in Chapter 2).

Exemptions

The following types of organizations are exempt from Pennsylvania's registration requirements under its charitable solicitations law. You are not required to apply for an exemption. However, if you believe your nonprofit is exempt, you may complete section B of Form BCO-2, *Non-Renewal Notice Form* (available on the state website) and postal mail it to the Bureau of Charitable Organizations. That way the Bureau would have a record that your organization is exempt.

> ### CAUTION
> **Even if your nonprofit is exempt, you may still have to file a report with the Bureau of Charitable Organizations.** See "Additional Requirements," below.

$25,000 exemption. Any charitable organization that receives gross national contributions of $25,000 or less annually is exempt as long as it does not pay anyone to conduct solicitations. The nonprofit can have salaried staff and hire independent contractors as long as they don't perform fundraising-related functions.

When calculating your $25,000 limit, you don't need to count government grants or contracts or membership dues or similar payments.

Religious institutions. Any religious institution, and any separate group or corporation that forms an integral part of a religious institution, is exempt provided it is primarily supported by government grants or contracts, funds solicited from its own membership, congregation, or previous donors, or fees charged for services. Such religious organizations are excluded from Pennsylvania's definition of a "charitable organization." Thus, the state's charitable solicitations law does not apply to them at all.

Educational institutions. Accredited educational institutions and auxiliary associations, foundations, and support groups that are directly responsible to educational institutions, are exempt. Publicly supported nonprofit libraries are also exempt if they file annual reports with the Pennsylvania State Library System.

PTAs. Local parent-teacher organizations are exempt if they are recognized in a notarized letter from a school district.

Hospitals. Hospitals and hospital foundations are exempt if they are regulated by the Pennsylvania Department of Health or the Department of Public Welfare.

Other exemptions. The following organizations and their auxiliaries or affiliates are exempt if no one is paid to do fundraising:

- veterans' organizations chartered under federal law
- volunteer firemen
- ambulance associations
- rescue squad associations, and
- nonprofit, tax-exempt senior citizen centers and nursing homes.

Registration Procedure

Application form. You may register online from the state website or by visiting http://efile.form990.org. Alternatively, you may use the URS or state application Form BCO-10, *Charitable Organization Registration Statement,* available from the state website.

Documents to be included with application. Include copies of the following documents with your application:

- articles of incorporation (or other founding document)
- bylaws
- IRS determination letter, and
- IRS Form 990 (including Schedule A) filed with the IRS for the immediately preceding fiscal year.

If your nonprofit doesn't file IRS Form 990 with the IRS—for example, because it files Form 990-EZ, 900-N, or 990-PF—you must file the state BCO-23 Form, *Pennsylvania Public Disclosure Form*, which is available from the state website. You will also need to provide a financial statement for the immediately preceding fiscal year. The type of statement required will depend on your nonprofit's nationwide gross contributions for the previous fiscal year. To determine your gross contributions, add Part VIII Lines 1a, 1b, 1c, 1d, 1f, 8a, and 9a from your IRS Form 990, or see Line 6 from your state BCO-23 Form if you do not file a Form 990. If you filed a Form 990-EZ, add Lines 1 and 6a and subtract any government grants.

Gross Contributions	Type of Financial Statement Required
Less than $50,000	Internally prepared, compiled, reviewed, or audited financial statements
$50,001 to $99,999	Compiled, reviewed, or audited financial statements
$100,000 to $299,999	Reviewed or audited financial statements
$300,000 or more	Audited financial statements

Internally prepared financial statements must contain a balance sheet and statement of revenue, expenses, and changes in fund balances. Compiled financial statements must be prepared by a licensed CPA or licensed public accountant in accordance with Statements on Standards for Accounting and Review Services issued by the American Institute of Certified Public Accountants. Reviews and audits must be performed by an independent, licensed public accountant or an independent, licensed CPA. Reviews must be performed in accordance with the American

Institute of Certified Public Accountants' Statements on Standards for Accounting and Review Services. Audits must be performed in accordance with the American Institute of Certified Public Accountants' Statements on Auditing Standards.

Signatures required. Two signatures must be provided—one from the chief fiscal officer, and one from another authorized officer. Notarization is not required.

Fee. Sliding scale based on gross annual contributions. Your check should be made payable to "Commonwealth of Pennsylvania."

Gross Contributions	Fee
$25,000 or less	$15
$25,001 to $99,999	$100
$100,000 to $499,999	$150
$500,000 and more	$250

Filing procedure. If you are not filing electronically, mail the application, accompanying documents, and fee to:

Office of the Secretary of the Commonwealth
Bureau of Charitable Organizations
207 North Office Building
Harrisburg, PA 17120

Renewal Registration

You must renew your registration annually for each fiscal year you solicit contributions from Pennsylvania residents.

Time for renewal. Your renewal must be filed within 135 days (4½ months) after the close of your nonprofit's fiscal year. If you use the calendar year, it is due by May 15. This is the same deadline as for filing IRS Form 990 or 990-EZ.

If you cannot meet this deadline, the Bureau can grant an extension of up to 180 days. Complete the state Form BCO-2 and have it postmarked on or before the date your registration is due. An organization failing to file a registration or an extension request by the due date must pay late fees of $25 per month.

Pennsylvania

Procedure. The procedure for renewal is the same as for initial registration above, except you need not file copies of your articles of incorporation, bylaws, or IRS determination letter.

Fee. The fee is the same as for initial registration.

Annual Financial Report

The annual financial report is included with the annual renewal.

Other Requirements

If your nonprofit is located in Pennsylvania and is exempt from registering under the state's charitable solicitations laws (see "Exemptions," above), you may still be required to register annually under another Pennsylvania law called the Purely Public Charity Act, 10 Pa. Statutes, sections 371 through 385. This law requires a nonprofit organization receiving or claiming exemption from Pennsylvania property or sales taxes to file a one page annual report and a copy of its IRS Form 990 with the Department of State's Bureau of Charitable Organization and pay a $15 fee. You must file the report with the Bureau within 135 days after the close of your nonprofit's fiscal year, unless you are granted an extension. See the state website for the report form and instructions.

Your nonprofit need not file this report if your nonprofit has already registered under the state charitable solicitations laws.

You should still file the annual report, but need not provide copies of any IRS forms or pay a fee if your nonprofit is a religious organization or receives less than $25,000 in contributions per year.

In addition, all nonprofits in Pennsylvania must include the following disclosure statement on every printed solicitation and every written confirmation, receipt, or reminder of a contribution:

> The official registration and financial information of [*insert the legal name of the charity as registered with the department*] may be obtained from the Pennsylvania Department of State by calling toll-free, within Pennsylvania, 1-800-732-0999. Registration does not imply endorsement.

Rhode Island

Governing Law

Rhode Island has a charitable solicitations law codified at Rhode Island General Laws, sections 5-53.1-1 through 5-53.1-18. The law is administered by the Department of Business Regulation and can be accessed from its website.

State Website

The Rhode Island Department of Business Regulation website has information on charitable solicitations at www.dbr.state.ri.us/divisions/securities/charitable.php.

Registration Requirements

All charitable organizations must register with the State of Rhode Island before soliciting charitable contributions in the state.

Exemptions

The following types of organizations are exempt from Rhode Island's registration requirements:

$25,000 exemption. Any nonprofit that does not intend to solicit, and does not actually raise, contributions over $25,000 during its fiscal year is exempt, provided none of its fundraising functions are carried on by professional fundraisers. Paid employees or salaried staff, however, can perform fundraising work. Contributions received from corporations, charitable foundations, government agencies, or a duly registered federated fund, incorporated community appeal, or United Way, are not counted toward the $25,000 limit. In addition, officers and directors, including those performing fundraising-related work, must be unpaid.

Religious organizations. Religious organizations, including churches or recognized denominations, are exempt. Also exempt are societies and institutions operated, supervised, or controlled by a religious organization.

Educational institutions. All accredited or government approved educational institutions are exempt, as are parent teacher organizations.

Appeals for individuals. People and organizations who solicit charitable contributions for a named individual are exempt, provided all the money collected is turned over to the individual.

Membership organizations. Organizations which solicit only from their own membership are exempt.

Foundations. Foundations or associations created exclusively for the benefit of religious organizations, education institutions, non-profit or charitable hospitals, and public libraries are exempt.

Other exemptions. Rhode Island also exempts:

- nonprofit, charitable hospitals
- homes for the aged, orphanages, and homes for unwed mothers affiliated with, but not operated or controlled by, religious organizations
- people soliciting contributions solely from corporations, charitable foundations, or governmental agencies
- chartered veterans' organizations and their auxiliaries
- public libraries
- Rhode Island historical societies
- free, nonprofit public art museums
- grange organizations and their auxiliaries
- volunteer fire and rescue associations, and
- land trusts organized under Rhode Island law.

Registration Procedure

Application form. You may use the URS or the state form, *Charitable Organizations Application*, available from the state website.

Documents to be included with application. Include an electronic copy of your IRS determination letter with your application and copies of any fundraiser contracts.

In addition, if your nonprofit's annual gross income was less than $500,000, include a copy of IRS Form 990 or a compiled financial statement for the immediately preceding fiscal year. If your nonprofit's annual gross income was more than $500,000, file an audited financial statement prepared by an independent certified public accountant. You need not file a copy of your Form 990.

Signatures required. Two authorized officials, one of whom is a director or trustee, must sign the application. Notarized signatures are not required.

Fee. $90, payable to "Rhode Island Secretary of State."

Filing procedure. All documents must be submitted on a CD-ROM. Paper filings are not accepted. The CD-ROM must use the PDF format or be Windows 2000 compatible. Mail the CD-ROM to:

State of Rhode Island and Providence Plantations
Department of Business Regulation
Securities Division
Charitable Origination Section
1511 Pontiac Avenue, John O. Pastore Complex Bldg 69-1
Cranston, RI 02920

Renewal Registration

Your registration expires one year after it is issued. You must renew it within 30 days prior to its expiration. The renewal process is the same as for initial registration.

Annual Financial Report

The annual financial report is included with your annual renewal.

South Carolina

Governing Law

South Carolina has a charitable solicitations law codified at South Carolina Code of Laws, sections 33-56-10 through 33-56-200. The law is administered by the South Carolina Secretary of State, Division of Public Charities, and can be accessed from its website.

State Website

The South Carolina secretary of state Division of Public Charities has a website with information on charitable solicitations at www.scsos.com/Public_Charities/Public_Charities_Info.

Registration Requirements

All charitable organizations that solicit contributions or have contributions solicited on their behalf must register with the South Carolina Secretary of State's Office prior to any solicitation activity.

Exemptions

The following types of organizations are exempt from South Carolina's registration requirements. Exempt nonprofits other than religious organizations and political groups must file an annul *Application for Exemption* with the secretary of state within 4½ months after the close their fiscal year. There is no fee for this filing. You can file online through the state website or postal mail the application. The application is available from the state website.

$20,000 exemption. Any IRS tax-exempt organization that does not intend to solicit or receive contributions over $20,000 during the calendar year is exempt if (1) it does not employ any professional fundraisers, and (2) no one who works for the organization is paid more than $500 per year.

$7,500 exemption. Any organization that does not solicit or receive contributions over $7,500 during a calendar year is exempt, regardless of whether or not it uses professional fundraisers.

Religious organizations. Any bona fide religious organization is exempt if it is supported primarily by government grants or contracts, funds solicited from its own membership, congregation, or previous donors, or fees charged for services rendered in furtherance of its tax-exempt purposes.

Groups affiliated with exempt religious organizations are also exempt. Such religious organizations are excluded from South Carolina's definition of a "charitable organization." Thus, the state's charitable solicitations law does not apply to them at all.

Political groups and candidates. Candidates for elective office, political parties, and other groups required to file information with the Federal Election Commission or State Election Commission are exempt.

Educational institutions. Provided that it does not use professional fundraisers, an educational institution that solicits contributions from only its students and their families, alumni, faculty, friends, and other constituencies, trustees, corporations, foundations, and individuals who are interested in and support its programs is exempt.

Appeals for individuals. A person requesting contributions for the relief of a specified individual is exempt if all the money collected is turned over to the individual. Professional fundraisers may not be used for such appeals.

Other exemptions. Provided they don't use professional fundraisers, the following organizations are also exempt:

- any organization that solicits exclusively from its membership
- any veterans' organization with a congressional charter, and
- state agencies subject to the disclosure provisions of the Freedom of Information Act.

Registration Procedure

Application form. You can file online through the state website. Alternatively, you can file the URS or state application form by postal mailing the form to the Division of Public Charities. The state application, *Registration Statement for a Charitable Organization*, is available at the state website.

Documents to be included with application. Include a copy of your IRS determination letter with your application.

Signatures required. The application must be signed by your nonprofit's chief executive officer and chief financial officer. The signatures need not be notarized.

Fee. $50, payable to "Secretary of State."

Filing procedure. If you are not filing online, postal mail the application, accompanying documents, and fee to:

South Carolina Secretary of State
Attn: Division of Public Charities,
Post Office Box 11350
Columbia, SC 29211

Renewal Registration

You must renew your registration each year.

Time for renewal. Your annual renewal must be filed no later than 4½ months after the end of your nonprofit's fiscal year. If you use the calendar year, the renewal is due May 15.

Procedure. You may file online or use the state form, *Registration Statement for a Charitable Organization*, available from the state website. If you haven't filed your annual financial report for the preceding fiscal year (see below), you must include the report with your renewal.

Fee. $50.

Annual Financial Report

Every registered nonexempt nonprofit must file an annual financial report with the secretary of state. You can do this separately, or include it with your renewal. If you don't have the necessary financial information available when your renewal is due, you can obtain an extension and file the financial report later.

Time to file. The report is due 4½ months after the end of your nonprofit's fiscal year. If you use the calendar year, it is due May 15. This is the same deadline for filing IRS Form 990 or 990-EZ. You can request up to two three-month extensions of the time to file the report. If you file the secretary of state's *Annual Financial Report Form*, you must send an extension request in writing to the Division of Public Charities. If you file IRS Form 990 or 990-EZ, send in a copy of IRS Form 8868, *Request for Extension in Filing Form 990.*

Procedure. You may file online at the state website. Alternatively, you may postal mail either the secretary of state's *Annual Financial Report Form* (available from the state website), or copies of your IRS Form 990, 990-EZ, or 990-PF filed with the IRS for the prior fiscal year.

Fee. None.

South Dakota

South Dakota does not have a charitable solicitations law and does not require nonprofits to register with a state agency before soliciting contributions in the state. However, an out-of-state nonprofit corporation may have to register to do business in the state if it conducts intrastate business there. See Chapter 6 for detailed information on registering as an out-of-state business.

Tennessee

Governing Law

Tennessee has a charitable solicitations law codified at Tennessee Code sections 48-101-501 through 48-101-520. The law is administered by the Tennessee Secretary of State, Division of Charitable Solicitation and Gaming, and may be accessed through its website.

State Website

The Tennessee Secretary of State, Division of Charitable Solicitation and Gaming, has information on charitable fundraising registration on its website at www.state.tn.us/sos/charity/co-info.htm.

Registration Requirements

Any charitable organization which intends to solicit charitable contributions in Tennessee must register with the secretary of state before making any such solicitation.

Impact of websites on registration. Tennessee has adopted the Charleston Principles to help out-of-state nonprofits determine whether they must register in Tennessee solely because they have a website. Of course, an out-of-state nonprofit that directly solicits Tennessee residents by other means—for example, sending fundraising materials to residents—would have to register on that basis, whether or not it has a website.

The Charleston Principles are discussed in detail in Chapter 2. Under these principles and Tennessee law, nonprofit websites are divided into two categories: interactive and noninteractive. A website is interactive if donors can make contributions or purchase products by electronically completing the transaction through the website, even if completion requires the use of a linked or redirected site. Noninteractive websites do not have this capacity.

An out-of-state nonprofit must register if it maintains an interactive website and either (1) targets people in Tennessee, or (2) receives contributions on a repeated and ongoing basis or a substantial basis through its website. "Repeated and ongoing basis" means 100 or more online contributions at any time in a year and "substantial basis" means $25,000 in online contributions in a year.

If a nonprofit solicits contributions through a website that is not interactive, it must register if:

- it satisfies the same requirements as an interactive website above, and
- it specifically invites further offline activity to complete a contribution—for example, by including an address to send contributions—or establishes other contacts with Tennessee, such as sending email messages or other communications that promote the website.

Exemptions

The following types of organizations are exempt from Tennessee's registration requirements.

$30,000 exemption. Any nonprofit that does not intend to solicit, and does not actually receive, more than $30,000 in gross contributions during its fiscal year is exempt. Gross contributions include the entire value of noncash items raised by an outside fundraiser, not just the amount actually received by the charity. Membership fees and similar fees need not be counted toward the limit. To qualify for this exemption, your nonprofit must file an *Exemption Request Form* with the secretary of state. You can do this online at the state website or by postal mailing the form to the Division of Charitable Solicitation and Gaming.

Religious institutions. Religious institutions are exempt. This includes:

- ecclesiastical or denominational organizations, or churches
- established physical places for worship in Tennessee at which nonprofit religious services and activities are regularly conducted
- bona fide tax-exempt religious groups which do not maintain specific places of worship, and
- any separate tax-exempt group or corporation that forms an integral part of a religious institution, provided that (1) it is not required to file a Form 990 with the IRS, and (2) it is supported primarily by funds solicited from the religious institution's membership or congregation.

Such religious organizations are exempt from application of all the provisions of Tennessee's charitable solicitations law. However, religious organizations that file a Form 990 with the IRS are not exempt and must register.

Educational institutions. Educational organizations are exempt. This includes:

- any accredited educational organization which normally maintains a regular faculty, curriculum, and student body
- any parent-teacher organization or other organization created to support the school or its extracurricular activities, and
- private foundations soliciting contributions exclusively for educational organizations.

Other exemptions. Also exempt are:

- volunteer fire departments, rescue squads, local civil defense organizations
- community fairs, county fairs, district fairs, and division fairs, that have been qualified by the Tennessee Commissioner of Agriculture to receive state aid grants
- political parties, candidates for federal or state office, and political action committees required to file financial information with federal or state election commissions
- hospitals and nursing homes that are subject to regulation by the Tennessee Department of Health, and
- congressionally chartered corporations.

Registration Procedure

Application form. You may file online at the state website. Alternatively, you may file by postal mail and use the URS or the state application form, *Application for Registration of a Charitable Organization*, available from the state website.

Documents to be included with application. Include copies of the following documents with your application:

- articles of incorporation (or other organizing documents)
- bylaws
- IRS determination letter, if any (if IRS application is pending, include a copy of your filed IRS Form 1023 and any letters received from the IRS acknowledging receipt), and
- fundraiser contracts, if any.

If your nonprofit has completed an accounting year, it must also file:

- the state *Summary of Financial Activities* form (available from the state website),
- a copy of your latest filed IRS form 990, 990-EZ or 990-N, and
- an audited financial statement if your revenues exceed $500,000, excluding government grants and grants from private foundations.

Signatures required. Signatures of two authorized officers are required. The signatures need not be notarized.

Fee. $50, payable to "Secretary of State."

Filing procedure. If you don't register online, postal mail the application, accompanying documents, and fee to:

State of Tennessee Department of State
Division of Charitable Solicitation and Gaming
William R. Snodgrass Tennessee Tower
312 Rosa L. Parks Avenue, 8th Floor
Nashville, TN 37243

Renewal Registration

Time for renewal. The deadline for renewal is the last day of the sixth month after the end of your nonprofit's accounting year. If you use the calendar year, the deadline is June 30. You can obtain an extension of time to file the renewal of up to 90 days by filing the state *Extension Request* form. You can do this online at the state website or by postal mail.

Procedure. You can renew online at the state website. Alternatively, you may postal mail the state *Application to Renew Registration of a Charitable Organization* form. You must also provide:

- a completed state *Summary of Financial Activities* form
- a copy of your IRS Form 990, Form 990-EZ, or 990-N for the most recently completed accounting year
- an audited financial statement if your nonprofit grossed more than $500,000 in revenue, excluding grants from government agencies and 501(c)(3) private foundations, and
- copies of any fundraiser contracts.

Fee. The fee is on a sliding scale based on your nonprofit's gross revenue.

Annual Financial Report

If your nonprofit registers during its first year of operation, it must complete a quarterly financial report at the end of each quarter of its current fiscal year and submit it to the Division of Charitable Solicitation and Gaming. The report is due within thirty (30) days of the end of each quarter. You may file online at the state website or postal mail the *Quarterly Financial Report* form, which is available from the state website. There is no fee for this filing.

Texas

Texas has no charitable solicitations law and most nonprofits are not required to register with a state agency. However, some organizations that solicit contributions for law enforcement, public safety, or veterans' causes are subject to a registration requirement. For details, see the Texas attorney general's website at www.oag.state.tx.us/consumer/nonprofits.shtml.

Texas

Utah

Governing Law

Utah has a charitable solicitations law codified at Utah Code Annotated sections 13-22-1 through 12-22-23. The law is administered by the Utah Division of Consumer Protection and may be accessed from its website.

State Website

The Utah Division of Consumer Protection has a website with information on registering charities at http://consumerprotection.utah.gov/registrations/charities.html.

Registration Requirements

A charitable organization may not solicit, request, promote, advertise, or sponsor a charitable solicitation that originates in Utah, is received in Utah, or is made through business operations located in Utah, unless it is registered with the Division of Consumer Protection.

Exemptions

The following types of organizations are exempt from Utah's registration requirement. The exemption is not automatic. You must submit a notice of claim of exemption to the Utah Division of Consumer Protection. There is no form for this purpose. You should draft a letter to the Division containing:

- a detailed description of your organization and its purposes
- a citation to the claimed exemption and a detailed explanation of why it applies (citations are provided below)
- any documents supporting your notice of claim of exemption—for example, articles of incorporation, and
- a notarized statement from you certifying that the statements are true and made to the best of your knowledge.

There is no fee for this filing.

Religious organizations. Bona fide religious, ecclesiastical, or denominational organizations are exempt if they are:

- a church, society, religious corporation, or other institution with an established physical place of worship

- a tax-exempt bona fide religious group that does not maintain specific places of worship and is not required to file an IRS Form 990, or
- a separate group or corporation that is an integral part of a section 501(c)(3) organization and is not primarily supported by funds solicited outside its own membership or congregation.

Only solicitations made for a church, missionary, religious, or humanitarian purpose are exempt.

Educational institutions. Educational organizations are exempt. This includes:

- accredited schools or institutions of higher learning
- clubs or parent, teacher, or student organizations authorized by a school to support its operations or extracurricular activities, or
- public or higher education foundations established under Utah law.

Membership solicitations. An organization need not register if it only solicits donations from its own membership exclusively through the voluntarily donated efforts of other members or officers of the organization. (Utah Code section 13-22-9(1)(a).)

Appeals for individuals. People or organizations soliciting donations for the relief of a named individual sustaining a life-threatening illness or injury are exempt, provided that the entire amount collected is turned over to the named person. (Utah Code section 13-22-9(1)(d).)

Political groups. Political parties, candidates, and campaign workers need not register as long as they make it clear that all solicitations are for the benefit of a political party or candidate. (Utah Code section 13-22-9(1)(e).)

Political action committees or groups soliciting funds relating to issues or candidates on the ballot are exempt if they are required to file financial information with a federal or state election commission. (Utah Code section 13-22-9(1)(f).)

Other exemptions. There are also exemptions for:

- broadcast media owned or operated by educational institutions or governmental entities (Utah Code section 13-22-9(1)(d))
- television stations, radio stations, or newspapers of general circulation that donate free air time or print space as part of a cooperative solicitation effort on behalf of a charitable organization (Utah Code section 13-22-9(1)(i))

- a volunteer fire department, rescue squad, or local civil defense organization whose financial oversight is under the control of a local governmental entity (Utah Code section 13-22-9(1)(j))
- any state or federal agency (Utah Code section 13-22-9(1)(k)), and
- Congressionally chartered corporations (Utah Code section 13-22-9(1)(l)).

Registration Procedure

Application form. You may use the URS or the state application form, *Charitable Organization Permit Application Form*, available from the state website. If you use the URS, you must also provide a completed *Supplement to Unified Registration Statement* form, available from the state website.

Documents to be included with application. Include copies of the following documents with your application:

- articles of incorporation (or other founding document)
- bylaws
- IRS determination letter, if any (if none, attach IRS Form 1023)
- your most recent IRS Form 990, if any, and
- current contracts with professional fundraisers, professional fundraising counsel, or professional fundraising consultants.

If you don't have an IRS Form 990 to file, you must complete and file the state *Statement of Functional Expenses* form, available from the state website. File this form if your nonprofit is new or you file IRS Forms 990-EZ, 990-PF, or 990-N.

Signatures required. One signature of any authorized person. The signature need not be notarized.

Fee. $100, payable to "State of Utah—Consumer Protection Division."

Filing procedure. Mail the application, accompanying documents, and fee to:

Division of Consumer Protection
160 East 300 South
P.O. Box 146704
Salt Lake City, UT 84114-6704

Renewal Registration

Your registration (called a charitable solicitation permit) expires each year on the earlier of January 1, April 1, July 1, or October 1 following the end of 12 months after the date it was initially issued. For example, if your permit was issued on March 15, 2011, it will expire on April 1, 2012. You must renew before the date of expiration. The renewal process is the same as applying for initial registration.

Annual Financial Report

The annual financial report is included with the annual renewal.

Utah

Vermont

Vermont

Vermont has a charitable solicitation law, but it applies only to paid fundriasers who are required to register with the Attorney General's office before soliciting contributions in the state. The law does not require charitable organizations to register before soliciting contributions in the state. For more information, refer to the Vermont attorney general's website at http://www.atg.state.vt.us/issues/consumer-protection/charities.php.

Virginia

Governing Law

Virginia has a charitable solicitations law codified at Virginia Code sections 57-48 through 57-69. The law is administered by the Virginia Department of Agriculture and Consumer Services, Office of Consumer Affairs, and can be accessed from its website.

State Website

The Virginia Department of Agriculture and Consumer Services has a website with information on charitable solicitation at www.vdacs.virginia. gov/allforms.shtml.

Registration Requirements

No charitable organization may solicit charitable contributions in Virginia without first registering with the Virginia Department of Agriculture and Consumer Services.

Exemptions

Organizations falling within the first three categories listed below are not subject to the Virginia charitable solicitations law at all, and need not make any filing to obtain their exemption.

Religious organizations. This includes any church, or convention or association of churches, primarily operated for nonsecular purposes that does not file a Form 990 with the IRS. Such religious organizations are exempt from application of all the provisions of Virginia's charitable solicitations law.

Political groups. These include all political parties or political action committees registered with the Federal Election Commission or any similar state agency.

Red Cross. The American Red Cross and its chapters are exempt.

The organizations listed below are exempt, but they must file an application with the Office of Consumer Affairs to have their exemption officially recognized. To do so, you must file the state Form 100 and pay a $10 fee. The form is available from the state website. You must also include the same documents as are required for initial registration, plus documentation showing your organization is exempt. Parent organizations may file consolidated applications for exemptions for any chapters, branches, or affiliates. If your claim of exemption is granted, you will be issued a letter of exemption which remains in effect until you no longer qualify for the exemption.

$5,000 exemption. Your nonprofit is exempt if (1) it raises less than $5,000 in contributions from the public during its three preceding calendar years, and (2) you intend to raise less than $5,000 during the current year. In addition, all your nonprofit's functions, including fundraising activities, must be carried out by unpaid volunteers.

Nonprofits supported solely by grants. Tax-exempt nonprofits are exempt from registration if they solicit contributions only through grant proposals submitted to:

- for-profit corporations
- other tax-exempt nonprofit organizations, or
- private foundations.

Solicitations confined to five or fewer counties. Your organization is exempt in any year in which it:

- solicits in only five or fewer contiguous cities and counties in Virginia, and
- has registered under the charitable solicitations ordinance, if any, of each such city and county.

If you solicit through a local publication or radio or television station, you still qualify for this exemption even if the circulation extends beyond the five cities or counties.

However, you don't qualify for this exemption if, during the preceding fiscal year, you paid more than 10% of your gross receipts to any person located outside the five cities and counties. But this doesn't apply to the purchase of real property or tangible personal property or personal services to be used within the cities and counties.

Educational institutions. Educational institutions are exempt. This includes:

- any fully accredited educational institution
- any foundation that has an established identity with an accredited educational institution, and
- any educational institution whose solicitations are confined to its student body, faculty, alumni, trustees, and their families.

Appeals for individuals. People who request contributions for the relief of specified individuals are exempt, provided all the contributions are turned over to the individual.

Membership organizations. Organizations that solicit only from members by members are exempt.

Non-resident organizations. Any organization that does not have an office within Virginia is exempt if it has a chapter, branch, or affiliate within Virginia that has registered. If such an organization solicits within Virginia from outside the state, it may do so only by telephone or telegraph, direct mail, or advertising in national media. Presumably, the Internet would fall under "telephone or telegraph" solicitations.

Health care institutions. These include:

- any licensed tax-exempt section 501(c)(3) health care institution
- designated federally qualified health centers
- rural health clinics certified by the Health Care Financing Administration
- Virginia health education centers
- tax-exempt regional emergency medical services councils
- free clinics, or
- any other organization that exists solely to support licensed health care institutions.

Civic organizations. This includes any nonprofit local service club, veterans' post, fraternal society or association, volunteer fire or rescue group, or local civic league or association of ten or more people. Such organizations must be operated exclusively for educational or charitable purposes, including the promotion of community welfare.

Other exemptions. Also exempt are:

- tax-exempt labor unions, labor associations, and labor organizations
- tax-exempt trade associations
- Virginia licensed nonprofit debt counseling agencies, and
- Virginia agencies on aging.

Registration Procedure

Application form. You can use the URS or the state application form, *Remittance Form Charitable Organization Form 102*, which is available from the state website.

Documents to be included with application. Include copies of the following documents with your application:

- articles of incorporation, if any
- bylaws
- IRS determination letter or copy of IRS Form 1023 or 1024 if your exemption is pending, and
- contracts with professional fundraisers.

If your organization is new, you must also submit a copy of a board-approved budget for the current year. If your organization has been in existence for more than one fiscal year, you must provide a copy of (1) the previous fiscal year's Form 990, Form 990-EZ, or 990-PF, or (2) certified audited financial statements. Organizations with income under $25,000 may file a certified treasurer's report containing a balance sheet and income and expense statement.

Signatures required. Two signatures are required—one from the chief fiscal officer and one from the president or other authorized officer. The signatures need not be notarized.

Fee. The fee is $100 if your nonprofit has no prior financial history. If you have a financial history, you must pay an initial registration fee of $100, plus an annual registration fee on a sliding scaling based on gross contributions for the prior year. Your check should be made payable to "Treasurer of Virginia."

Gross contributions for prior year	Fee
$25,000 or less	$30
$25,001 through $50,000	$50
$50,001 through $100,000	$100
$100,001 through $500,000	$200
$500,001 through $1,000,000	$250
over $1,000,000	$325

Filing procedure. Mail the application, accompanying documents, and fee to:

Virginia Department of Agriculture and Consumer Services
Office of Consumer Affairs
P.O. Box 526
Richmond, VA 23218-0526

Renewal Registration

Your registration must be renewed each year. This is called "annual registration" in Virginia.

Time for renewal. The renewal is supposed to be filed no later than 4½ months after the end of your fiscal year. If you use the calendar year, the deadline is May 15. This is the same deadline as the deadline for filing IRS Form 990. You may obtain an extension of time to file of up to three months by sending a letter to the Office of Consumer Affairs.

Procedure. The procedure for renewal is the same as for initial registration described above.

Fee. The fee is on a sliding scale based on your nonprofit's gross contributions for the year. See the table above.

Annual Financial Report

This is included with the renewal registration.

Other Requirements

All nonprofits in Virginia must include the following disclosure statement on every printed solicitation and every written confirmation, receipt, or reminder of a contribution:

Financial statements are available from the State Division of Consumer Affairs, Department of Agricultural and Consumer Services, P.O. Box 1163, Richmond, VA 23218.

Washington

Governing Law

Washington has a charitable solicitations law codified at Revised Code of Washington sections 19.09.020 through 19.09.560. The law is administered by the Washington Secretary of State, Charities Program, and can be accessed from the Washington State Legislature's website at http://apps.leg. wa.gov/rcw.

State Website

The Washington secretary of state, Charities Program has a website with information on charitable solicitation registration at www.sos.wa.gov/charities/Default.aspx.

Registration Requirements

All charitable organizations must register with the Office of the Washington secretary of state before conducting any charitable solicitations in the state.

The State of Washington has created a helpful Self-Assesment Guide flowchart you can use to determine if your organization must register in the state (see www.sos.wa.gov/charities/SelfAssessmentGuide.aspx).

Exemptions

The following types of organizations are exempt from Washington's registration requirements. Organizations that are exempt are encouraged to submit an *Optional Statement for an Exempt Organization* with the Charities Program (available on the state website). The application is not required, but does allow the Office of the Secretary of State to respond to customer inquiries regarding your organization.

$25,000 exemption. Charitable organizations that are run entirely by unpaid volunteers are exempt if they raise less than $25,000 from the public during their fiscal year. Use of the phrase "from the public" in this definition is apparently meant to exclude government grants or contracts from the annual limit.

Religious organizations. The following types of religious organizations are exempt from application of all the provisions of Washington's charitable solicitations law:

- all churches and their integrated auxiliaries

- nondenominational ministries
- interdenominational and ecumenical organizations
- mission organizations
- speakers' organizations
- faith-based social agencies, and
- other entities whose principal purpose is the study, practice, or advancement of religion.

However, religious organizations that file a Form 990 with the IRS are not exempt and must register.

Educational institutions. This includes:

- any public school, college, or university, or
- any private nonprofit educational institution offering secondary or collegiate instruction comparable to that of a public school or college.

Political groups. This includes any political party, committee, or group whose activities are subject to the public reporting requirements of the Federal Election Commission or its State of Washington counterpart.

Appeals for individuals. People or groups who make charitable appeals on behalf of a specific named individual are exempt provided that all the money collected is turned over to the individual.

Registration Procedure

Application form. You may use the URS or the state application form, *Charitable Solicitations Registration/Renewal Form*, available from the state website. If you use the URS, you must also file the *Washington State Unified Registration Addendum* form, which contains a financial report called *Solicitation Report*. It is available from the state website.

Documents to be included with application. Include copies of the following documents with your application:

- IRS determination letter, if any, and
- IRS Form 990 or Form 990-EZ filed for the preceding fiscal year, if any (include all schedules except for the list of contributors).

If your nonprofit contracts with professional fundraisers, it must submit:

- a completed state *Fundraising Service Contract Registration Form* (available from the state website)
- copies of the written contracts, and

- an additional $10 filing fee.

If (1) your nonprofit had more than $1 million in annual gross revenue averaged over the past three fiscal years, and (2) your Form 990 was not prepared by an independent third party CPA or other tax professional, then you must file the state *Confirmation of Independent Third-Party Review* form, available from the state website. This form must be signed by a CPA or other professional independent third party who normally prepares such returns. By signing, the CPA or other tax professional certifies that he or she has reviewed the Form 990.

If your nonprofit has more than $3 million in annual gross revenue averaged over the past three fiscal years, you also must submit audited financial statements prepared by a CPA. This is in addition to the *Confirmation of Independent Third-Party Review* form.

Signatures required. One signature from your organization's president, treasurer, or a comparable officer or someone responsible for the organization. The signature need not be notarized.

Fee. $20, payable to "The State of Washington."

Filing procedure. Mail the application, accompanying documents, and fee to:

> Secretary of State
> Charities Program
> P.O. Box 40234
> 801 Capitol Way S.
> Olympia, WA 98504-0234

Renewal Registration

Your Washington registration must be renewed each year. Upon the completion of each successful renewal, you will receive a written confirmation, including your nonprofit's "extended" renewal date.

Time for renewal. You are required to renew by the 15th day of the fifth month after the end of your fiscal or accounting year end. If you use the calendar year, the renewal is due by May 15. This is the same deadline as for filing IRS Form 990. You are also entitled to an automatic six and a half month extension. This gives you until November 1 to file your renewal. Due to an extremely high volume of extension requests, registrants are not required to submit an extension request to the Washington State Charities Program.

Procedure. The renewal procedure is the same as for filing your initial registration (except you need not file another copy of your IRS determination letter). You should mail your renewal seven business days before the due date to allow sufficient time for postal delivery and receipt validation.

Fee. $10.

Annual Financial Report

This is included with the annual renewal.

Other Requirements

All nonprofits in Washington must include the following disclosure statement at every point of solicitation and on every printed solicitation and every written confirmation, receipt, or reminder of a contribution:

> The notice of solicitation required by the State Office of Consumer Affairs is on file with the Washington Secretary of State, and information relating to financial affairs of [name of charity] is available from the Secretary of State, and the toll-free number for Washington residents: 800-332-4483.

West Virginia

Governing Law

West Virginia has a charitable solicitations law codified at West Virginia Code sections 29-19-1 through 29-19-16. The law is administered by the West Virginia Secretary of State, Charitable Organizations Division, and can be accessed from its website.

State Website

The West Virginia Secretary of state has a website with information on charitable solicitations at www.sos.wv.gov/business-licensing/charities/Pages/default.aspx.

Registration Requirements

Every charitable organization must register with the West Virginia secretary of state before soliciting charitable contributions in the state.

Exemptions

The following types of organizations are exempt from West Virginia's registration requirements. If you think your organization is exempt, send a letter to the West Virginia Secretary of State, Charities Division, describing your organization, how you raise money, and how much revenue you expect in a year. The secretary of state will notify you whether you are exempt or have to register based on the information provided.

$25,000 exemption. Your nonprofit is exempt if you intend to solicit, and actually receive, less than $25,000 from the public during the calendar year. You may not employ professional fundraisers although you can have employees or salaried staff perform fundraising-related work. Unlike most states, West Virginia requires that grants be included toward the annual limit.

Religious institutions. These include all churches, synagogues, associations or conventions of churches, and religious orders. Also exempt are tax-exempt religious organizations that are an integral part of a church and are not required to file Form 990 with the IRS. However, religious institutions that file Form 990 with the IRS are not exempt and must register.

Educational institutions. This includes all accredited educational institutions and auxiliary associations, foundations, and support groups responsible to the educational institution.

Hospitals. All nonprofit, charitable hospitals, and licensed nursing homes are exempt.

Membership organizations. Organizations that solicit only from their participating (voting) membership are exempt.

Appeals for individuals. People and organizations who request contributions for the relief of a specific named individual are exempt, provided all the money collected is turned over to the individual.

Special fundraising events for registered charity. Any person, firm, corporation, or organization that holds a single fundraising event for the benefit of a named charity that is registered is exempt provided:

- all or part of the funds collected are donated to the charity
- the charity reports each of these donations individually, and
- the charity certifies that no funds were withheld by the organization that solicited the funds.

Registration Procedure

Application form. You may use the URS or the state form, *Registration Statement of Charitable Organizations*, available from the state website. If you file the URS, you must also complete and file the state *Unified Registration Statement Supplement* form.

Documents to be included with application. Include copies of the following documents with your application:

- IRS determination letter, if any
- your most recently filed IRS Form 990 or 990-EZ, if any, and
- current contracts with professional fundraisers.

You must also provide a balance sheet and financial statement audited by an independent public accountant if your organization raised more than $100,000 from all sources, not including government grants and grants from private foundations.

Signatures required. The application must be signed by two authorized officers, one of whom should be the chief fiscal officer. The signatures must be notarized.

Fee. See the chart below. Your check should be made payable to "West Virginia Secretary of State."

Type of Organization	Fee
Independent organizations collecting under $1 million per year	$15
Organizations collecting over $1 million per year	$50
Parent organizations with affiliates operating under the same registration	$50

Filing procedure. Mail the application, accompanying documents, and fee to:

Charities Division
Secretary of State Bldg. 1, Suite 157-K
1900 Kanawha Blvd.
East Charleston, WV 25305-0770

Renewal Registration

You must renew your registration every year.

Time for renewal. Your renewal is due by the anniversary date of your initial registration.

Procedure. The renewal procedure is same as the procedure for initial registration.

Fee. The fee is the same as the fee for initial registration.

Annual Financial Report

This report is included with the annual renewal.

Other Requirements

All nonprofits in West Virginia must include the following disclosure statement on every printed solicitation and every written confirmation, receipt, or reminder of a contribution:

West Virginia residents may obtain a summary of the registration and financial documents from the Secretary of State, State Capitol, Charleston, WV 25305.

Wisconsin

Governing Law

Wisconsin has a charitable solicitations law codified at Wisconsin Statutes sections 440.41 through 440.48. The law is administered by the Wisconsin Department of Regulation and Licensing and may be accessed through the Wisconsin State Legislature's website at www.legis.state.wi.us/rsb.

State Website

The Wisconsin Department of Regulation and Licensing has a website with information for charitable organizations at www.drl.state.wi.us. Click on "Choose Profession" and then "Charitable Organizations."

Registration Requirements

No charitable organization may solicit charitable contributions in Wisconsin without first registering with the Department of Regulation and Licensing. The state has created a *Checklist to Determine Exemption from Registration as a Charitable Organization*, that summarizes the exemptions in Wisconsin. It is available on the state website.

Exemptions

The following types of organizations are exempt from Wisconsin's registration requirements:

$5,000 exemption. Your organization is exempt if it does not intend to raise more than $5,000 in contributions in a fiscal year. Your nonprofit must be run entirely by unpaid volunteers and may not use any professional fundraisers. You don't have to count the following toward the annual limit:

- the value of donated used clothing or household goods
- income from bingo or raffles
- government grants, or
- bona fide fees or dues paid by members of your organization.

Religious institutions. Any tax-exempt religious institution that doesn't have to file a Form 990 with the IRS is exempt. This includes all churches, their integrated auxiliaries, and conventions or associations of churches. However, religious institutions that file Form 990 with the IRS are not exempt and must register.

Educational institutions. This includes:

- all accredited nonprofit, postsecondary educational institutions,
- private schools, and
- educational institutions that solicit contributions only from their students and their families, alumni, faculty, trustees, corporations, foundations, and patients.

Membership organizations. Any fraternal, civic, benevolent, patriotic, or social organization that solicits contributions solely from its membership is exempt.

Political groups and candidates. Candidates for elective office are exempt, as are political parties, groups, or committees that file financial information with the federal elections commission or the State of Wisconsin.

Appeals for individuals. People and organizations who request contributions for the relief of a specific named individual are exempt, provided all the money collected is turned over to the individual.

Veterans organizations. State or federally chartered veterans organizations and their service foundations are exempt.

State agencies. Wisconsin state agencies and local governments are exempt.

Registration Procedure

Application form. You may use the URS or the state *Charitable Organization Registration Statement* (Form 296), available from the state website.

Documents to be included with application. Include copies of the following documents with your application:

- articles of incorporation
- bylaws
- if your nonprofit is an out-of-state corporation, the Certificate of Incorporation issued by your home state, and
- IRS determination letter (if your application is pending, submit a copy of your filed IRS Form 1023).

If your organization solicited contributions in Wisconsin during its most recently completed fiscal year, you will also have to submit a financial report or a signed affidavit in lieu of filing such a report. See the discussion in "Annual Financial Report," below.

Signatures required. Two notarized signatures are required: one from the president or any other authorized officer and one from the chief fiscal officer.

Fee. $30, payable to "Department of Regulation and Licensing."

Filing procedure. Mail the application, accompanying documents, and fee to:

Wisconsin Department of Regulation & Licensing
P.O. Box 8935
Madison, WI 53708-8935

Renewal Registration

Your are required to renew your Wisconsin registration every year by July 31 and pay a $15 renewal fee. This can be accomplished online through the state website. Renewal notices are sent out each year on June 15.

Annual Financial Report

In addition to filing a renewal, registered nonprofits must file an annual financial report if they have received contributions over $5,000 during their most recently completed fiscal year. If your nonprofit is not required to file a financial report, it must file a signed affidavit stating that you are not required to file a report. This requirement is totally separate from the renewal.

Time to file. The report is due within six months after the end of your nonprofit's fiscal year. If you use the calendar year, it is due by June 30. The Department of Regulation and Licensing does not grant extensions of the time to file this report. Failure to meet the financial report deadline may affect your ability to renew your registration.

Procedure. You need to complete and file with the Department of Regulation and Licensing one of three state forms:
- Form 1943, *Affidavit in Lieu of Annual Financial Report*
- Form 308, *Charitable Organization Annual Report*, or
- Form 1952, *Wisconsin Supplement to Financial Report on Form Other Than Form #308*.

The chart below shows what type of form must be filed.

Type of organization	Form to be filed
Contributions during preceding fiscal year of $5,000 or less	*Affidavit in Lieu of Annual Financial Report* (Form 1943)
Contributions during preceding fiscal year of over $5,000	*Charitable Organization Annual Financial Report* (Form 308) or IRS Form 990, 990-EZ, 990-PF plus *Wisconsin Supplement to Financial Report on Form Other Than Form #308* (Form 1952)
Contributions during preceding fiscal year of less than $50,000 and you only solicited in your county of residence	*Affidavit in Lieu of Annual Financial Report* (Form 1943)

All reports require submission of a list of the officers and directors and their titles, addresses, term dates, and the compensation they receive. The compensation must be explicitly stated.

Audit requirement. You must also provide a CPA audit with an expressed opinion if your nonprofit received $400,000 or more in contributions during the fiscal year for which a report is being filed. A CPA review, instead of an audit, is required if your organization received between $200,000 and $399,999 in contributions. No additional documentation is required if your nonprofit took in less than $200,000 in contributions.

Fee. None.

Wyoming

Wyoming does not have a charitable solicitation law, and does not require charitable organizations to register with a state agency before soliciting contributions in the state. However, an out-of-state nonprofit corporation may have to register to do business in the state if it conducts intrastate business there. See Chapter 6 for detailed information on registering as an out-of-state business.

Supplemental State Forms for the URS

hirteen jurisdictions (twelve states plus the District of Columbia)
accept the Uniform Registration Statement (the "URS") but also
have their own supplemental forms that must be filed with the
application. These are state-specific charitable registration forms that are
required in addition to any governing or other documents that you may
have to submit with your application, such as articles of incorporation or
Form 990. The thirteen jurisdictions that have a supplemental form for
charitable registration are: Arkansas, the District of Columbia, Georgia,
Kansas, Maine, Minnesota, Mississippi, North Dakota, Tennessee, Utah,
Washington, West Virginia, and Wisconsin.

Forms in This Appendix (continued)		
Form		**Page #**
Tennessee	Summary of Financial Activities of a Charitable Organization	325
Utah	Supplement to Unified Registration Statement	327
Washington	Washington State Unified Registration Statement Addendum	331
West Virginia	Unified Registration Statement Supplement	334
Wisconsin	Affidavit in Lieu of Annual Financial Reporting	335
	Wisconsin Supplement to Financial Report on Form Other Than Form #308	339

CAUTION

Check that these forms are still up-to-date before using them. These forms were up-to-date at the time this book was published but make sure they are still the most current version available before using a copy of any of them. You can check for the most current version on the state's website which is listed in Appendix A.

Unified Registration Statement (URS) for Charitable Organizations (v. 4.0)

___ **Initial registration**   ___ **Renewal/Update**

This URS covers the reporting year which ended (day/month/year) _____

Filer EIN _____

State _____

State ID _____

1. Organization's legal name_____

   If changed since prior filings, previous name used _____

   All other name(s) used_____

2.

   (A) Street address _____

   City _____

   County _____

   State _____

   Zip Code _____

   (B) Mailing address (if different) _____

   City _____

   County _____

   State _____

   Zip Code _____

3. Telephone number(s) _____

   Fax number(s) _____

   E-mail _____

   Web site _____

4. Names, addresses (street & P.O.), telephone numbers of other offices/chapters/branches/affiliates (*attach list*).

5. Date incorporated _____ State of incorporation _____

   Fiscal year end: day/month _____

6. If not incorporated, type of organization, state, and date established _____

   _____

7. Has organization or any of its officers, directors, employees or fund raisers:

   A. Been enjoined or otherwise prohibited by a government agency/court from soliciting?   Yes ___   No ___

   B. Had its registration denied or revoked?   Yes ___   No ___

   C. Been the subject of a proceeding regarding any solicitation or registration?   Yes ___   No ___

   D. Entered into a voluntary agreement of compliance with any government agency or in a case before a court or administrative agency?

      Yes ___   No ___

   E. Applied for registration or exemption from registration (but not yet completed or obtained)?   Yes ___   No ___

   F. Registered with or obtained exemption from any state or agency?   Yes ___   No ___

   G. Solicited funds in any state?   Yes ___   No ___

   If "yes" to 7A, B, C, D, E, *attach explanation*.

   If "yes" to 7F & G, *attach list* of states where registered, exempted, or where it solicited, including registering agency, dates of registration, registration numbers, any other names under which the organization was/is registered, and the dates and type (mail, telephone, door to door, special events, etc.) of the solicitation conducted.

8. Has the organization applied for or been granted IRS tax exempt status?   Yes ___   No ___

   If yes, date of application _____ OR date of determination letter _____.

   If granted, exempt under 501(c) _____.   Are contributions to the organization tax deductible?   Yes ___   No ___

9. Has tax exempt status ever been denied, revoked, or modified?   Yes ___   No ___

10. Indicate all methods of solicitations:

    Mail ___   Telephone ___   Personal Contact ___   Radio/TV Appeals ___

    Special Events ___   Newspaper/Magazine Ads ___   Other(s) ___ (specify) _____

11. List the NTEE code(s) that best describes your organization   _____, _____, _____

12. Describe the purposes and programs of the organization and those for which funds are solicited *(attach separate sheet if necessary)*.

    _____

    _____

    _____

    _____

13. List the names, titles, addresses, (street & P.O.), and telephone numbers of officers, directors, trustees, and the principal salaried executives of organization *(attach separate sheet)*.

14.

   (A) (1) Are any of the organization's officers, directors, trustees or employees related by blood, marriage, or adoption to:
   (i) any other officer, director, trustee or employee OR
   (ii) any officer, agent, or employee of any fundraising professional firm under contract to the organization OR
   (iii) any officer, agent, or employee of a supplier or vendor firm providing goods or services to the organization?
   Yes ___   No ___

(2) Does the organization or any of its officers, directors, employees, or anyone holding a financial interest in the organization have a financial interest in a business described in (ii) or (iii) above OR serve as an officer, director, partner or employee of a business described in (ii) or (iii) above? Yes ___ No ___
(If yes to any part of 14A, *attach sheet* which specifies the relationship and provides the names, businesses, and addresses of the related parties). Yes ___ No ___

(B) Have any of the organization's officers, directors, or principal executives been convicted of a misdemeanor or felony? (If yes, attach a complete explanation.) Yes ___ No ___

15. *Attach separate sheet listing names and addresses (street & P.O.) for all below:*

Individual(s) responsible for custody of funds.

Individual(s) responsible for distribution of funds.

Individual(s) responsible for fund raising.

Individual(s) responsible for custody of financial records.

Individual(s) authorized to sign checks.

Bank(s) in which registrant's funds are deposited (*include account number and bank phone number*).

16. Name, address (street & P.O.), and telephone number of accountant/auditor.

Name _____

Address _____

City _____ State _____

Zip Code _____ Telephone _____

Method of accounting _____

17. Name, address (street & P.O.), and telephone number of person authorized to receive service of process. *This is a state-specific item. See instructions.*

Name _____

Address _____

City _____ State _____

Zip Code _____ Telephone _____

18.

(A) Does the organization receive financial support from other nonprofit organizations (foundations, public charities, combined campaigns, etc.)? Yes ___ No ___

(B) Does the organization share revenue or governance with any other non-profit organization? Yes ___ No ___

(C) Does any other person or organization own a 10% or greater interest in your organization OR does your organization own a 10% or greater interest in any other organization? Yes ___ No ___

(If "yes" to A, B or C, *attach an explanation* including name of person or organization, address, relationship to your organization, and type of organization.)

19. Does the organization use volunteers to solicit directly?   Yes ___ No ___

Does the organization use professionals to solicit directly?   Yes ___ No ___

20. If your organization contracts with or otherwise engages the services of any outside fundraising professional (such as a "professional fundraiser," "paid solicitor," "fund raising counsel," or "commercial co-venturer"), *attach list* including their names, addresses (street & P.O.), telephone numbers, and location of offices used by them to perform work on behalf of your organization. Each entry *must include* a simple statement of services provided, description of compensation arrangement, dates of contract, date of campaign/event, whether the professional solicits on your behalf, and whether the professional at any time has custody or control of donations.

21. Amount paid to PFR/PS/FRC during previous year: $ _____

22. For the most recent fiscal year, please provide the following:

    (A) Total contributions: $ _____

    (B) Program service expenses: $ _____

    (C) Management & general expenses: $ _____

    (D) Fundraising expenses: $ _____

    (E) Total Expenses: $ _____

    (F) Fundraising expenses as a percentage of funds raised: _____%

    (G) Fundraising expenses plus management and general expenses as a percentage of funds raised: _____%

    (H) Program services as a percentage of total expenses: _____%

Under penalty of perjury, we certify that the above information and the information contained in any attachments or supplement is true, correct, and complete.

    Sworn to before me on (or signed on) _____, 20 _____

_____
Notary public (if required)

_____
Name (printed)

_____
Name (signature)

_____
Title (printed)

_____
Name (printed)

_____
Name (signature)

_____
Title (printed)

Consult the state-by-state appendix to the URS to determine whether supporting documents, supplementary state forms or fees must accompany this form. Before submitting your registration, *make sure you have attached or included everything required by each state to the respective copy of the URS.*

Attachments may be prepared as one continuous document or as separate pages for each item requiring elaboration. In either case, please number the response to correspond with the URS item number.

© 2010 MULTI-STATE FILER PROJECT

DUSTIN McDANIEL
ATTORNEY GENERAL
OFFICE OF THE ATTORNEY GENERAL
323 CENTER STREET, Suite 200
LITTLE ROCK, AR 72201-2610 (501) 682-2007

CONSENT FOR SERVICE
CHARITABLE ORGANIZATION

_____, a Charitable Organization, hereby appoint(s) the Attorney General of the State of Arkansas as agent for service in case of any and all lawsuits, proceedings and actions growing out of the violation of any provisions of Ark. Code Ann. § 4-28-401 *et seq.*, or as a result of any activities conducted in the State of Arkansas giving rise to a cause of action.

It is hereby agreed that consent for service is irrevocable, and service on the Attorney General of the State of Arkansas shall be binding on this organization as if due service has been made on its agents in person.

_____

Date Signed

_____

Legal Name of Charitable Organization

_____

Signature

_____

Printed Name

_____

Title/Official Position

NOTARY

STATE OF_____   )
) SS.
COUNTY OF _____   )

Subscribed and sworn to, before me, a Notary Public in, and for, said County and State, this _____ day of _____, 20_____.

My Commission Expires:
_____/_____/_____

_____

Signature of Notary Public

County of Residence
_____

_____

Printed Name

STAMP or SEAL:

Basic Business License Information:
Charitable Solicitation

NAICS CODE: 813000-1

NAICS DESCRIPTION: Charitable Solicitation means the request directly or indirectly for any contribution on the plea or representation that such contribution will or may be used for any charitable purpose.

Endorsement Class: General Business

Legal Authority: DC Code: 44-1700; 47-2851   DC Municipal Regulations, Title 16, Chapter 13

License Duration: Two (2) Years	**Category License Fee:** $208.00
License Available Online: No	**Application Fee:** $70.00
Online Processing Fee: N/A	**Endorsement Fee:** $25.00

Payment Method

If applying in person, you can pay for your Basic Business License (BBL) by cash, check, money order, or credit card at the Department of Consumer and Regulatory Affairs, Business License Center, 1100 4th Street, SW, 2nd Floor, Washington, DC 20024.

If applying by mail you can pay for your Basic Business License (BBL) by check or money order payable to "DC Treasurer" and submitted to:

Bank of America Lockbox Services
Attention: DC Government Wholesale Lockbox #91360
Bank of America Lockbox Services
11333 McCormick Road
Hunt Valley, MD 21031

Application Requirements

All applicants for a Basic Business License must comply with the following DC Code requirements:

Basic Business License Application
To make sure you get your BBL as quickly as possible, you must submit a properly completed BBL EZ Form. All of your responses should be printed clearly in English.

- Fillable Downloadable BBL EZ FORM*
- Barrill nuevo BBL EZ Form en Español*

Note on PDF Forms: To download and fill out BBL EZ form you should open the form and save to your desktop. We recommend you also rename the form as you save to your desktop. For most users, you should be able to save your work. If you cannot, you should print the form before closing.

Certificate of Occupancy / Compliance for Zoning Regulations
Before applying for your BBL, you'll need a Certificate of Occupancy (C of O) for the location where your business is conducted to demonstrate that your business does not conflict with building and zoning codes. (If your business is located in an office building, you may operate under the umbrella of the C of O issued to the owner of the building, as long as the C of O was issued for the entire building; check with your building owner or management company for the C of O holder name, number, and issue date.) If you have any questions about Certificates of Occupancy, please call the Building & Land Regulation Administration at (202) 442-4589.

Clean Hands Certification
You'll also need to certify that you don't owe more than $100 to the District of Columbia government as a result of fees, penalties, interest, or taxes through completion of a Clean Hands form provided in your BBL application package.

- DCRA Clean Hands Form*

Office of Tax & Revenue (OTR) Registration
Before applying for your BBL, you'll also need to register your business with OTR and submit a copy of your tax registration certificate with your application. If you're not already registered, simply complete and file a Tax Exemption Registration Form (FR-164). You get all the necessary forms and submit your application online at the Business this can also be done online at the Business Tax Service Center. For more information, please call the Tax Customer Center at (202) 727-4829.

Internal Revenue 501 Exemption
A copy of the 501(c)3 document from the Internal Revenue Service citing the exemption must be submitted. Each applicant, who claims his or her tax status is pending, must submit a certified copy of the application from the Internal Revenue Service. This certified copy must be provided in order to process the Charitable Solicitation application.

Charter and By-Laws
A copy of the organization's charter and by-laws must be submitted.

Uniform Registration Statement
A Uniform Registration Statement is required. A list of professional fund raisers and solicitors is required as part of the Uniform Registration Statement.

Statement Requirement
A full statement of the character and extent of the charitable work being done.

Resolution
A certified Resolution authorizing a corporate officer to make application in the District of Columbia is required of all corporations.

Itemized Financial Statement
Each application should be occupied by an itemized financial statement for the last preceding calendar or fiscal year.

Solicitor Information Cards
Each registrant or applicant for a charitable solicitation registration may obtain solicitor information cards for a fee of $3.00. A list of the names and addresses of the persons who will be soliciting on behalf of the organization must be submitted in triplicate (3 copies).

Professional Fundraisers or Solicitors
Each professional fund raisers and professional solicitors shall provide a copy of the contract, if any, made by or on behalf of each applicant with each professional fund raiser and professional solicitor.

....

Special Instructions
If your business falls into one of the following categories, there are additional requirements for your BBL application, as described below.

Corporation Division Requirements
If you are a corporation, partnership or limited liability company you must be registered in the District and in good standing. For instructions on how to register, please go to DCRA Corporate Registration Information Center. For more information, please call the Corporation Division at (202) 442-4432.

Non-Resident of the District of Columbia (including Foreign Corporations)
If you are not a resident of the District of Columbia, you'll need to appoint a Resident Agent or an Attorney-in-Fact who lives or works in an office in the District, who will be the official recipient of any financial, process, or legal notices that we need to send to you. If you are not a DC resident, please complete the Certified Resident Agent Appointment Form.

Corporate Registered Agents
Every corporation needs to have a registered agent office in the District of Columbia. This office can but does not need to be the same as your place of business. Foreign corporations doing business in DC need to certify that their named registered agent is duly authorized to represent that corporation.

Trade Name Operative (Use of Fictitious Business Name)
If your business uses a Trade Name, you'll need to register the name with DCRA and indicate both the trade name and the official business name (including its corporation, LLC, or partnership classification) if applicable.

Other District or Federal Agencies Involved for this Basic Business License

1. Department of Consumer and Regulatory Affairs
2. Office of Tax and Revenue

Additional Business Activities (BBL Endorsements)

If you conduct more than one business activity (endorsement type), you'll need to indicate those activities on your BBL application. You might have any number of additional business activities connected to this particular license endorsement.

Special Notes: If your business includes any of the above endorsement activities, you can get additional fact sheets and application forms by contacting DCRA's License Center at (202) 442-4311, or by email at bbl.infocenter@dc.gov.

SECURITIES AND BUSINESS REGULATION
2 Martin Luther King, Jr. Drive, S.E.
Ste 802, West Tower
Atlanta, Georgia 30334
(404) 656-3920
http://www.sos.state.ga.us/securities/

Brian P. Kemp
Secretary of State

Georgia Charitable Solicitations Act
Charitable Organization Registration

Robert D. Terry
Division Director

EXECUTION PAGE

Statutory Fees
(Nonrefundable)
Make Check Payable to Georgia Secretary of State

☐	INITIAL APPLICATION $35.00	☐	AMENDMENT (No Fee Required)	☐	REINSTATEMENT Registration #: _____ $35.00

WARNING: Failure to keep this form current and file accurate supplemental information on a timely basis, or failure to keep accurate books and records or otherwise comply with provisions of the Georgia Charitable Solicitations Act of 1988, is a violation of said Act and may result in disciplinary, administrative, injunctive or criminal action. **INTENTIONAL MISSTATEMENTS OR OMISSIONS OF FACT MAY CONSTITUTE CRIMINAL VIOLATIONS.**

1. Official Name and Mailing Address of Applicant (Charitable Organization):

2. Other Names under which solicitations will be made:

3. Contact Person: | Telephone:

Contact Person Email Address for Official Correspondence:

4. Location of Books and Records:

EXECUTION: On behalf of the applicant identified above, for the purpose of complying with the Charitable Solicitations Act of 1988, as amended (O. C. G. A. 43-17-1 et seq.) ("Act"), I hereby certify that the applicant is in compliance with said Act and irrevocably appoints the Secretary of State of the State of Georgia the agent for the applicant upon whom may be served any notice, process or pleading in any action or proceeding against the applicant arising out of, or founded upon, a violation or an alleged violation of said Act. The applicant hereby consents that any such action or proceeding against said applicant may be commenced in any court of competent jurisdiction and proper venue within the State of Georgia by service of process upon Secretary of State with the same effect as if the applicant was a resident of the State of Georgia and had been personally served with process. The undersigned hereby verifies that he had executed this form on behalf of, and with the authority of, said applicant. The undersigned and applicant represent that the information and statements contained herein, including the exhibits attached hereto, and other information filed herewith, all of which are made a part hereof, are current, true and complete. The undersigned and applicant further represent that to the extent any information previously submitted is not amended, such information is currently accurate and complete.

Name of authorized Executive Officer (please type or print): | Date:

Signature of Executive Officer: | Title:

Official Witness (Notary)

THIS PAGE MUST ALWAYS BE COMPLETED IN FULL with original manual signature and notarization with seal. To amend, circle number(s) being amended. To explain answers attach additional sheets identifying the questions and provide explanation.

Form C100 Rev. **Jan 2010**   Page 1

APPLICANT'S NAME:

To amend, circle numbers being amended and file with a completed execution page (C100 page 1)

5. Status of registration in other jurisdictions
Enter "1" for pending registrations, "2" if already registered, and leave blank if not registered.

AL		AK		AR		AZ		CA		CO		CT		DC		DE
FL		GA		HI		IA		ID		IL		IN		KS		KY
LA		MA		MD		ME		MI		MN		MO		MS		MT
NC		ND		NE		NH		NJ		NM		NV		NY		OH
OK		OR		PA		PR		RI		SC		SD		TN		TX
UT		VA		VT		WA		WI		WV		WY				

ORGANIZATION

6. Fiscal Year Ends on (Month/Day):	Date of Formation:	Place of Filing:

7. Applicant is a:

	Corporation	Proprietorship
Partnership	Limited Liability Company	Other:

8. If FOREIGN Corporation, date qualified to transact business in Georgia:

9. **The following financial information must accompany the application in order for registration to become effective:**
   An IRS Form 990 or 990 E-Z dated within one year of filing AND one of the following types of financial statements dated within one year of filing:
a. **Organizations that received or collected more than $1,000,000 in the preceding fiscal year must submit a financial statement certified by an independent certified public accountant.**
b. **Organizations that received or collected more than $500,000 but less than $1,000,000 must submit a financial statement reviewed by an independent certified public accountant**
c. **Organizations that received or collected less than $500,000 must submit a financial statement. The financial statement does not have to be reviewed or certified.**
d. **If no funds have been received or collected, attach a signed statement to that effect.**

10. State the general purpose for which the charitable organization is organized (attach additional sheets if necessary):

SOLICITATION INFORMATION

11. Specify the purpose or object for which funds solicited will be used (attach additional sheets if necessary):

12. Specify the method and period of time of solicitation:

Form C100 Rev. **Jan 2010**   Page 2

13. Does the charitable organization have a contract with a fund raising counsel or paid solicitor to solicit contributions in Georgia?　　　　　Yes　　No

If the answer to the above question is yes:
(a) list the name and address of the fund raising counsel or paid solicitor to be used in connection with the solicitations in Georgia:

(b) Terms of remuneration for paid solicitor:

(c) Is the paid solicitor registered with the Secretary of State to solicit contributions in Georgia?　　　　Yes　　No

BACKGROUND INFORMATION

To amend, circle questions being amended and file with a completed Execution page (C100 page 1)
NOTE: (1) For the purpose of the following questions the term **"executive officer" means the chief executive officer, the president, the principal financial officer, the principal operation officer, each vice president with responsibility involving policy-making, the treasurer or any other person performing similar functions.**
(2) All YES answers to questions must be fully explained. Attach additional sheets as needed.

	YES	NO
14. In the past ten years has the applicant, executive officer, or control person been convicted of or pled guilty or nolo contendere (no contest) to a felony or misdemeanor which:		
(a) Involves the solicitation or acceptance of charitable contributions or the making of a false oath, the making of a false report, bribery, perjury, burglary, or conspiracy to commit any of the foregoing offenses?	——	——
(b) Arises out of the conduct of solicitation of contributions for a charitable organization?	——	——
(c) Involves the larceny, theft, robbery, extortion, forgery, counterfeiting, fraudulent concealment, embezzlement, fraudulent conversion, or misappropriation of funds?	——	——
(d) Involves murder or rape?	——	——
(e) Involves assault or battery if such person proposes to be engaged in counseling, advising, housing, or sheltering individuals? Or	——	——
(f) Pled guilty or nolo contendere (no contest) to any other felony offense?	——	——
15. Has any court:		
(a) in the past ten years enjoined the applicant or an executive officer in connection with any aspect of the fundraising business?		
(b) ever found that the applicant or executive officer was involved in a violation of any state or federal law regarding fundraising or any other deceptive practice?		
16. Has any local, state or federal government agency:		
(a) ever found the applicant or executive officer to have made a false statement or omission or been dishonest, unfair or unethical?		
(b) ever found the applicant or executive officer to have been involved in a violation of a fundraising law?		
(c) ever found the applicant or executive officer to have been a cause of any fundraising organization having its authorization to do business denied, suspended, revoked or restricted?		
(d) in the past ten years entered an order or consent order against the applicant or an executive officer in connection with any fundraising statute or deceptive practices?		
(e) ever denied, suspended, or revoked the applicant's or an executive officer's registration or license, prevented it from association with a fundraising organization, or otherwise disciplined it by restricting its activities?		
(f) ever revoked or suspended the applicant's or an executive officer's license as an attorney or accountant?		
17. Is the applicant or executive officer now the subject of any proceeding that could result in a yes answer to any question contained herein?		
18. Does the applicant have any unsatisfied judgments or liens against it or has it filed for any type bankruptcy?		
19. Has any governmental agency, including the United States Internal Revenue Service determined that the organization is tax exempt? **If yes, attach copy of determination letter.** If applicable, indicate employer identification number here:		
20. Has a tax exemption status been denied or cancelled at any time by any governmental agency or official?		

**List the name and address of each affiliated branch or chapter
located within the State of Georgia and
the directors of each such branch or chapter.**
Attach additional sheets as needed.

Name	Address	Director(s)
Name	Address	Director(s)
Name	Address	Director(s)
Name	Address	Director(s)
Name	Address	Director(s)

OTHER OFFICERS, DIRECTORS AND TRUSTEES

List the names and address of all officers, directors, and trustees
Attach additional sheets as needed.

Name	Address	Title
Name	Address	Title
Name	Address	Title
Name	Address	Title
Name	Address	Title

ACKNOWLEDGEMENTS

By submitting this application, the applicant acknowledges the following statutory requirements:

(a) SOLICITATION CONTRACT REQUIRED. [OCGA 43-17-3(e)(1)] There must be a written contract between the charitable organization and paid solicitor.

(b) SOLICITATION NOTICE. [OCGA 43-17-3(f)] Paid solicitor must file a solicitation notice and a copy of each solicitation contract with the Secretary of State in order to commence a solicitation campaign in Georgia.

(c) POINT OF SOLICITATION DISCLOSURE. [OCGA 43-17-8] Every charitable organization, paid solicitor, or solicitor agent required to be registered under this Code section, at the time of any solicitation that occurs in or from this state, shall include the following disclosures: (1) The name and location of the paid solicitor and solicitor agent, if any; (2) The name and location of the charitable organization for which the solicitation is being made; (3) That the following information will be sent upon request: (A) A full and fair description of the charitable program for which the solicitation is being carried out and, if different, a full and fair description of the programs and activities of the charitable organization on whose behalf the solicitation is being carried out; and (B) A financial statement or summary which shall be consistent with the financial statement required to be filed with the Secretary of State pursuant to Code Section 43-17-5; and (4) If made by a solicitor agent or paid solicitor, that the solicitation is being made by a paid solicitor on behalf of the charitable organization and not by a volunteer and inform the person being solicited that the contract disclosing the financial arrangements between the paid solicitor and the charity is on file with and available from the Secretary of State.

(d) ACCOUNTING TO CHARITABLE ORGANIZATION. [OCGA 43-17-3(g)] Within 90 days after a solicitation campaign has been completed, and on the anniversary of the commencement of a solicitation campaign lasting more than one year, the paid solicitor shall account in writing to the charitable organization with whom it has contracted and to the Secretary of State, for all contributions received and expenses paid. The accounting shall be in the form of a written report, submitted to the charitable organization and to the Secretary of State, and shall be retained by the charitable organization for three years.

(e) COLLECTIONS AND DEPOSITS. [OCGA 43-17-3(h)] Each monetary contribution received by the paid solicitor shall, in its entirety and within three business days of its receipt, be deposited in an account at a federally insured financial institution. The account shall be in the name of the charitable organization with whom the paid solicitor has contracted and the charitable organization shall have sole control of all withdrawals from the account.

(f) EXPIRATION. [OCGA 43-17-5(b)(9)] Registration as a charitable organization, if granted, shall be valid for a period of 24 months, and if not renewed shall expire without further notice to the applicant.

(g) COMMERCIAL CO-VENTURERS. [OCGA 43-17-6] Every charitable organization which agrees to permit a charitable sales promotion shall obtain, prior to the commencement of the sales promotion, a written agreement from the commercial coventurer, signed by the charity and the commercial coventurer.

(h) AMENDMENTS TO REGISTRATION. [OCGA 43-17-5(b)(5)] Registration must be current and up to date at all times and must be amended within 30 days to reflect any material changes in operations of the charitable organization.

(i) RECORDS. [OCGA 43-17-5(d)] Records must be prepared and maintained for no less than three years and be available for inspection by representatives of the Secretary of State.

(j) MISAPPROPRIATION OF FUNDS AND FRAUDULENT CONDUCT. [OCGA 43-17-12] The Georgia Charitable Solicitations Act of 1988, as amended O.C.G.A. 43-17-1 et seq. ("Act"), establishes that it is a felony to engage in fraudulent conduct or to misappropriate, convert or illegally withhold contributions collected pursuant to the Act.

APPLICANT'S NAME:

CONTROL PERSONS

The applicant must provide the following information for **each person** who directly or indirectly, has the power to direct or cause the direction of the management and policies of the applicant. The term control person includes, but is not limited to, each executive officer or person holding similar position.
Make additional copies of this form as needed.
(Please type or print)

Name:	Title:	
Address:		
City:	State:	Zip Code:
Date of Birth:	Social Security Number:	

The person named above MUST provide a ten year employment history
beginning with the most recent employment.
Attach separate sheets if needed.

All persons who have custody of charitable donations must submit to a criminal background check. By signing this form, the person named above authorizes the Secretary of State to conduct a criminal history check pursuant to the charitable organization's registration in the State of Georgia.

Signature of Control Person _____

This _____ Day of _____

Official Witness (Notary)   Signature _____

<table>
<tr><td>

Contact Information
Kansas Secretary of State
Ron Thornburgh
Memorial Hall, 1st Floor
120 S.W. 10th Avenue
Topeka, KS 66612-1594
(785) 296-4564
kssos@kssos.org
www.kssos.org

</td><td>

KANSAS SECRETARY OF STATE
Charitable Solicitation Financial Statement

All information must be completed or this document will not be accepted for filing.

FS

53-10

</td></tr>
</table>

Tax year beginning _____ **and ending** _____ .

Total contributions, gifts, grants and other
amounts given: _____
(Attach a listing of total receipts and income
 for each separate solicitation project/source)

Cost of fundraising: (_____)

Net amount to charity: _____

Administrative expenses: (_____)

Operating income: _____

Educational/informational program expenses: (_____)

Other expenses: (_____)

Net income: _____

Charitable distributions in Kansas: (_____)

Charitable distributions outside of Kansas:
(Attach a listing of non-Kansas recipients of
distributions and such recipients' purposes) (_____)

Other distributions: (_____)

Balance this period: _____

Beginning balance: _____

Ending balance: _____

Do not write in this space

I declare under penalty of perjury under the laws of the state of Kansas that the foregoing is true and correct.

Executed on _____ _____ , _____ .
                Month   Day   Year

_____   _____
Authorized officer   Chief fiscal officer

K.S.A. 17-1763

Rev. 2/09/05 jls

**STATE OF MAINE
DEPARTMENT OF PROFESSIONAL
AND FINANCIAL REGULATION
OFFICE OF LICENSING AND REGISTRATION
CHARITABLE SOLICITATIONS APPLICATION**

APPLICANT INFORMATION (please print)

FULL LEGAL NAME			
FEIN OR SSN			
PHYSICAL ADDRESS			
CITY	STATE	ZIP	COUNTY
MAILING ADDRESS			
CITY	STATE	ZIP	COUNTY
PHONE # ( )	FAX # ( )	E-MAIL	

By my signature, I hereby certify that the information provided on this application is true and accurate to the best of my knowledge and belief. By submitting this application, I affirm that the Office of Licensing and Registration will rely upon this information for issuance of my license and that this information is truthful and factual. I also understand that sanctions may be imposed including denial, fines, suspension or revocation of my license if this information is found to be false.

SIGNATURE   **DATE**

CHARITABLE SOLICITATIONS PROGRAM

Charitable Organization Application
Required Fee: $50.00

☐   CHARITABLE ORGANIZATION - NON-PROFIT & TAX-EXEMPT (CO1421)

Office Use Only:

1421 - $25.00
1446 - $25.00

Office Use Only:
Check #_____
Amount:_____
Cash #_____
Lic. #_____
Issue Date_____
Exp. Date_____

PAYMENT OPTIONS:
Make checks payable to "Maine State Treasurer" - If you wish to pay by Mastercard or Visa, fill out the following:

NAME OF CARDHOLDER (please print)	*FIRST*	*MIDDLE INITIAL*	*LAST*

I authorize the Department of Professional and Financial Regulation, Office of Licensing and Registration to charge my

☐ VISA   ☐ MASTERCARD   the following amount: $_____

Card number: *XXXX-XXXX-XXXX-XXXX*   Expiration Date   *mm* / *yyyy*

SIGNATURE   **DATE**

STATE OF MAINE   DEPARTMENT OF PROFESSIONAL & FINANCIAL REGULATION - OFFICE OF LICENSING & REGISTRATION
Mailing Address: 35 State House Station, Augusta, Maine 04333 **Courier/Delivery address:** 122 Northern Avenue, Gardiner, Maine 04345
Phone: (207) 624-8603   Fax: (207) 624-8637   Hearing Impaired: (888) 577-6690 web: www.maine.gov/professionallicensing

Frequently Asked Questions

- **Where do I send my application?** Our mailing address is 35 State House Station, Augusta, Maine 04333-0035

- **Where are you located?** 76 Northern Avenue, Gardiner, Maine.

- **What hours are you open?** 8:00 AM to 5:00 PM weekdays

- **Can I come to Gardiner to drop off my application?** Yes. You will not leave with a license, though.

- **Can I come to Gardiner to pick up my license?** No. Your license will be mailed to you.

- **How long does it take to process an application?** You can check our website: www.maine.gov/professionallicensing. Your license will show up as PENDING at first; as soon as your status is ACTIVE you are authorized to practice.

What if I have other questions? Visit our website at: http://www.maine.gov/pfr/professionallicensing/ professions/charitable/organization.htm or contact Marlene McFadden, Office Specialist I, Tel. 207/624-8624, e-mail: Marlene.M.McFadden@Maine.gov or Elaine Thibodeau, Program Administrator, Tel. 207/624-8617, e-mail: Elaine.M.Thibodeau@Maine.gov

NOTICE

PUBLIC RECORD: This application is a public record for purposes of the Maine Freedom of Access Law (1 MRSA §401 et seq). Public records must be made available to any person upon request. This application for licensure is a public record and information supplied as part of the application (other than social security number and credit card information) is public information. Other licensing records to which this information may later be transferred will also be considered public records. Names, license numbers and mailing addresses listed on or submitted as part of this application will be available to the public and may be posted on our website.

Before you seal the envelope, did you:

- Complete every item on the application (incomplete applications may be returned)
- Sign and date your application
- Include correct amount (payable to Maine State Treasurer) *or* credit card information (plus signature)
- Make a copy of your application to keep for your records
- DO NOT SEND CASH.

For Your Information

The State of Maine accepts, and you may submit, either the Unified Registration Statement or this State of Maine Charitable Organization Application.

What is the Unified Registration Statement?

The Unified Registration Statement (URS) represents an effort to streamline the collection of information and data by states that require licensure/registration of nonprofit organizations performing charitable solicitations within their jurisdictions. The National Association of State Charities Officials and the National Association of Attorneys General together have established the Standardized Reporting Project to facilitate and simplify compliance with State laws.

The Unified Registration Statement form and instructions can be downloaded from the following Internet website (Please be sure to complete the entire form.):
http://www.multistatefiling.org/

If you decided to use the URS, then please note that --

- The first page of this form should be attached to the front of the URS, and the information on the second page, noted.

- A notarized signature is required.

What is the Charitable Organization Application?

This State of Maine's Charitable Organization Application is an alternative to the Unified Registration Statement. It can be downloaded from the Charitable Solicitations website:

http://www.maine.gov/pfr/professionallicensing/professions/charitable/

Application, Renewal, and Annual Fundraising Activity Report forms are available at that site.

Fees

The fees which must accompany the application are:

- $25 application

- $25 license

Regulations

Please read the laws and rules governing Charitable Solicitations prior to submitting your application. These are available at the following website:
http://www.maine.gov/pfr/professionallicensing/professions/charitable/laws.htm

Definitions

A Charitable Organization must be licensed with this office prior to conducting solicitation activities, or having contributions solicited on its behalf, in the State of Maine. Qualification as a "Tax Exempt Organization" under IRS regulations <u>does not exempt</u> a Charitable Organization from the licensure requirement.

"Charitable Organization" is defined as: "Any person or entity, including any person or entity organized in a foreign state, that is or holds itself out to be organized or operated for any charitable purpose or that solicits, accepts or obtains contributions from the public for any charitable purpose <u>and by any means, including, but not limited to, personal contact, telephone, mail, newspaper advertisement, television or radio. Status as a tax-exempt entity does not necessarily qualify that entity as a charitable organization</u>. A chapter, branch, area office or similar affiliate or any person soliciting contributions for any charitable purpose within the State for a charitable organization that has its principal place of business outside the State is considered a charitable organization.
However, an organization established for and serving bona fide religious purposes is not a charitable organization."

"Contribution" is defined as: "The promise or grant of any money or property of any kind or value, including the payment or promise to pay in consideration of a sale, performance or event of any kind which is advertised in conjunction with the name of any charitable organization. <u>This definition does not include</u>:

A. Payments by members of an organization for membership fees, dues, fines or assessments, or for services rendered to individual members, if membership in the organization confers a bona fide right, privilege, professional standing, honor or other direct benefits, other than the right to vote, elect officers or hold offices;

B. Money or property received from any governmental authority; or money or property received from a foundation established for charitable or educational purposes."

Instructions for Application

- Licenses will not be issued to prospective licensees who submit incomplete applications, or whose applications omit required documentation. All questions on the application must be answered, and supporting documentation must be provided, where requested. Otherwise, the application will be considered incomplete and returned for completion. If you need additional room to answer a question, then please attach a separate sheet of paper to the application and state on the application that you have done so.

- The principal officer of the organization must sign this document. Signatures must be original, and all applications must be notarized.

- Please submit a photocopy of the organization's IRS Determination Letter.

- If your organization contracts with, or otherwise engages the services of, any outside fundraising professional (such as a paid "Professional Solicitor," "Fundraising Counsel," or Commercial Co-venturer"), then attach a list, including their names, addresses (street & P.O.), telephone numbers, e-mail addresses and the physical location of offices used by them to perform work on behalf of your organization. Also include fees, expenses and any other costs paid to the fund-raising professional(s). Each entry must include a simple statement of: services provided, dates of contract, date of campaign/ event, whether the professional solicits on your behalf, and whether the professional at any time has custody or control of donations.

- Before you enter into a contract with an entity to provide fundraising services on your behalf in the State of Maine, please confirm that it is properly licensed here. (You can verify the entity's license status at: http://pfr.informe.org/almsonline/almsquery/welcome.aspx?board=4076.)

  It is illegal for a Charitable Organization to enter into a contract with an unlicensed Professional Solicitor, Professional Fundraising Counsel, or Commercial Co-venturer, and doing so could subject you to disciplinary action (9 M.R.S.A., Section 5005-B(3)). Note: An entity that, in exchange for a fee or other compensation, solicits contributions from the public on behalf of a Charitable Organization, exercises custody or control over contributions, or employs someone who does so, must become licensed as a Professional Solicitor, and not as a Professional Fundraising Counsel.

- Licenses expire on 11/30 of each year, so you will need to submit a renewal application by next 11/30, even if this falls within the same calendar year as the effective date of the license for which you are currently applying. If your renewal license application is postmarked after that date, then it will be considered late, and you will be charged a $50 late fee. This would make the total renewal fee $75. In this event, you would remain eligible to be considered for renewal only until March 1st, or within the first 90 days after your license has lapsed. During the interim (November 30th to March 1st), you may not conduct activities in Maine. Thereafter, you would be required to make application to become a new licensee, as you would not be eligible for renewal. The renewal application is different from this one, and it can be downloaded at: http://www.maine.gov/pfr/professionallicensing/professions/charitable/organization.htm#renewal

- An application for a license or renewal of a license can be denied for fraud, misrepresentation or deception on an application, or for a violation of any provision of the Charitable Solicitations Act or rules adopted under authority of the Act.

REQUIRED INFORMATION

1. License Period of one year to begin on November 30, 20_____ and end on November 30, 20_____

2. If the Legal Name has changed since prior filings, provide the name previously used:

   _____

   All other name(s) under which Charity intends to solicit contributions:

   _____
   _____
   _____

3. Does your organization have other offices/chapters/branches/affiliates within the State of Maine?

   ☐ Yes   ☐ No

   Contact Person: _____

   Street or P. O. Box: _____

   City: _____ County: _____

   State: <u>Maine</u>   Zip Code: _____-_____

   Telephone number(s): _____ _____

   Fax number (if available): _____

   E-mail (if available): _____

   Web site (if available): _____

4. Person having custody of financial records:

   _____

   Title: _____

   Street or P. O. Box: _____

   City: _____ County: _____

   State: _____ Zip Code: _____-_____

   Telephone number(s): _____ _____

   Fax number (if available): _____

   E-mail (if available): _____

   Web site (if available): _____

5. Fiscal year begins / ends: ____/____/_____ - ____/____/_____

6. Date incorporated: _____ State of incorporation: _____

   If not incorporated, indicate legal structure (type of organization), jurisdiction, and date established:

   _____

   _____

7. Has the organization been granted IRS tax-exempt status?

   ☐ Yes   ☐ No

   Please specify section of IRS Tax Code under which exempt status was granted, if other than 501 (C) (3): _____

   (If this is your initial application for license in Maine as a Charitable Organization, please attach a photocopy of the IRS Determination Letter.)

8. Has your organization been licensed or registered to solicit funds in any other State? Please attach list.)

   ☐ Yes   ☐ No

9. Indicate all methods of solicitation:

   ☐ Mail   ☐ Phone   ☐ E-mail   ☐ Website   ☐ Personal Contact   ☐ Radio/TV Appeals

10. Identify the <u>primary</u> purpose of your organization (check one):

CH	CHILDREN'S ASSISTANCE	☐
CU	CULTURAL	☐
ED	EDUCATIONAL	☐
EM	EMERGENCY RELIEF	☐
EN	ENVIRONMENTAL	☐
HE	HEALTHCARE	☐
HI	HISTORIC PRESERVATION	☐
HU	HUMANITARIAN RELIEF	☐
LA	LEGAL ASSISTANCE	☐
PH	PHILOSOPHICAL	☐
PO	POLITICAL	☐
RE	RELIGIOUS	☐
SA	SAFETY PROMOTION	☐
SP	SPORTS PROMOTION	☐
TR	TRAINING & DEVELOPMENT	☐
VA	VETERANS' ASSISTANCE	☐
WP	WILDLIFE PRESERVATION	☐
OT	OTHER	☐

11. Describe the programs for which funds are solicited. (Attach a separate sheet, if necessary.)

_____

_____

12. On a separate sheet, list the names, titles, addresses (street or P.O. Box), telephone numbers and E mail addresses (if available) of current officers, directors, trustees and principal salaried executive staff officer of your organization.

13. On a separate sheet, list the names, titles, addresses (street or P.O. Box), telephone numbers and E-mail addresses (if available) of individual(s) –

- Responsible for custody of contributions received

- Responsible for final distribution of contributions received

14. Does the organization use volunteers to solicit directly from the public?

☐ Yes   ☐ No

15. Does the organization use contract professionals (who are not employees) to solicit directly from the public?

☐ Yes   ☐ No

16. On a separate sheet, list the name and address of any Professional Solicitor, Professional Fund-raising Counsel or Commercial Co-venturer who acts, or will act, on behalf of the organization, and the terms of remuneration for each.

17. Total Dollar Amount received as contributions (as defined on page #4 of this application) in the last fiscal year: $ _____

18. Has your organization ever been enjoined by any court from soliciting contributions?

☐ Yes *   ☐ No

19. Has your organization ever been the subject of a criminal conviction?

☐ Yes *   ☐ No

20. Has your organization ever been the subject of a revocation, suspension or other disciplinary action taken in this or any other jurisdiction against any occupational or professional license held by the applicant or licensee?

☐ Yes *   ☐ No

* If you answered "Yes," to questions 18, 19 or 20, then please attach a detailed explanation and copies of all documents.

===

<u>Principal Officer(s):</u>

_____   _____
Name (printed / typed)   Name (printed / typed)

_____   _____
Name (signature)   Name (signature)

_____   _____
Title (printed / typed)   Title (printed / typed)

_____   _____
Date   Date

Sworn and subscribed to before me this _____ day of _____, 20_____.

_____   _____
Notary Signature   Jurisdiction in which Signed

STATE OF MINNESOTA
Supplement To Unified Registration Statement
FOR CHARITABLE ORGANIZATION INITIAL REGISTRATION & ANNUAL REPORTING

ATTORNEY GENERAL LORI SWANSON
SUITE 1200, BREMER TOWER
445 MINNESOTA STREET
ST. PAUL, MN 55101-2130
(651) 757-1311
(651) 296-1410 (TTY)
www.ag.state.mn.us

☐ **Annual Reporting**   ☐ **Initial Registration**

FEDERAL EIN NUMBER:

FOR YEAR ENDING:

SECTION ONE: REQUIRED INFORMATION FOR INITIAL REGISTRATION & ANNUAL REPORTING
All organizations MUST complete questions 1 & 2.

1. *Legal Name of Organization*: _____

2. Complete the following for the most recent twelve-month accounting year. *While this information should reflect the financials on the IRS For 990, this section is required to be completed even if an IRS Form 990 is attached. Before completing this section, please refer to the Annual Report Instructions.*

INCOME   **For Year Ending:** _____

Contributions from the public	$_____
Government Grants	$_____
Other revenue	$_____
TOTAL REVENUE	$_____

EXPENSES

Amount spent for program or charitable purposes	$_____
Management/general expense	$_____
Fund-raising expense	$_____
TOTAL EXPENSES	$_____

EXCESS or DEFICIT	$_____
TOTAL Assets	$_____
TOTAL Liabilities	$_____

END OF YEAR FUND BALANCE/NET WORTH (Assets minus Liabilities) $_____

SECTION TWO: REQUIRED FOR INITIAL REGISTRATION ONLY

1. Please attach a copy of the organization's IRS determination letter and formation documents (i.e. Articles of Incorporation).

2. **Attach** a list of organization's officers, directors, trustees, and chief executive officer, including their titles, addresses, and total annual compensation paid to each.   ☐ Attached

<u>SECTION THREE: REQUIRED FOR ANNUAL REPORTING ONLY</u>

All annual report filers must complete questions 1 and 2.

1. List the **five** highest paid directors, officers and employees of the organization and its related organization(s) who receive total compensation of **$50,000** or more, indicating their titles and total compensation paid to each. Total compensation includes salaries, fees, bonuses, fringe benefits, severance payments and deferred compensation paid by the organization and all related organizations. A "related organization" is an organization that controls, is controlled by or is under common control with another corporation. "Control" can exist through stock ownership or membership interests, the authority to appoint members, or the ability to direct the policies and management of other corporations. *See* Minn. Stat. § 317A.011, subd. 18.

	Name/Title	Compensation
1		
2		
3		
4		
5		

2. **Attach a GAAP audit** if total revenue exceeds $750,000 or other threshold set by Minn. Stat. § 309.53. ☐ Attached ☐ Audit not included under the Food Shelf Exemption (excluding from total revenue the value of food donated to a nonprofit food shelf for redistribution at no cost).

3. **Complete the Statement of Functional Expenses on the next page if NOT filing an IRS Form 990 that contains a *completed* Statement of Functional Expenses.**

*Complete this section only if **NOT** filing an IRS Form 990 that contains a Statement of Functional Expenses.*

Statement of Functional Expenses

		(A) Total expenses	(B) Program service expenses	(C) Management and general expenses	(D) Fundraising expenses
1	Grants and other assistance to governments and organizations in the U.S.				
2	Grants and other assistance to individuals in the U.S.				
3	Grants and other assistance to governments, organizations, and individuals outside the U.S.				
4	Benefits paid to or for members				
5	Compensation of current officers, directors, trustees, and key employees				
6	Compensation not included above, to disqualified persons (as defined under section 4958(f)(1) and persons described in section 4958(c)(3)(B)				
7	Other salaries and wages				
8	Pension plan contributions (include section 401(k) and section 403(b) employer contributions)				
9	Other employee benefits				
10	Payroll taxes				
11	Fees for services (non-employees):				
a	Management				
b	Legal				
c	Accounting				
d	Lobbying				
e	Professional fundraising services				
f	Investment management fees				
g	Other				
12	Advertising and promotion				
13	Office expenses				
14	Information technology				
15	Royalties				
16	Occupancy				
17	Travel				
18	Payments of travel or entertainment expenses for any federal, state, or local public officials				
19	Conferences, conventions, and meetings				
20	Interest				
21	Payments to affiliates				
22	Depreciation, depletion, and amortization				
23	Insurance				
24	Other expenses. Itemize expenses not covered above. (Expenses grouped together and labeled miscellaneous may not exceed 5% of total expenses shown on line 25 below.)				
a	....				
b	....				
c	....				
d	All other expenses				
25	**Total functional expenses.** Add lines 1 through 24d				
26	**Joint costs.** Check here ► ☐ if following SOP 98-2. Complete this line only if the organization reported in column (B) joint costs from a combined educational campaign and fundraising solicitation				

Must be prepared in accordance with generally accepted accounting principles.
Column A, Line 25 should equal line 17 of IRS Form 990-EZ
The total of lines 1 through 24d should equal line 25.
The total of lines 25b, 25c and 25d, should equal line 25a.

Minnesota—Supplement to Unified Registration Statement for Charitable
Organization Initial Registration and Annual Reporting

Page 3 of 4

<u>**SECTION FOUR: REQUIRED FOR INITIAL REGISTRATION & ANNUAL REPORTING**</u>

BOARD OF DIRECTORS
<u>*SIGNATURES AND ACKNOWLEDGMENT*</u>

We, the undersigned, state and acknowledge that we are duly constituted officers of this organization, being the _____(Title) and _____(Title) respectively, and that we execute this document on behalf of the organization pursuant to the resolution of the _____(Board of Directors, Trustees, or Managing Group) adopted on the _____ day of _____, 20____, approving the contents of the document, and do hereby certify that the _____(Board of Directors, Trustees or Managing Group) has assumed, and will continue to assume, responsibility for determining matters of policy, and have supervised, and will continue to supervise, the finances of the organization. We further state that the information supplied is true, correct and complete to the best of our knowledge.

_____
Name   (Print)

_____
Name   (Print)

_____
Signature

_____
Signature

_____
Title

_____
Title

_____
Date

_____
Date

✷ NOTICE ✷

Documents required to be filed are public records. Please do not include *social security numbers*, *driver's license numbers* or *bank account numbers* on the documents filed with this Office as they are not required, but could become part of the public records. A charitable organization is not required to file a list of its donors. If it is included, it may become part of the public file.

MISSISSIPPI SECRETARY OF STATE

CHARITABLE ORGANIZATION REGISTRATION

INSTRUCTIONS

Charitable Organizations must submit a **Unified Registration Statement (URS)** and an **Annual Financial Statement Report Form (FORM FS)** for the organization's most recently completed fiscal year end.

All questions must be answered or the forms will be considered deficient and will not satisfy the filing requirement(s). If a question does not apply, answer "no" or "not applicable". When attachments are necessary, indicate the question number on the attachment.

A $50 filing fee made payable to the Mississippi Secretary of State must be enclosed.

Return the registration statement (URS), financial form (Form FS) and $50 filing fee to:

Mississippi Secretary of State's Office
Charities Registration
Post Office Box 136
Jackson, Mississippi 39205-0136

(601) 359-1371 or 888-236-6167

A copy of the completed registration should be kept by the organization.

REGISTRATION IS REQUIRED *PRIOR* TO ANY SOLICITATIONS.

The laws and rules that govern the solicitation of contributions may be viewed at the Secretary of State's website at www.sos.state.ms.us.

RENEWAL OF REGISTRATION

All registrations must renew annually. A complete Unified Registration Statement (URS) along with the Supplement to Unified Registration Statement - Annual Financial Statement Report Form (FORM FS) is due by the date on the Certificate of Registration issued by this Office.

NOTICE: MISSISSIPPI LAW DOES NOT ALLOW AN EXTENSION.

This copy of the Unified Registration Statement is intended for Mississippi filers only. A complete Unified Registration Statement (URS) for all states is posted at the website *http://www.nonprofits.org/library/gov/urs*.

Revised 7/1/08

WHO NEEDS TO REGISTER AS A CHARITABLE ORGANIZATION?

Any organization which collects contributions from the public to be used for charitable purposes. This includes health and welfare, humane, philanthropic, patriotic organizations educational, humane, scientific, public health, environmental conservation, civic or law enforcement personnel, fire fighters, or other public safety organization, or any person employing in any manner a charitable appeal as the basis of any solicitation or an appeal that suggests that there is a charitable purpose to any solicitation.

WHAT IS A CONTRIBUTION?

A contribution is the promise or grant of any money or property. Professional Membership dues are not considered contributions.

WHO IS EXEMPT UNDER THIS LEGISLATION?

A. Accredited educational institutions and foundations associated therewith;
B. Fraternal, patriotic, social, educational, alumni organizations and historical societies who use only their memberships to solicit contributions;
C. Persons who are soliciting contributions for specified individuals in need, if the solicitations are made solely by persons who are unpaid;
D. Organizations which do not intend to solicit or receive and do not actually receive more than $4000 per year in contributions;
E. Organizations which receive allocations from registered united funds or community chests and receive less than $4000 from other sources;
F. All volunteer fire departments and rescue units which are chartered as nonprofit organizations by the State of Mississippi;
G. Any humane society which contracts with counties or municipalities for the care and keeping of strays.

HOW DOES AN EXEMPT ORGANIZATION FILE?

1. Fill out a "Charitable Organization Notice of Exemption" (FORM CE). Answer each question completely and have the application notarized. The Form CE is available on the Mississippi Secretary of State's website at www.sos.state.ms.us.

2. Return completed application and required attachments to:

Mississippi Secretary of State's Office
Charities Registration
Post Office Box 136
Jackson, Mississippi   39205-0136

Exempt organizations must file the FORM CE __and__ receive approval by the Mississippi Secretary of State PRIOR to any solicitations.

INSTRUCTIONS AND CHECKLIST
FOR UNIFIED REGISTRATION STATEMENT (URS)

Preliminary identifying information:

Indicate whether registration is initial or renewal in the appropriate box.

Fill in your organization's federal Employer Identification Number (EIN).

Enter Mississippi in blank next to State.

Enter registration number issued on the Certificate of Registration for a renewal application in the State ID blank. Leave blank for initial registration.

_____ **Questions #1 - #6** are answered.

_____ **Question #7**: If A, B, C, D, and/or E is answered yes, **attach a written explanation**. If F and/or G is answered yes, **attach** a listing of all states where registered, or from whom an exemption was obtained, or in which the organization solicited contributions. (Include agencies, dates of registration, registration numbers, any other names organization was/is registered under, and the dates and types of solicitation conducted).

VERY IMPORTANT: In answering 7G for an initial registration, make sure a specific date when solicitation began is provided. OR, if 7G is "no" but the organization intends to begin soliciting, give the approximate date solicitations will begin.

_____ **Questions #8 – 10 are answered.**

_____ **Question 11 NTEE Codes.** The National Taxonomy of Exempt Entities (NTEE) is a system for classifying nonprofits developed by the National Center for Charitable Statistics. Select the code letter that best describes the organization's primary purpose or field (enter a second or third code letter if no single code seems adequate):

A Arts, culture, humanities	**J** Employment, job related	**S** Community improvement, capacity building
B Educational institutions & related activities	**K** Food, nutrition, agriculture	**T** Philanthropy, voluntarism and grantmaking foundations
C Environmental quality, protection & beautification	**L** Housing, shelter	**U** Science and technology
D Animal related	**M** Public safety, disaster preparedness & relief	**V** Social science research
E Health-general & rehabilitative	**N** Recreation, sports, leisure, athletics	**W** Public affairs, society benefit
F Mental health, crisis Intervention	**O** Youth development	**X** Religion, spiritual development
G Disease, disorders, medical Disciplines	**P** Human services	**Y** Mutual/membership benefit
H Medical research	**Q** International, foreign affairs, national security	**Z** Unknown, unclassifiable
I Crime, legal related	**R** Civil rights, social action advocacy	

_____ **Question #12**: Explain purposes and programs of organization for which funds are solicited. Attach a separate sheet if necessary.

_____ **Question #13:** Attach a list of officers, directors and executives of organization complete with their addresses and telephone numbers.

_____ **Question #14:** (A) (1&2) If "yes" is answered to any of the relationships described, **attach the requested information for all the related parties.** 14 (B): If answered "yes," **attach a written explanation.** A "misdemeanor or felony" is a crime but does not include minor traffic offenses.

_____ **Question #15:** Attach a list to provide the names and addresses of the people with the specified responsibilities. Please clearly indicate the respective responsibility for each name listed. Also include the names, addresses, and phone numbers of all banks, and all accounts (provide numbers), in which organization's funds are deposited. "Custody" means legal custody of the organization's funds, typically the charge of the treasurer. Person responsible for "distribution" means the person, typically the president or chief executive, who has primary day-to-day authority over disposing of the organization's funds.

_____ **Questions #16 – 22 are answered.**

_____ **Question #17** This item should be left blank for Mississippi corporations. Any organization that does not maintain an office within the State should appoint a registered agent upon which process may be served in the State of Mississippi. If no designation is made, then service of process shall be upon the Secretary of State of Mississippi.

_____ **Question #20** Attach a list of all professional fund-raisers and/or fund-raising counsel that provide fundraising services to the organizations in Mississippi. *This list must include a complete address (street & P.O.), phone number and dates of contract.* NOTE: Copies of *current* contracts not already on file must be submitted with the registration statement. *Do not include copies of contracts that have expired.* (If a contract is executed after the filing of the registration statement, a copy must be filed within 10 days of the date of execution.)

_____ **Question #22** Lines (A) thru (E) should be taken from the IRS Form 990.

> Signatures: The URS must be signed by the **President** or other authorized officer *AND* the *Chief Financial Officer*. **BOTH** signatures must be notarized.

Initial Filing Only:

_____ A copy of the organization's Articles of Incorporation
_____ A copy of the organization's by-laws
_____ A copy of the organization's IRS Determination Letter.

(Copies of the above documents are not required with renewals)

IMPORTANT: Each answer on every form must be completed, and all required documents must be included in the filing.

Failure to submit a complete filing may result in denial of the registration.

_____ **ANNUAL FINANCIAL STATEMENT REPORT FORM IS INCLUDED**

Unified Registration Statement (URS) for Charitable Organizations© (v. 3.10)

☐ **Initial registration** ___   ☐ **Renewal/Update**

This URS covers the reporting year which ended (day/month/year)_____

Filer EIN_____

State_____ State ID_____

1. Organization's legal name_____

If changed since prior filings, previous name used_____

All other name(s) used_____

2. (A) Street address _____

City_____ County _____

State_____ Zip Code _____

(B) Mailing address (if different) _____

City_____ County _____

State_____ Zip Code _____

3. Telephone number(s)_____ Fax number(s) _____

E-mail_____ Web site _____

4. Names, addresses (street & P.O.), telephone numbers of other offices/chapters/branches/affiliates (*attach list*).

5. Date incorporated _____ State of incorporation_____

Fiscal year end: day/month _____

6. If not incorporated, type of organization, state, and date established_____

_____

7. Has organization or any of its officers, directors, employees or fund raisers:
A. Been enjoined or otherwise prohibited by a government agency/court from soliciting? Yes __ No __
B. Had its registration denied or revoked?   Yes __ No __
C. Been the subject of a proceeding regarding any solicitation or registration?   Yes __ No __
D. Entered into a voluntary agreement of compliance with any government agency or in a case before a court or administrative agency? Yes ____ No ____

E. Applied for registration or exemption from registration (but not yet completed or obtained)?
Yes _____ No _____

F. Registered with or obtained exemption from any state or agency? Yes _____ No _____

G. Solicited funds in any state? Yes _____ No _____
        If "yes" to 7A, B, C, D, E, *attach explanation.*

If "yes" to 7F & G, *attach list* of states where registered, exempted, or where it solicited, including registering agency, dates of registration, registration numbers, any other names under which the organization was/is registered, and the dates and type (mail, telephone, door to door, special events, etc.) of the solicitation conducted.

8. Has the organization applied for or been granted IRS tax exempt status? Yes _____ No _____
If yes, date of application_____ OR date of determination letter_____.
If granted, exempt under 501(c)_____. Are contributions to the organization tax deductible? Yes __ No __

9. Has tax exempt status ever been denied, revoked, or modified? Yes _____ No _____

10. Indicate all methods of solicitations:
Mail___   Telephone___   Personal Contact___   Radio/TV Appeals___
Special Events___   Newspaper/Magazine Ads___   Other(s)
(specify)_____

11. List the NTEE code(s) that best describes your organization. _____, _____, _____

12. Describe the purposes and programs of the organization and those for which funds are solicited *(attach separate sheet if necessary).*

13. List the names, titles, addresses, (street & P.O.), and telephone numbers of officers, directors, trustees, and the principal salaried executives of organization *(attach separate sheet).*

14. (A) (1)   Are any of the organization's officers, directors, trustees or employees related by blood, marriage, or adoption to:
         (i) any other officer, director, trustee or employee OR

         (ii) any officer, agent, or employee of any fundraising professional firm under contract to the organization OR

         (iii) any officer, agent, or employee of a supplier or vendor firm providing goods or services to the organization? Yes _____ No _____

(2)   Does the organization or any of its officers, directors, employees, or anyone holding a financial interest in the organization have a financial interest in a business described in (ii) or (iii) above OR serve as an officer, director, partner or employee of a business described in (ii) or (iii) above?   Yes _____ No _____

(If yes to any part of 14A, *attach sheet* which specifies the relationship and provides the names, businesses, and addresses of the related parties).

(B) Have any of the organization's officers, directors, or principal executives been convicted of a misdemeanor or felony?

(*If yes, attach a complete explanation.*) Yes _____ No _____

15. *Attach separate sheet listing names and addresses (street & P.O.) for all below:*

Individual(s) responsible for custody of funds.   Individual(s) responsible for distribution of funds.

Individual(s) responsible for fund raising.   Individual(s) responsible for custody of financial records.

Individual(s) authorized to sign checks.   Bank(s) in which registrant's funds are deposited (*include account number and bank phone number*).

16. Name, address (street & P.O.), and telephone number of accountant/auditor.

Name _____

Address _____

City_____ State_____ Zip Code_____ Telephone _____

Method of accounting _____

17. Name, address (street & P.O.), and telephone number of person authorized to receive service of process. *This is a state-specific item. See instructions.*

Name _____

Address _____

City_____ State_____ Zip Code_____ Telephone _____

18. (A) Does the organization receive financial support from other nonprofit organizations (foundations, public charities, combined campaigns, etc.)?   Yes _____ No _____

(B) Does the organization share revenue or governance with any other non-profit organization?
Yes _____ No_____

(C) Does any other person or organization own a 10% or greater interest in your organization OR does your organization own a 10% or greater interest in any other organization?   Yes _____ No _____

(If "yes" to A, B or C, *attach an explanation* including name of person or organization, address, relationship to your organization, and type of organization.)

19. Does the organization use volunteers to solicit directly?   Yes _____ No _____

Does the organization use professionals to solicit directly?   Yes _____ No _____

20. If your organization contracts with or otherwise engages the services of any outside fundraising professional (such as a "professional fundraiser," "paid solicitor," "fund raising counsel," or "commercial co-venture"), *attach list* including their names, addresses (street & P.O.), telephone numbers, and location of offices used by them to perform work on behalf of your organization. Each entry *must include* a simple statement of services provided, description of compensation arrangement, dates of contract, date of campaign/event, whether the professional solicits on your behalf, and whether the professional at any time has custody or control of donations.

21. Amount paid to PFR/PS/FRC during previous year: $_____

22. (A) Total contributions: $

    (B) Program service expenses: $

    (C) Management & general expenses: $

    (D) Fundraising expenses: $

    (E) Total expenses: $

    (F) Fundraising expenses as a percentage of funds raised: _____%

    (G) Fundraising expenses plus management and general expenses as a percentage of funds raised: _____%

    (H) Program services as a percentage of total expenses: _____%

Under penalty of perjury, we certify that the above information and the information contained in any attachments or supplement is true, correct, and complete.

_____

SIGNATURE OF PRESIDENT OR   **DATE**
OTHER AUTHORIZED OFFICER

Sworn to and subscribed before me this the

_____ day of _____, 20____

_____

PRINTED OR TYPED NAME AND TITLE

_____
NOTARY PUBLIC

NOTARY SEAL

_____

CHIEF FINANCIAL OFFICER   **DATE**

Sworn to and subscribed before me this the

_____ day of _____, 20____

_____

PRINTED OR TYPED NAME AND TITLE

_____
NOTARY PUBLIC

NOTARY SEAL

Consult the state-by-state appendix to the URS to determine whether supporting documents, supplementary state forms or fees must accompany this form. Before submitting your registration, *make sure you have attached or included everything required by each state to the respective copy of the URS.*

Attachments may be prepared as one continuous document or as separate pages for each item requiring elaboration. In either case, please number the response to correspond with the URS item number.

© 2007 M U L T I - S T A T E F I L E R P R O J E C T

FORM FS

MISSISSIPPI SECRETARY OF STATE

SUPPLEMENT TO UNIFIED REGISTRATION STATEMENT
ANNUAL FINANCIAL STATEMENT REPORT FORM

INSTRUCTIONS

The Supplement to Unified Registration Statement – Annual Financial Statement Report (FORM FS) must be filed with the Unified Registration Statement.

This form must be completed for the most recently completed fiscal year end.

FORM FS should be completed using the financial information on either the IRS Form 990 or the financial statement. (If you have filed an extension or are not required to complete the IRS Form 990, the Form FS should be completed using the organization's financial statements.)

Complete the Name of Organization, Mississippi Registration number, contact person and the fiscal year the report covers.

1) *IF COMPLETING FORM FS USING THE IRS FORM 990:*

        RECEIPT AND INCOME (REVENUE) - use Line 1 thru 11

        TOTAL RECEIPTS AND INCOME – use Line 12

        EXPENSES:
        PROGRAMS SERVICES – use Line 13   Break out any funds expended for public education.

        ADMINISTRATION (MANAGEMENT & GENERAL) – use Line 14

        FUNDRAISING – use Line 15

        PAYMENTS TO AFFILIATES – use Line 16

2) *IF COMPLETING FORM FS USING THE FINANCIAL STATEMENT –*

        RECEIPTS AND INCOME (REVENUE) - use Support and Revenue

        TOTAL RECEIPTS AND INCOME - use Total Support and Revenue

        EXPENSES - use Statement of Functional Expenses

            PROGRAM SERVICES: Program expense on financial statement – break out any funds expended for public education and research.

            ADMINISTRATION (MANAGEMENT & GENERAL) – use Management and general

            FUNDRAISING – use Fundraising

NOTE: The Other category should not be used for any expense that would be considered program services, management and general or fund-raising.

> ## THE FOLLOWING INSTRUCTIONS SET OUT THE SUPPORTING DOCUMENTS REQUIRED TO BE FILED *WITH THE FORM FS*. PLEASE REVIEW AND SUBMIT THE REQUIRED DOCUMENTATION.

1) **CONTRIBUTIONS OVER $500,000**
A financial statement **audited** by an independent certified public accountant and IRS Form 990 must be filed along with the Unified Registration Statement and Annual Financial Statement Report if the organization:
A) Received contributions over **$500,000**; or
B) Engaged the services of a professional fund-raiser or fund-raising counsel; or if fundraising was conducted by persons who were paid for performing these services.

   The report must be signed by two officers - the president (or other authorized officer) and chief financial officer and the signatures must be notarized.

2) **CONTRIBUTIONS OF $250,000 to $500,000**
A financial statement **reviewed** by an independent certified public accountant and the IRS Form 990 must be filed with the Unified Registration Statement and Annual Financial Statement Report if the organization:
A) Received contributions of **$250,000 to $500,000**; and
B) Did not engage the services of a professional fund-raiser /fund-raising counsel and if fundraising was conducted by persons who were unpaid for performing these services.

   The report must be signed by the president or other authorized officer and the signature must be notarized).

3) **CONTRIBUTIONS LESS THAN $250,000**
A financial statement and the IRS Form 990 or 990EZ must be filed with the Unified Registration Statement and Annual Financial Statement Report Form if the organization:
A) Received contributions **less than $250,000**; and
B) Did not engage the services of a professional fund-raiser /fund-raising counsel and if fundraising was conducted by persons who were unpaid for performing these services.

   The report must be signed by the president or other authorized officer and the signature must be notarized.

4) **NEW ORGANIZATIONS**
The Annual Financial Statement Report must be completed using zeros.

   The report must be signed by the president or other authorized officer and the signature must be notarized

A separate Annual Financial Statement Report must be filed for each local division, chapter or affiliate the Organization has included under its registration (See Miss. Code Ann. Section 79-11-503(7)).

MISSISSIPPI LAW DOES NOT ALLOW FOR AN EXTENSION TO FILE.

Mississippi Secretary of State's Office
Charities Registration
Post Office Box 136
Jackson, Mississippi 39205-0136
(601) 359-1371 or 888-236-6167

FORM FS

MISSISSIPPI SECRETARY OF STATE
ANNUAL FINANCIAL REPORT FORM

____ Initial
____ Renewal

____**Final Report**

NAME OF ORGANIZATION   **MISSISSIPPI REGISTRATION #**

CHARITY CONTACT PERSON:

PERSON COMPLETING FORM:

FORM FS must be completed and be in agreement with financial information reported on IRS Form 990 or the filed financial statement.

FORM COMPLETED USING: _____ IRS 990   _____ FINANCIAL STATEMENT

FISCAL YEAR END   _____

1. **RECEIPTS AND INCOME**

   CONTRIBUTIONS (LIST SEPARATELY FOR EACH PROJECT OR SOURCE)

   1._____ $_____

   2._____   _____

   3._____   _____

   4._____   _____

   SUBTOTAL CONTRIBUTIONS ....$_____

   OTHER INCOME (MEMBERSHIP DUES, ENDOWMENTS, ETC.)

   1._____ $_____

   2._____   _____

   3._____   _____

   SUBTOTAL OTHER INCOME ....$_____

   TOTAL RECEIPTS AND INCOME: ....$_____

2. EXPENSES –

    1. PROGRAM SERVICES .... $_____

       Itemize by category the amount disbursed for each major purpose.

          PUBLIC EDUCATION $_____

          _____ $_____

          _____ $_____

    2. ADMINISTRATION (MANAGEMENT & GENERAL) .... $_____

    3. FUNDRAISING .... $_____

    4. PAYMENTS TO AFFILIATES .... $_____

    5. OTHER .... $_____

TOTAL EXPENSES .... $_____

List joint costs reported in Program Services from a combined educational campaign and fundraising solicitation:

Total Amount before allocation : _____   Amount allocated to Program Services: _____
                                                                      Amount allocated to Fundraising: _____
                                                                      Amount allocated to Management & General: _____

Under penalty of perjury, we certify that the above information and the information contained in any attachments or supplement is true, correct, and complete.

_____   Sworn to and subscribed before me this the
SIGNATURE OF PRESIDENT OR   **DATE**
OTHER AUTHORIZED OFFICER   _____ day of _____, 20____

_____
PRINTED OR TYPED NAME AND TITLE   _____
                                                                   NOTARY PUBLIC

                                                                 NOTARY SEAL

_____   Sworn to and subscribed before me this the
CHIEF FINANCIAL OFFICER   **DATE**
                                                _____ day of _____, 20____

_____
PRINTED OR TYPED NAME AND TITLE   _____
                                                                   NOTARY PUBLIC

                                                                 NOTARY SEAL

**CHARITABLE ORGANIZATION
REGISTRATION STATEMENT**
SECRETARY OF STATE
SFN 11300 (07-09)

FEE: $25.00

FOR OFFICE USE ONLY
ID Number
WO Number
Approved By
Issued By

Instructions:

1. For reference, see North Dakota Century Code, Section 50-22.
2. Please type or print, complete all blanks, enter "None" when appropriate.
3. Any omission or failure to report complete and/or accurate information in this application may result in an investigation by the Secretary of State and/or the Attorney General and may result in forfeiture of your registration.
4. Once the registration process has started and the requirements are not completed or perfected within 90 days, the filing fee submitted will be retained and the file closed.

Secretary of State
State of North Dakota
600 E Boulevard Ave Dept 108
Bismarck ND 58505-0500
Telephone 701-328-3665
Toll Free 800-352-0867 Ext 83665
Fax 701-328-1690
Web Site: www.nd.gov/sos

1. Legal Name of Organization:

   Name(s) under which the organization solicits contributions:

Street & mailing address of principal office:	Federal ID Number

City	State	Zip Code	Telephone Number

   The business is a:
   ☐ Unincorporated association   ☐ Non-profit Corporation   ☐ Trust
   ☐ State of Origin _____   First Year Organized _____

2. Is the organization exempt from federal income taxes? If yes, attach a copy of your IRS determination letter. If the application is pending attach a copy of the first page of the application.

   ☐ Yes   ☐ No   ☐ Application Pending   Status: 501(c)(_____)

3. Check one or more methods of soliciting the organization anticipates using.
   ☐ Direct Mail   ☐ Radio   ☐ Telemarketing
   ☐ Personal Contact   ☐ Television ☐ National ☐ Local   ☐ Newspaper
   ☐ Vending Business   ☐ Show or Concert   ☐ Magazines or Periodicals
                          ☐ Grant Writing   ☐ Membership Enrollment
   ☐ Other (please describe)_____

4. Period of time during which solicitation is to be conducted? _____

5. General Purposes for which organized:

6. General Purposes for which contributions to be solicited will be used?

7. Name of auditor in charge of organization's books & records if not kept at the organizations office. | Telephone Number

Address	City	State	Zip Code

8. Attach a list of names & addresses of all directors officers and trustees. Indicate the individuals having the final discretion or authority as to the distribution and use of contributions received.

9. Attach a list of total compensation, including salaries, fees, bonuses, fringe benefits, severance payments, and deferred compensation, paid to employees by the charitable organization and all its affiliated organizations.

(continue on reverse side)

SFN 11300 (07-09) Page 2

10. Month and day accounting year ends_____.

11. State the total contributions the organization received during the last ended accounting year: $_____.

12. Attach financial statement or IRS Form 990. If neither is available, complete the following for the most recent twelve-month accounting year.

INCOME		EXPENSES	
Contributions from the public	$_____	Amount spent for program or charitable purposes	$_____
Government Grants	$_____	Management / general expense	$_____
Fees for program service	$_____	Fund-raising expense	$_____
Other Revenue	$_____	Amounts paid to affiliated organizations	$_____
TOTAL INCOME	**$_____**	**TOTAL EXPENSES**	**$_____**
EXCESS or Deficit	$_____	**END OF YEAR FUND BALANCE / NET WORTH**	
TOTAL Assets	$_____	(Assets minus Liabilities)	**$_____**
TOTAL Liabilities	$_____		

13. Will the solicitation be conducted by ☐ voluntary unpaid solicitors ☐ paid solicitors ☐ both

If in whole or part by paid solicitors, list the name and address of each professional fundraiser supplying the solicitors and a copy of the agreement. Attach an additional sheet if necessary. If a contract, written agreement, or statement of any arrangement is made between an applicant and professional fundraiser/solicitor after a solicitation registration, the applicant agrees to file a copy of such contract or agreement with the Secretary of State.

Name of Professional Fundraiser		Telephone Number	
Address	City	State	Zip Code
Name of Professional Fundraiser		Telephone Number	
Address	City	State	Zip Code

14. Has your organization or a member thereof been involved in any civil or criminal litigation in the past year?
☐ Yes - attach a statement of your summary of the litigation, the outcome, and the parties involved. ☐ No

15. Has your organization been denied the right to solicit contribution, at any time, by any government? or any court?
☐ Yes - attach an explanation ☐ No

SIGNATURE AND CERTIFICATION

I, the undersigned, state and certify that I am a duly constituted officer of this organization, being the _____(Title) and that this Registration Statement is executed on behalf of the organization by me pursuant to resolutions of the _____ (Board of Directors, Trustees, or Managing Group) adopted on the_____day of _____, 20_____, approving the contents of the Registration Statement, and do hereby certify that the _____(Board of Directors, Trustees or Managing Group) has assumed, and will continue to assume responsibility for determining matters of policy, and have supervised, and will continue to supervise, the finances of the organization, and I, the undersigned, state that the information supplied is true, correct and complete to the best of my knowledge.

_____
Name   (PRINT)

_____ / _____
Signature   Date

State of Tennessee

Department of State

Division of Charitable Solicitations & Gaming
William R. Snodgrass Tennessee Tower
312 Rosa L. Parks Avenue, 8th Floor
Nashville, TN 37243
(615) 741-2555   FAX (615) 253-5173

WARNING: False or misleading statements
Subject to maximum $5,000 civil penalty. T.C.A. §48-101-514

SUMMARY OF FINANCIAL ACTIVITIES
OF A
CHARITABLE ORGANIZATION

INSTRUCTIONS: Complete this form with financial information from the most recently completed accounting year. The form must be signed by two (2) authorized officers.

Name of Organization: _____

Address: _____ City: _____ State: _____ Zip Code _____

Federal ID: _____ State ID: _____ Telephone: _____

Accounting Year End: _____ Has your accounting year changed?   Yes _____   No _____

A.   Gross Revenue

1.   Public contributions ....$ _____
2.   Government grants ....$ _____
3.   Program service revenue ....$ _____
4.   Special events and activities ....$ _____
5.   Gross sales of inventory..$ _____
6.   Other revenue ....$ _____
7.   **Total Revenue** [add line 1 through line 6] ....$ _____

B.   Expenses

8.   Total program expenses ....$ _____
9.   Direct expenses from special events ....$ _____
10. Cost of goods ....$ _____
11. Management and general expenses.......................................$ _____
12. Fund raising expenses ....$ _____
13. Other Expenses..$ _____
14. **Total Expenses** [add line 8 through line 13] ....$ _____
15. **Excess / Deficit for the year** [line 7 minus line 14].............$ _____

C.   Changes in Net Assets or Fund balances

16. Net assets / fund balances at beginning of year ....$ _____
17. Other changes in net assets or fund balances......................$ _____
18. **Net assets / fund balances** [add line 15 through line 17] ....$ _____
19. Total assets ....$ _____
20. Total liabilities...$ _____
21. **Net assets / fund balances** [line 19 minus line 20].............$ _____

D.   Accounting Method Used:

CASH:_____   ACCRUAL: _____   OTHER: _____

SIGNATURES

I certify that the information furnished in this summary and all supplemental forms, documents and continuation sheets is true and correct to the best of my knowledge and belief.

_____

Signature of Authorized Officer

_____

Print Name

_____

Title

_____

Date

_____

Signature of Authorized Officer

_____

Print Name

_____

Title

_____

Date

State of Utah

DEPARTMENT OF COMMERCE
DIVISION OF CONSUMER PROTECTION

SUPPLEMENT TO
UNIFIED REGISTRATION STATEMENT

(To be used only when the Unified Registration Statement is filed in place of the
Charitable Organization Permit Application Form)

Annual Application fee: $100.00 (Non-refundable)

_____

Name of Charitable Organization

_____

Date of Application

OFFICE USE ONLY
Date Issued: _____
Permit Number: _____
Approved: _____
Exempt: _____
Denied: _____
Expiration: _____
Percentage of total contributions that are available for the charitable purpose:_____

Please mark the appropriate box:

☐ INITIAL
  APPLICATION

☐ RENEWAL
  APPLICATION

If you have any questions, please contact the Division at (801) 530-6601.

Please make application fee check or money order payable to the **State of Utah**.

Please return the completed application form and check or money order to:

Department of Commerce
Division of Consumer Protection
160 East 300 South
Box 146704
Salt Lake City, Utah 84114-6704

NOTE: The Charitable Solicitation permit will expire annually on the earlier of January 1, April 1, July 1, or October 1 following the completion of 12 months after the date of initial issuance.

April 2010

STATE OF UTAH

SUPPLEMENT TO UNIFIED REGISTRATION STATEMENT

If the Unified Registration Statement (URS) for Charitable Organizations is filed in lieu of the Charitable Organization Permit Application Form, this supplement must be completed in its entirety and attached to the URS. Use additional sheets if necessary. For definitions of professional fundraiser, professional fund raising counsel or consultant, commercial co-venturer, vending device, contributions, etc. refer to the Charitable Solicitations Act, U.C.A. § 13-22-2 (1953, as amended). This form does not need to be completed if the Division's Charitable Organization Permit Application form is used.

1. Contact Name: _____ Phone: _____

2. State the percentage of contributions that remained available in previous year for application to the charitable purposes declared in the URS, paragraph 22 (100% minus line 22(g) of the URS): _____%
   An initial applicant with no previous financial information is required to complete this Part using pro forma financial statements or budgets.

3. For each method of solicitation described in paragraph 10 of the URS, state the projected length of time that each solicitation will be conducted during the **upcoming** year. If any method of solicitation is ongoing, please indicate so.

4. Paragraph 17 of the URS must be completed by stating the name, address and telephone number of the Charitable Organization's registered agent. (The registered agent does not need to reside in Utah.)

5. Is your organization the parent foundation of a local unit or does your organization associate with a parent foundation? ☐ Yes ☐ No

If "yes", complete questions 6, 7, and 8. If "no", go to question 9.

6. List the following information concerning your parent foundation or local unit:

Name: _____

Address: _____

        Street

_____

        City   State   Zip Code

Contact Person: _____

Telephone Number: _____ Facsimile Number: _____

7. List the state(s) where your parent foundation is currently registered.

_____

_____

2

8. Please provide a copy of your current contract with the parent foundation with this application.

9. If your organization uses vending devices, state the following information:

   a. Type of vending devices used:_____

   b. Location(s) of vending devices:_____

   c. Length of time vending devices will be used: _____

10. In addition to the documents requested in the URS and its Appendix, please enclose copies of the following documents:

    a. Statement of Functional Expenses form, only if you are filing IRS Forms 990 EZ, 990PF, 990N, or other financial information other than IRS Form 990 (this form is available at www.dcp.utah.gov).
    b. Most recent IRS Form 990 or annual financial report filed with the IRS **(with signature).**
    c. Telephone transcript to be used in solicitation, if applicable.
    d. Current contract with Parent Foundation, if applicable. Parent foundation is defined in Utah Admin. Code R152-22-2(2)(a).
    e. Any order or judgment resulting from an injunction or criminal conviction disclosed in the URS.
    f. Any voluntary agreement of compliance disclosed in the URS.
    g. A copy of the IRS determination letter granting exempt status.
    h. The Applicant's articles of incorporation or other organizational documentation showing its current legal status **(initial application only, unless amended).**
    i. The Applicant's current by-laws or other policies and procedures governing its day-to-day operations **(initial application only, unless amended).**
    j. The Applicant's IRS Section 501(c)(3) or 501 (c)(4) tax exemption letter, if applicable **(initial application only, unless amended).**

11. If this is an initial application or a renewal application of an organization which has let its permit expire, has the applicant conducted activities regulated by the Charitable Solicitations Act, Utah Code Title 13, Chapter 22, without being duly registered with the Division?

This includes soliciting, requesting, promoting, advertising, or sponsoring a charitable solicitation in the state of Utah without being duly registered with the Division.

☐ Yes ☐ No

12. If "yes", please explain in detail, including how much was collected, who actually coordinated and scheduled the solicitation(s), the dates of the solicitation(s), and the number of pieces mailed and/or the number of solicitations made for each date indicated.

_____

_____

_____

3

The person signing this application on behalf of the charitable organization:
- affirms that this application is complete and not misleading;
- understands that this application is subject to audit; and
- acknowledges that fund raising in Utah will not commence until both the charitable organization, its parent foundation, if any, and the professional fund raiser or professional fund raising counsel or consultant are registered and in compliance with the Utah Charitable Solicitations Act.

DATED: _____   APPLICANT:

BY _____

ITS

4

DO NOT
STAPLE

STATE of WASHINGTON SECRETARY of STATE

Charities Program • 801 Capitol Way South • PO Box 40234 • Olympia, WA 98504-0234
Phone: 360-725-0378 • Fax: 360-664-4250 • E-mail: charities@sos.wa.gov
Web Address: www.sos.wa.gov/charities

WASHINGTON STATE UNIFIED REGISTRATION STATEMENT ADDENDUM

☐ Check here to request **EXPEDITED MAIL SERVICE** *(optional)*. If checked, please enclose an additional **$20** fee.

Make fees payable to "State of Washington"

Please complete entire form or write "n/a" if not applicable. Incomplete forms will not be accepted.
All documents must be typewritten or printed legibly in ink. **DO NOT** staple or bind form or attachments.

SECTION 1 - ORGANIZATION INFORMATION
Organization's Full Legal Name:

WA State Registration Number:	UBI *(Unified Business Identifier)* Number *(if located in WA)*:

SPECIFIC BENEFICIARIES
In the event of dissolution, will assets be distributed to a specific beneficiary whom the organization supports? ☐ Yes ☐ No If yes, attach a list containing the names and addresses of specific, named beneficiaries.

SECTION 2 - FINANCIAL, ADMINISTRATIVE & FUNDRAISING INFORMATION
THE NEXT TWO QUESTIONS PERTAIN TO FINANCIAL INFORMATION PROVIDED IN SOLICITATION REPORT
Did the organization solicit or collect contributions in Washington during the fiscal/accounting year reported below? (check one) ☐ Yes ☐ No If no, please check reason: ☐ New organization ☐ No activity in Washington State ☐ Other: _____ <div align="right">(describe)</div>If new organization, please provide the fiscal/accounting year end date of the first year during which solicitations will be conducted in WA and proceed to Three Highest Paid Officers Or Employees Of The Organization section: ____/____/____ **(REQUIRED)** <div align="center">month day year</div>
Did/will the organization submit a Federal tax return to the Internal Revenue Service for the fiscal/accounting year reported below? (check one) ☐ Yes ☐ No If yes, check type of return: ☐ Form 990 ☐ Form 990 EZ ☐ Form 990PF ☐ 990-T ☐ 1120 ☐ Other: _____ <div align="right">(describe)</div>If no, check reason: ☐ Church/church-affiliated ☐ Government-affiliated ☐ Covered by group return ☐ Annual gross receipts less than $25,000 ☐ Organization not tax-exempt ☐ Other (describe): _____
REQUIRED ATTACHMENT
If the organization has/will file an IRS Form 990, 990EZ or 990PF with the Internal Revenue Service for the fiscal/accounting year reported below...a complete copy of the tax return **MUST** be provided with this addendum. Be sure to include Schedule A and all attachments except contributor lists/Schedule B. Do not enclose the organization's bank statements or annual report. **DO NOT staple** or bind Form 990, 990EZ or 990PF, Schedule A, or their attachments.
NOTE: If the organization's tax return for the fiscal/accounting year reported below has not yet been completed, please contact our office for instructions. **DO NOT** submit the URS, URS Addendum or filing fee without a copy of the Form 990, 990EZ or 990PF.
SOLICITATION REPORT
Please supply fiscal/accounting beginning/ending dates and complete line items 1 - 8 (REQUIRED)
Suggested guidelines for completing the Solicitation Report using the organization's federal tax return can be obtained at http://www.sos.wa.gov/charities/charities_forms.aspx or by contacting the Charities Program directly.

Fiscal/accounting year begin date: (Mo/Day/Year)	**Fiscal/accounting year end date:** (Mo/Day/Year)

URS Addendum/Rev 11/09   1

1. The total gross dollar value of all contributions received from solicitations: "Solicitations" include, but are not limited to, special events, sale of inventory, and amounts collected on behalf of the charitable organization by a commercial fundraiser or commercial coventurer.	$
2. The total gross dollar value of revenue from all other sources (not the result of a solicitation):	+ $
3. The total dollar value of gross receipts: "Gross receipts" include, but are not limited to, contributions, gross revenue from special events, sales of inventory, goods or services (including tickets to events), and all other revenue from solicitations, regardless of custody of funds. Amounts collected on behalf of the charitable organization by a commercial fundraiser or commercial coventurer must be included on line 3.	= $ *(line 1 + line 2 = line 3)*
4. The total gross dollar value of expenditures used directly for charitable program services: *Payments to affiliates may be included if costs involved are not connected with the administrative or fundraising functions of the reporting organization.*	$
5. The total gross dollar value of expenditures used for administrative and fundraising: "Administrative and fund-raising costs" include, but are not limited to, the following expenses if not directly related to program services: salaries, wages, compensation, legal, accounting, occupancy, equipment costs, printing and publications, telephone, postage, supplies, travel, meetings, fees for services, and cost of goods or inventory sold that are not directly related to program services. Amounts paid to or retained by a commercial fundraiser or fundraising counsel must be included on line 5.	+ $
6. The total dollar value of program service, administrative and fundraising expenditures: Enter on line 6 the sum of the expenditures reported on lines 4 and 5. This includes, but is not limited to, amounts paid to or retained by a commercial fundraiser or fundraising counsel, amounts expended for charitable program services, administrative expenses, fees for services, and fundraising costs incurred by the charitable organization.	= $ *(line 4 + line 5 = line 6)*
7. Beginning assets (gross):	$
8. Ending assets (gross):	$

CHARITY'S COMMENTS REGARDING SOLICITATION REPORT *(OPTIONAL)*
Attach additional information or provide an explanation, if any, which the organization believes would be of assistance in understanding the financial information provided in Solicitation Report or IRS tax return, or to provide context for reported information. Be sure to clearly label attachment as "Solicitation Comments".

THREE HIGHEST PAID OFFICERS OR EMPLOYEES OF THE ORGANIZATION	
Officer or Employee Name	Title
1.	
2.	
3.	

NOTE: If no one is compensated, write "None". If less than three persons are compensated, write "n/a" on the appropriate row(s).

REQUIRED ATTACHMENTS FOR FIREFIGHTER, POLICE, SHERIFF OR VETERANS' SERVICE ORGANIZATIONS
Attach written authorization, signed by two officials from a bona fide police, sheriff, or fire fighter department, if your organization uses "police," "sheriff," "fire fighter," "firemen" or a similar name during the conduct of solicitations.
Attach written authorization, signed by the highest ranking official in WA State of a Federally chartered or nationally recognized military veterans' service organization (as determined by the United States Veterans' Administration), if your organization uses the name of said military veterans' service organization during the conduct of solicitations.

REQUIRED ATTACHMENTS
Please clearly label the attachments that correspond with the following questions
(A) Does the organization, or a commercial fundraiser operating on its behalf, use any other mailing, street, electronic or Internet addresses (excluding those provided above) to conduct solicitations in Washington State? (check one) ☐ Yes - Attach a list of other addresses used, including those used by commercial fundraisers, if any. ☐ No
(B) Is the charitable organization a chapter, subsidiary, branch, affiliate, related foundation or supporting organization of a superior or parent organization? (check one) ☐ Yes - Attach a list of superior or parent organizations. Include the Federal EIN, mailing address, email address, and web address for each superior/parent listed. ☐ No

SECTION 3 - SIGNATURE *(Required)*

By signing this addendum, the applicant: (a) certifies that the information contained in the application and in the attachments are accurate and true to the best of the applicant's knowledge; (b) irrevocably appoints the Secretary of State to receive process (notice of lawsuits) in non-criminal cases against the applicant, and under the conditions set out in RCW 19.09.305; and (c) certifies that neither the organization nor any of its officers, directors, and principals have been convicted of a crime involving charitable solicitations, nor been subject to permanent injunction or administrative order under the Washington Consumer Protection Act (Chapter 19.86 RCW) in the past ten years.

Signature of applicant	Printed name	Title	Date

This form may be signed by the President, Treasurer or a comparable officer or, in the absence of officers, person responsible for the organization.

NOTE: Expedited Mail Service is available for registration documents requiring 48-hour turnaround. To utilize Expedited Mail Service, please enclose **$20** per registration document (in addition to regular fees), check (√) the box on page one of this document, <u>and</u> write the word **"EXPEDITE"** in large, bold letters on the outside of the envelope. Your request will be processed and mailed within **TWO** business days of receipt by the Charities Program.

STATE OF WEST VIRGINIA

UNIFIED REGISTRATION STATEMENT SUPPLEMENT

This supplement must be completed in its entirety, attached to the Unified Registration Statement and filed with the Secretary of State.

1. Actual amount of funds raised in West Virginia during the last fiscal reporting year [see §29-19-5(a)(6)]:$_____.

2. Amount disbursed for program services in West Virginia during the period covered in this report [see §29-19-5(a)(6)]:$_____.
   Explain:_____.

3. Amount disbursed for charitable purposes outside West Virginia during the same period:$_____.
   Explain:_____.

Wisconsin Department of Regulation & Licensing

YES	NO	
☐	☐	During the past year has your organization had its authority to solicit contributions denied, suspended, revoked or enjoined by a court or other governmental authority? If YES, attach an explanation.
☐	☐	Does your organization solicit contributions under any name other than the name of the organization at the top of this form? If YES, list the other name or names here:

DESCRIBE THE CHARITABLE PURPOSE OR PURPOSES FOR WHICH CONTRIBUTIONS WILL BE USED OR ATTACH A DOCUMENT WHICH PROVIDES SUCH INFORMATION.

Complete either affidavit Form 1 or Form 2 below, or both, if true of your charitable organization's operations and revenues.

FORM 1: AFFIDAVIT OF ORGANIZATION WITH CONTRIBUTIONS LESS THAN $5,000

We swear that the organization identified on the other side of this form will not be submitting Form #308, Charitable Organization Annual Report, for its most recently-completed fiscal year, ending _____, _____, because contributions received during that fiscal year did not exceed $5,000.

CERTIFICATION-TWO DIFFERENT SIGNATURES ARE REQUIRED BY LAW.

_____   _____
(Signature of President)   (Date)

_____   _____
SIGNATURE OF NOTARY PUBLIC   (Seal)   DATE COMMISSION EXPIRES

Subscribed and sworn before me this _____ day of _____, _____.

_____   _____
(Signature of Chief Fiscal Officer)   (Date)

_____   _____
SIGNATURE OF NOTARY PUBLIC   (Seal)   DATE COMMISSION EXPIRES

Subscribed and sworn before me this _____ day of _____, _____.

Wisconsin Department of Regulation & Licensing

YES	NO	
☐	☐	During the past year has your organization had its authority to solicit contributions denied, suspended, revoked or enjoined by a court or other governmental authority? If YES, attach an explanation.
☐	☐	Does your organization solicit contributions under any name other than the name of the organization at the top of this form? If YES, list the other name or names here:

DESCRIBE THE CHARITABLE PURPOSE OR PURPOSES FOR WHICH CONTRIBUTIONS WILL BE USED OR ATTACH A DOCUMENT WHICH PROVIDES SUCH INFORMATION.

Complete either affidavit Form 1 or Form 2 below, or both, if true of your charitable organization's operations and revenues.

FORM 1: AFFIDAVIT OF ORGANIZATION WITH CONTRIBUTIONS LESS THAN $5,000

We swear that the organization identified on the other side of this form will not be submitting Form #308, Charitable Organization Annual Report, for its most recently-completed fiscal year, ending _____, _____, because contributions received during that fiscal year did not exceed $5,000.

CERTIFICATION-TWO DIFFERENT SIGNATURES ARE REQUIRED BY LAW.

_____   _____
(Signature of President)   (Date)

_____   _____
SIGNATURE OF NOTARY PUBLIC   (Seal)   DATE COMMISSION EXPIRES

Subscribed and sworn before me this _____ day of _____, _____.

_____   _____
(Signature of Chief Fiscal Officer)   (Date)

_____   _____
SIGNATURE OF NOTARY PUBLIC   (Seal)   DATE COMMISSION EXPIRES

Subscribed and sworn before me this _____ day of _____, _____.

Wisconsin Department of Regulation & Licensing

FORM 2: AFFIDAVIT OF ORGANIZATION WHICH SOLICITED CONTRIBUTIONS SOLELY IN ONE COMMUNITY AND RECEIVED LESS THAN $50,000 IN CONTRIBUTIONS

We swear that the organization identified on the other side solicits contributions solely within the county in which its principal office is located and that it received less than $50,000 in contributions during its most recently completed fiscal year, ending _____, _____. Therefore, by filing this affidavit, we are:

☐ seeking exemption from filing a financial report for that fiscal year/ and/or
☐ seeking exemption, for the current fiscal year, from the solicitation disclosure requirements reproduced on the back side of this page.

Our organization solicits contributions in the following county. (Please identify the county in which you solicit in person, by telephone or by mail.) If you solicit in more than one county, your organization is not qualified for this affidavit.

```
┌──────────────────────────────────────┐
│                                      │
└──────────────────────────────────────┘
```

CERTIFICATION--TWO DIFFERENT SIGNATURES ARE REQUIRED BY LAW.

_____   _____
(Signature of President)   (Date)

_____   _____
SIGNATURE OF NOTARY PUBLIC   (Seal)   DATE COMMISSION EXPIRES

Subscribed and sworn before me this _____ day of _____, _____.

_____   _____
(Signature of Chief Fiscal Officer)   (Date)

_____   _____
SIGNATURE OF NOTARY PUBLIC   (Seal)   DATE COMMISSION EXPIRES

Subscribed and sworn before me this _____ day of _____, _____.

Wisconsin Department of Regulation & Licensing

SOLICITATION DISCLOSURES

440.41 (10) "Unpaid solicitor" means a person who solicits in this state and who is not a professional fund-raiser

440.455 Solicitation disclosure requirements.

(1) Except as provided in sub. (4), if a professional fund–raiser or unpaid solicitor solicits a contribution for a charitable organization that is required to be registered under s. 440.42 (1), the professional fund–raiser or unpaid solicitor shall, at the time of the solicitation or with a written confirmation of a solicitation, prior to accepting a contribution, make the following disclosures to the person from whom the contribution is solicited:

(a) The name and location of the charitable organization.

(b) That a financial statement of the charitable organization disclosing assets, liabilities, fund balances, revenue and expenses for the preceding fiscal year will be provided to the person upon request.

(c) A clear description of the primary charitable purpose for which the solicitation is made.

(2) The financial statement under sub. (1) (b) shall, at a minimum, divide expenses into categories of management and general, program services and fund–raising. If the charitable organization is required to file an annual financial report under s. 440.42 (3) (a), the financial statement under sub. (1) (b) shall be consistent with that annual financial report.

(3) In addition to the requirements under subs. (1) and (2), except as provided in sub. (4), if a professional fund–raiser solicits on behalf of a charitable organization that is required to be registered under s. 440.42 (1), all of the following apply:

(a) If a solicitation is made orally, including a solicitation made by telephone, the professional fund–raiser shall send a written confirmation, within 5 days after the solicitation, to each person contributing or pledging to contribute. The written confirmation shall include a clear and conspicuous disclosure of the name of the professional fund–raiser and that the solicitation is being con-ducted by a professional fund–raiser.

(b) The professional fund–raiser may not represent that any part of the contributions received by the professional fund–raiser will be given or donated to a charitable organization unless that charitable organization has, prior to the solicitation, consented in writing, signed by 2 authorized officers, directors or trustees of that other charitable organization, to the use of its name.

(c) The professional fund–raiser may not represent that tickets to an event will be donated to an organization for use by others unless all of the following conditions are met:

1. The professional fund–raiser has a commitment, in writing, from the organization stating that the organization will accept donated tickets and specifying the number of donated tickets that the organization is willing to accept.

2. The professional fund–raiser solicits contributions for donated tickets from no more contributors than the number of tickets that the organization has agreed to accept under subd. 1.

(4) A charitable organization that operates solely within one community and that received less than $50,000 in contributions during its most recently completed fiscal year may apply to the department for an exemption from the disclosure requirements under this section. The department shall promulgate rules specifying the criteria for eligibility for an exemption under this paragraph, and shall grant exemptions from the disclosure requirements under this section to a charitable organization that satisfies those criteria.

History: 1991 a. 278, 315.
Cross Reference: See also ch. RL 5, Wis. adm. code.

Wisconsin Department of Regulation & Licensing

Mail To: P.O. Box 8935 Madison, WI 53708-8935	1400 E. Washington Avenue Madison, WI 53703
FAX #: (608) 261-7083 **Phone #:** (608) 266-2112	E-Mail: web@drl.state.wi.us Website: http://drl.wi.gov

DIVISION OF PROFESSIONAL CREDENTIAL PROCESSING

WISCONSIN SUPPLEMENT TO FINANCIAL REPORT ON FORM OTHER THAN FORM #308

This form requires a Federal Form 990 or other supporting document, and 2 different signatures.

PLEASE TYPE OR PRINT IN INK

NAME OF ORGANIZATION	WISCONSIN REGISTRATION NUMBER
ADDRESS (NUMBER AND STREET) OR P.O. BOX	FEDERAL EMPLOYER I.D. NUMBER
CITY OR TOWN, STATE, ZIP CODE	ORGANIZATION'S DAYTIME PHONE NUMBER ( )

INDICATE ORGANIZATION TYPE	ACCOUNTING METHOD
___ Civic & Social Action ___ Health Services ___ Culture ___ Education & Research ___ Human Services ___ Other	___ Cash ___ Other (Specify) ___ Accrual

ACCOUNTING PERIOD   Beginning Date _____   Ending Date _____

1.	Public Support	1	
	(Enter total direct public support such as: contributions, gifts, grants-**but not government grants**-and bequests received directly from the public. This line includes indirect public support, such as: contributions received through solicitation campaigns conducted by federated fund-raising agencies like United Way, or affiliate organizations.)		
2.	Other Revenues	2	
3.	Total Revenue (line 1 plus line 2)	3	
4.	Expenses:		
a	Expenses Allocated to Program Services	4a	
b	Expenses Allocated to Management and General	4b	
c	Expenses Allocated to Fund-raising	4c	
d	Expenses Allocated to Payments to Affiliates	4d	
e	Total Expenses	4e	
5.	Excess or Deficit (line 3 minus line 4e)	5	
6.	Net Worth at Beginning of Year	6	
7.	Other Changes in Net Assets	7	
8.	Net Worth at End of Year	8	

PLEASE TYPE OR PRINT IN INK

NAME OF INDIVIDUAL TO CONTACT REGARDING INFORMATION ON THIS FORM	DAYTIME TELEPHONE NUMBER ( )
ADDRESS (NUMBER AND STREET)	
CITY OR TOWN, STATE, ZIP CODE	

Wisconsin Department of Regulation & Licensing

ADDITIONAL QUESTIONS	YES	NO
9. Did your organization receive contributions over **$400,000** during the fiscal year? If so, you **must** file an **audited financial statement** and the opinion of an independent certified public accountant on the financial statement. If your organization received over **$200,000** in contributions, a **review** by an independent certified public accountant is required.		
10. Have you **attached a list** of all officers, directors, trustees and the principal salaried employees? Include their name, address, title, and the date their term ends. **Compensation must be clearly stated.**		
11. For solicitation in Wisconsin, did your organization use a professional fund-raiser or fund-raising counsel or did your organization pay a person to solicit contributions, other than a salaried officer or employee of your organization? **If yes, indicate name and address.**		
12. Has there been a **name change** of the organization, **change of address** of the principal office or any branch office located in Wisconsin, **change in the accounting period**, change in the names of the persons within the organization who have final authority for custody or final distribution of contributions, or change in the articles, by-laws or statement of purpose? If yes, and not already submitted within 30 days, as required, give changes and attach document. **If a corporation, and the name has changed, you must attach a copy of the name change amendment.**		
13. Is your organization authorized by any other governmental authority to solicit contributions? If yes, provide name and address of governmental authority.		
14. Has your organization ever had its authority to solicit contributions denied, suspended, revoked or enjoined by a court or other governmental authority? **If yes, attach an explanation.**		
15. Do you intend to accumulate an increasing surplus in net worth, rather than spend current revenue on the organization's stated purpose? **If yes, attach an explanation.**		
16. Did the organization make a grant, award, or contribution to any organization in which any of its officers or directors hold an interest; or was it a party to any transaction in which any of its directors, trustees or officers has a material financial interest; or did any officer or director receive anything of value not reported above as compensation? **If yes to any of the above, attach an explanation.**		
17. Does your organization solicit contributions under any name other than the name listed in the first blank space on the reverse side? **If yes, list here any additional name(s).**		

DESCRIBE THE CHARITABLE PURPOSES FOR WHICH CONTRIBUTIONS WILL BE USED OR ATTACH A DOCUMENT WHICH PROVIDES SUCH INFORMATION.

CERTIFICATION - TWO DIFFERENT SIGNATURES ARE REQUIRED BY LAW

We swear and affirm that we have reviewed this report, including the accompanying schedules and statements, and to the best of our knowledge the information furnished is true, correct and complete.

Date	Title	Signature of President or Authorized Officer

Date	Title	Signature of Chief Fiscal Officer

Index

NOLO® *Keep Up to Date*

1. Go to Nolo.com/newsletters to sign up for free newsletters and discounts on Nolo products.

   - **Nolo Briefs.** Our monthly email newsletter with great deals and free information.

   - **Nolo's Special Offer.** A monthly newsletter with the biggest Nolo discounts around.

   - **BizBriefs.** Tips and discounts on Nolo products for business owners and managers.

   - **Landlord's Quarterly.** Deals and free tips just for landlords and property managers, too.

2. Don't forget to check for updates at **Nolo.com.** Under "Products," find this book and click "Legal Updates."

Let Us Hear From You

3. Register your Nolo product and give us your feedback at Nolo.com/book-registration.

   - Once you've registered, you qualify for technical support if you have any trouble with a download or CD (though most folks don't).

   - We'll also drop you an email when a new edition of your book is released—and we'll send you a coupon for 15% off your next Nolo.com order!

NREG1

NOLO® *and* USA TODAY

Cutting-Edge Content, Unparalleled Expertise

The Busy Family's Guide to Money
by Sandra Block, Kathy Chu & John Waggoner • $19.99

The Work From Home Handbook
Flex Your Time, Improve Your Life
by Diana Fitzpatrick & Stephen Fishman • $19.99

Retire Happy
What You Can Do NOW to Guarantee a Great Retirement
by Richard Stim & Ralph Warner • $19.99

The Essential Guide for First-Time Homeowners
Maximize Your Investment & Enjoy Your New Home
by Ilona Bray & Alayna Schroeder • $19.99

Easy Ways to Lower Your Taxes
Simple Strategies Every Taxpayer Should Know
by Sandra Block & Stephen Fishman • $19.99

First-Time Landlord
Your Guide to Renting Out a Single-Family Home
by Attorney Janet Portman, Marcia Stewart & Michael Molinski • $19.99

Stopping Identity Theft
10 Easy Steps to Security
by Scott Mitic, CEO, TrustedID, Inc. • $19.99

The Mom's Guide to Wills & Estate Planning
by Attorney Liza Hanks • $21.99

Running a Side Business
How to Create a Second Income
by Attorneys Richard Stim & Lisa Guerin • $21.99

Nannies and Au Pairs
Hiring In-Home Child Care
by Ilona Bray, J.D. • $19.99

The Judge Who Hated Red Nail Polish
& Other Crazy But True Stories of Law and Lawyers
by Ilona Bray, Richard Stim & the Editors of Nolo • $19.99

NOLO Catalog

BUSINESS

Bankruptcy for Small Business Owners	$39.99
Business Buyout Agreements (Book w/CD)	$49.99
Business Loans From Family & Friends: How to Ask, Make It Legal & Make It Work	$29.99
The California Nonprofit Corporation Kit (Binder w/CD)	$69.99
California Workers' Comp: How to Take Charge When You're Injured on the Job	$39.99
The Craft Artist's Legal Guide (Book w/CD)	$39.99
The Complete Guide to Buying a Business (Book w/CD)	$24.99
The Complete Guide to Selling a Business (Book w/CD)	$34.99
Consultant & Independent Contractor Agreements (Book w/CD)	$34.99
The Corporate Records Handbook (Book w/CD)	$69.99
Create Your Own Employee Handbook (Book w/CD)	$49.99
Dealing With Problem Employees	$49.99
Deduct It! Lower Your Small Business Taxes	$34.99
The eBay Business Start-Up Kit (Book w/CD)	$24.99
Effective Fundraising for Nonprofits	$24.99
The Employer's Legal Handbook	$49.99
The Essential Guide to Family & Medical Leave (Book w/CD)	$49.99
The Essential Guide to Federal Employment Laws	$44.99
The Essential Guide to Handling Workplace Discrimination & Harassment	$39.99
The Essential Guide to Workplace Investigations (Book w/CD)	$44.99
Every Nonprofit's Guide to Publishing	$29.99
Every Nonprofit's Tax Guide	$34.99
Form a Partnership (Book w/CD)	$39.99
Form Your Own Limited Liability Company (Book w/CD)	$44.99
Healthy Employees, Healthy Business	$29.99
Hiring Your First Employee: A Step-by-Step Guide	$24.99
Home Business Tax Deductions: Keep What You Earn	$34.99
How to Form a Nonprofit Corporation (Book w/CD)—National Edition	$49.99
How to Form a Nonprofit Corporation in California (Book w/CD)	$49.99
How to Form Your Own California Corporation (Binder w/CD)	$39.99
How to Form Your Own California Corporation (Book w/CD)	$39.99
How to Run a Thriving Business: Strategies for Success & Satisfaction	$19.99
How to Write a Business Plan (Book w/CD)	$34.99
Incorporate Your Business (Book w/CD)—National Edition	$49.99
The Job Description Handbook (Book w/CD)	$29.99
Legal Guide for Starting & Running a Small Business	$39.99
Legal Forms for Starting & Running a Small Business (Book w/CD)	$29.99
LLC or Corporation?	$24.99
The Manager's Legal Handbook	$49.99
Marketing Without Advertising	$20.00
Music Law: How to Run Your Band's Business (Book w/CD)	$39.99
Negotiate the Best Lease for Your Business	$24.99
Nolo's Crash Course in Small Business Basics (Audiobook on 5 CDs)	$34.99
Nolo's Quick LLC	$29.99

Nonprofit Meetings, Minutes & Records (Book w/CD)..$39.99
The Performance Appraisal Handbook (Book w/CD)..$29.99
The Progressive Discipline Handbook (Book w/CD)..$34.99
Retire—And Start Your Own Business (Book w/CD)..$24.99
Running a Side Business: How to Create a Second Income $21.99
Save Your Small Business: 10 Crucial Strategies to Survive Hard Times or Close Down & Move On $29.99
Small Business in Paradise: Working for Yourself in a Place You Love $19.99
The Small Business Start-Up Kit (Book w/CD)—National Edition $29.99
The Small Business Start-Up Kit for California (Book w/CD) $29.99
Smart Policies for Workplace Technologies: Email, Blogs, Cell Phones & More (Book w/CD) $29.99
Starting & Building a Nonprofit: A Practical Guide (Book w/CD)...$29.99
Starting & Running a Successful Newsletter or Magazine..$29.99
Tax Deductions for Professionals $39.99
Tax Savvy for Small Business $39.99
The Women's Small Business Start-Up Kit (Book w/CD) $29.99
The Work From Home Handbook $19.99
Working for Yourself: Law & Taxes for Independent Contractors, Freelancers & Consultants $39.99
Working With Independent Contractors (Book w/CD) $34.99
Your Limited Liability Company (Book w/CD) $49.99
Your Rights in the Workplace..$29.99

CONSUMER
How to Win Your Personal Injury Claim..$34.99
The Judge Who Hated Red Nail Polish & Other Crazy but True Stories of Law and Lawyers $19.99
Nolo's Encyclopedia of Everyday Law $29.99
Nolo's Guide to California Law $34.99
Nolo's Plain-English Law Dictionary $29.99
The Sharing Solution: How to Save Money, Simplify Your Life & Build Community $24.99
Your Little Legal Companion $9.95

ESTATE PLANNING & PROBATE
8 Ways to Avoid Probate $21.99
Estate Planning Basics $24.99
Estate Planning for Blended Families: Providing for Your Spouse & Children in a Second Marriage $34.99
The Executor's Guide: Settling a Loved One's Estate or Trust...$39.99
Get It Together: Organize Your Records So Your Family Won't Have To (Book w/CD) $21.99
How to Probate an Estate in California $49.99
Living Wills & Powers of Attorney for California $29.99
Make Your Own Living Trust (Book w/CD) $39.99
The Mom's Guide to Wills & Estate Planning $21.99
Plan Your Estate $44.99
Quick & Legal Will Book (Book w/CD)..$21.99
Quicken Willmaker Plus (Book and Software) $49.99
Special Needs Trusts: Protect Your Child's Financial Future (Book w/CD) $34.99
The Trustee's Legal Companion $39.99

FAMILY MATTERS
Always Dad: Being a Great Father During & After a Divorce..$16.99
Building a Parenting Agreement That Works..$24.99
The Complete IEP Guide: How to Advocate for Your Special Ed Child $34.99
Divorce After 50...$29.99
Divorce & Money: How to Make the Best Financial Decisions During Divorce $34.99

Divorce Without Court: A Guide to Mediation & Collaborative Divorce $34.99
Every Dog's Legal Guide: A Must-Have for Your Owner $19.99
Get It Together: Organize Your Records So Your Family Doesn't Have To (Book w/CD)................................ $21.99
The Guardianship Book for California $44.99
A Judge's Guide to Divorce (Book w/CD)... $24.99
A Legal Guide for Lesbian & Gay Couples (Book w/CD) $34.99
Living Together: A Legal Guide for Unmarried Couples (Book w/CD) $34.99
Making It Legal: A Guide to Same-Sex Marriage, Domestic Partnerships & Civil Unions........................... $29.99
Nannies & Au Pairs: Hiring In-Home Childcare... $19.99
Nolo's Essential Guide to Divorce $24.99
Nolo's IEP Guide: Learning Disabilities $34.99
Parent Savvy.. $19.99
Prenuptial Agreements (Book w/CD) $34.99

GOING TO COURT
Beat Your Ticket: Go to Court & Win—National Edition $21.99
The Criminal Law Handbook: Know Your Rights, Survive the System.. $39.99
Everybody's Guide to Small Claims Court—National Edition.. $29.99
Everybody's Guide to Small Claims Court in California $29.99
Fight Your Ticket & Win in California... $29.99
How to Change Your Name in California (Book w/CD)... $34.99
Legal Research: How to Find & Understand the Law $49.99
Nolo's Deposition Handbook... $34.99
Represent Yourself in Court: How to Prepare & Try a Winning Case $39.99
Win Your Lawsuit: A Judge's Guide to Representing Yourself in California Superior Court $39.99

HOMEOWNERS, LANDLORDS & TENANTS
Buying a Second Home (Book w/CD) $24.99
The California Landlord's Law Book: Evictions (Book w/CD).. $44.99
The California Landlord's Law Book: Rights & Responsibilities (Book w/CD) $44.99
California Tenants' Rights $29.99
Deeds for California Real Estate.. $27.99
The Essential Guide for First-Time Homeowners $19.99
Every Landlord's Guide to Finding Great Tenants (Book w/CD)... $24.99
Every Landlord's Legal Guide (Book w/CD) $44.99
Every Landlord's Property Protection Guide (Book w/CD) $29.99
Every Landlord's Tax Deduction Guide $39.99
Every Tenant's Legal Guide... $34.99
First-Time Landlord: Your Guide to Renting Out a Single-Family Home.. $19.99
For Sale by Owner in California (Book w/CD) $29.99
The Foreclosure Survival Guide $24.99
Leases & Rental Agreements (Book w/CD) $29.99
Neighbor Law: Fences, Trees, Boundaries & Noise $29.99
Nolo's Essential Guide to Buying Your First Home (Book w/CD) $24.99
Renters' Rights: The Basics $24.99
Saving the Family Cottage: A Guide to Succession Planning for Your Cottage, Cabin, Camp or
    Vacation Home.. $29.99
Selling Your House in a Tough Market: 10 Strategies That Work.. $24.99

IMMIGRATION
Becoming a U.S. Citizen: A Guide to the Law, Exam & Interview $24.99
Fiancé & Marriage Visas.. $34.99

How to Get a Green Card $39.99
Student & Tourist Visas.. $29.99
U.S. Immigration Made Easy $44.99

MONEY MATTERS
101 Law Forms for Personal Use (Book w/CD)... $29.99
The Busy Family's Guide to Money $19.99
Chapter 13 Bankruptcy: Keep Your Property & Repay Debts Over Time......................... $39.99
Credit Repair (Book w/CD).. $24.99
Easy Ways to Lower Your Taxes $19.99
How to File for Chapter 7 Bankruptcy $39.99
The New Bankruptcy: Will It Work for You? $24.99
Nolo's Guide to Social Security Disability (Book w/CD)... $39.99
Solve Your Money Troubles: Debt, Credit & Bankruptcy $24.99
Stand Up to the IRS... $34.99
Stopping Identity Theft: 10 Easy Steps to Security $19.99
Surviving an IRS Tax Audit.. $24.95

RETIREMENT & SENIORS
Get a Life: You Don't Need a Million to Retire Well... $24.99
IRAs, 401(k)s & Other Retirement Plans: Taking Your Money Out $34.99
Long-Term Care: How to Plan & Pay for It $24.99
Nolo's Essential Retirement Tax Guide $24.99
Retire Happy: What You Can Do NOW to Guarantee a Great Retirement..................... $19.99
Social Security, Medicare & Goverment Pensions $29.99
Work Less, Live More: The Way to Semi-Retirement... $17.99
The Work Less, Live More Workbook (Book w/CD).. $19.99

PATENTS AND COPYRIGHTS
All I Need Is Money: How to Finance Your Invention... $19.99
The Copyright Handbook: What Every Writer Needs to Know (Book w/CD) $39.99
Getting Permission: How to License & Clear Copyrighted Material Online & Off (Book w/CD)...................... $34.99
How to Make Patent Drawings $29.99
The Inventor's Notebook $24.99
Legal Guide to Web & Software Development (Book w/CD) $44.99
Nolo's Patents for Beginners $29.99
Patent, Copyright & Trademark: An Intellectual Property Desk Reference $39.99
Patent It Yourself... $49.99
Patent Pending in 24 Hours $34.99
Patent Savvy for Managers: Spot & Protect Valuable Innovations in Your Company $29.99
Patent Searching Made Easy... $39.99
Profit From Your Idea (Book w/CD) $34.99
The Public Domain $34.99
Trademark: Legal Care for Your Business & Product Name... $39.99
What Every Inventor Needs to Know About Business & Taxes (Book w/CD) $21.99

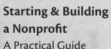

NOLO® *Lawyer Directory*

Find a Nonprofit Attorney

- *Qualified lawyers*
- *In-depth profiles*
- *A pledge of respectful service*

When you want professional help with crucial issues involving a nonprofit corporation, you don't want just any lawyer—you want an expert in the field, who can give you and your family up-to-the-minute advice. You need a lawyer who has the experience and knowledge to answer your questions about key issues such as deciding to incorporate, gaining 501(c)(3) tax-exempt status, dealing with board of directors disputes, and helping with legal issues raised by foundation, government and individual funders.

Nolo's Lawyer Directory is unique because it provides an extensive profile of every lawyer. You'll learn about not only each lawyer's education, professional history, legal specialties, credentials and fees, but also about their philosophy of practicing law and how they like to work with clients.

All lawyers listed in Nolo's directory are in good standing with their state bar association. Many will review Nolo documents, such as a will or living trust, for a fixed fee. They all pledge to work diligently and respectfully with clients—communicating regularly, providing a written agreement about how legal matters will be handled, sending clear and detailed bills, and more.

www.nolo.com